Volume 3
Beaches and Hills

Douglas Waitley

Pineapple Press, Inc.
Sarasota, Florida

Copyright © 2003 by Douglas Waitley

Photographs by the author.

All rights reserved. No part of this book may be reproduced in any form or by any means, electronic or mechanical, including photocopying, recording, or by any information storage and retrieval system, without permission in writing from the publisher.

Inquiries should be addressed to:

Pineapple Press, Inc.
P.O. Box 3889
Sarasota, Florida 34230

www.pineapplepress.com

Library of Congress Cataloging in Publication Data

Waitley, Douglas.
    Best Backroads of Florida. Douglas Waitley.
          p.   cm.
    Contents: v. 3. Upper Florida: beaches and hills
    ISBN 1-56164-283-5 (v. 3)
1. Florida—Tours. 2. Automobile travel—Florida—Guidebooks. 3. Scenic byways—Florida—Guidebooks. I. Title.

F309.3.W325 2000
917.5904'63—dc21

                                   2002152278

First Edition
10 9 8 7 6 5 4 3 2 1

Design by *Osprey Design Systems*
Text and Cover Composition by Shé Heaton

Printed in the United States of America

To all those who love the backroads

Light-hearted I take to the open road,
Healthy, free, the world before me . . . .
The earth expanding right and left hand,
The picture alive, every part in its best light . . . .
I inhale great draughts of space,
The east and the west are mine,
* and the north and the south are mine . . . .*
Forever alive, forever forward . . . .
I know not where they go,
But I know that they go toward the best . . . .

From *Song of the Open Road* in *Leaves of Grass*

—Walt Whitman

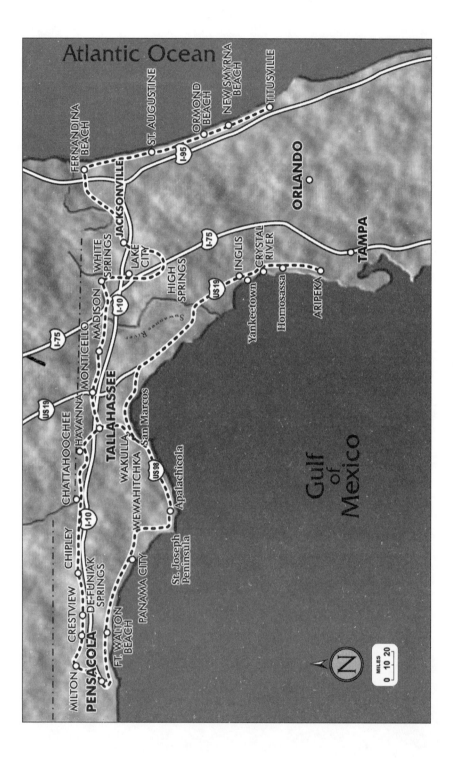

Contents

Introduction

The Lure of the Backroads

There is a feeling of wellbeing that comes over me every time I turn onto a backroad. The pavement stretches before me, beckoning, alluring, and promising new and exciting things. The horizon expands.

There's freedom on a backroad—a world out of the ordinary. There are truths eternal in the creeks, the dells, the forested glades, the grassy prairies—these are things that have always been and will always be.

Backroads take me closer to a mysterious essence that percolates

A backroad, such as this on Merritt Island,
challenges us to explore what's around the next bend.

1

through my memory. Backroads make the harsh glare of modernity dissolve into softer, more soothing tones.

The world hurries too much. Few motorists look farther than a few hundred feet in front of them or to the side. The leisurely pace along a backroad urges your vision to expand. Your gaze can drift over the landscape, and allow you, perhaps, to appreciate the beauty of that distant ridge quivering in the blue haze. Or, you can look closely at the plants growing along the road banks: there are wildflowers nearly everywhere. Often their fluorescences are so tiny you must consciously look for them.

Backroads do not disguise the sounds of nature. The symphony of the scenery accompanies the byways just as fragrance accompanies a rose. Slow down and listen to a bird in a wax myrtle, or a frog in a wetland, or perhaps, the rustling of a palmetto.

Yes, once you master the art of backroads driving, you'll find yourself in a fresh and appealing environment.

So why are we waiting? Let's get started!

A word about fishing licenses

Licenses are easy to obtain by calling 888-347-4356, which is a toll-free number. Have a major credit card ready. You'll be given a license number right over the phone.

For freshwater fishing, a nonresident's minimum purchase is a seven-day license, which costs $16.50. A Florida resident's minimum purchase is a twelve-month license, which costs $13.50.

For saltwater fishing, a nonresident's minimum three-day license costs $6.50 and a seven-day license costs $16.50. A Florida resident's minimum one-year license is $13.50.

For all licenses, there is an additional $3.95 processing fee.

Backroads often lead to enjoyable hideaways.

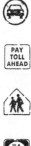

Icons

 Directions while driving

 Bridge and road tolls; admission fees

 Walking trails and paths

 Restaurants

Bike rentals, trails

Swimming areas

 Photo opportunities

Fishing

 Hotels, motels, bed and breakfasts

 Boat rides, cruises

Canoe rentals

 Boat ramp

The Upper Atlantic Coast

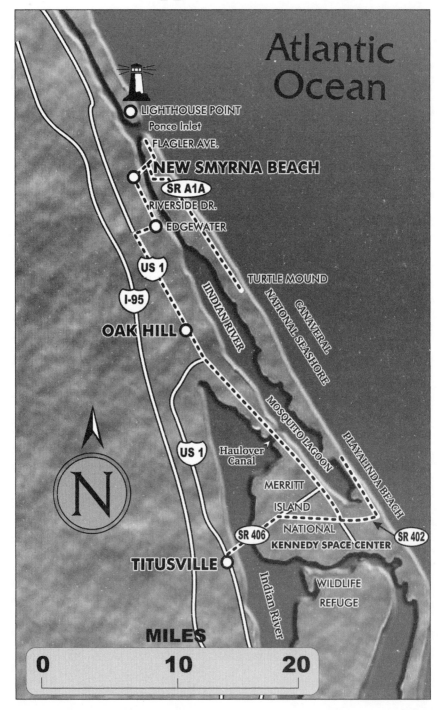

Birds, Beaches, and Blastoffs

Titusville to New Smyrna Beach • 74 Backroad Miles

The Song of the Road: Overview

Florida is a land of contrasts, as we'll see on this exploration. We begin at Titusville, famous for its close association with the Kennedy Space Center located directly across the Indian River on Merritt Island. In Veterans Memorial Park we can actually put our hands into the prints made by America's first astronauts. From there we'll cross onto Merritt Island where a large wildlife refuge has been created on NASA-owned acreage. After viewing the birds along Black Point Drive, we'll head out to the Atlantic coast, passing, on the way, the field where the space shuttle lands and perhaps seeing the shuttle in the distance being readied for flight. We can enjoy swimming at Playalinda Beach, where surf fishing is also popular.

Next we'll head north toward New Smyrna Beach along Riverside Drive and learn the story of the doomed Turnbull plantation. The fine beach at New Smyrna is ideal for surfers, who relish the rolling breakers. For those who prefer calmer waters, excursion boats ply the island-studded Indian River.

We'll end west of town where the haunting ruins of a slavery-era sugar mill provide a strange contrast to the glittering and noisy world of the twenty-first century.

On the Road

Our travels begin at Titusville, known as SpaceCity USA, directly across the Indian River from the Kennedy Space Center on Cape Canaveral. One of the best places to view a rocket launch is from Veterans Memorial Park at the corner of Indian River Avenue and Broad Street, two blocks south of the SR 406 bridge. Here, a series of piers protruding into the river affords unparalleled views of the launches.

In Titusville, this monument to NASA's first seven astronauts looks out across the Indian River to the Cape Canaveral launch pads.

Stairway to the Stars

A launch is impressive. When the shuttle blasts off, hot clouds billow from the site and thunder growls across the Indian River. The shuttle rises, ponderously at first, then with ever-accelerating speed. Soon it's a torch shooting heavenward, the fiery glow from its throbbing rockets turning the clouds molten-red. Behind the shuttle, smoke plumes as it is caught by high altitude winds. "Look!" an excited little girl shouted when I was there. "It's making its own stairs!"

But don't fret if you're not present during a launch. The park is of interest at other times due to its monument to the Mercury Project, America's initial entry into space. To appreciate Mercury's importance you must put yourself back into the days of the Cold War when concern over the power of the Soviet Union dominated American life. The Soviet leader was Nikita Khrushchev, a blunt, swaggering man with a passion for rough talk and strong vodka. When he launched Sputnik, the first man-made object to orbit the earth, in 1957, Americans were shocked. Two years later he sent a satellite racing to the moon, where it took pictures of the never-before-seen far side. President John Kennedy realized a race was on—not only for the international prestige of landing the first men on the moon, but for whatever military advantage might accrue from the scientific research involved. It was in this tense climate that the Mercury Project was launched.

On May 5, 1961, Alan Shepard became the first American in space. Yet he spent barely fifteen minutes aloft. Premier Khrushchev sneered that it was little more than "a flea jump," for he had just sent a man orbiting the earth for more than an hour and a half. Clearly America was way behind in space exploration. Nonetheless, the Mercury flights, which continued for two more years, would lay the groundwork for America's victory when the moon landing took place in 1969.

The Mercury Seven

The achievements of the Mercury Program are highlighted in Veterans Park. The monument's most prominent feature is a tall, stainless steel number 7 encircled by the astrological symbol for Mercury, the Roman god of travel. This structure once stood in the shuttle launch area and represented the seven astronauts involved with America's initial venture into space.

Around the base of the monument are the astronauts' actual handprints. It's a weird experience to place your own hand in a Mercury astronaut's print. As I put mine into Shepard's indentation, I pictured him at the controls of a Mercury capsule. The interior was so cramped that Shepard could hardly move. Journalists referred to him as "the man in the can." Waiting for the blastoff, he must have experienced deep concern, for another rocket had exploded on takeoff just eleven days earlier!

Each of the astronauts who followed Shepard had his own stressful experience. John Glenn made three orbits of the earth, but on his descent he feared he'd be incinerated as he saw chunks of his disintegrating heat shield flying past his window. Scott Carpenter overshot his landing site by 250 miles and spent three hours in a perilous life raft before rescue ships reached him. Wally Schirra had such a problem with his space suit that he was nearly ordered back after just one orbit. Gordon Cooper was forced to wait for more than six hours in his capsule in the torrid Florida sun while a fuel line was repaired.

One Mercury astronaut did not leave his handprint. This was

Virgil "Gus" Grissom, who burned to death when he and two other astronauts were trapped in a fire aboard an Apollo spacecraft.

When's a River Not a River?

 From Veterans Memorial Park take the SR 406 bridge over the broad Indian River. To the north, you'll see a fishing bridge and beyond that, the colorful Municipal Marina, where boats from the Space Coast Nature Tours conduct hour-and-a-half excursions along the river. These tours leave Monday through Saturday at 10:30 A.M. and 1:30 P.M. at the cost of $14 for adults and $12 for kids twelve and under. Call 321–267–4551 for more information.

The Indian River has long been famous for the luscious grapefruit grown near its shores farther south. But, despite the hoopla, the Indian River is not a river. It doesn't have a source, a mouth, or even a current. It is actually a 156-mile-long lagoon between the mainland and a string of barrier islands that extends halfway to Miami. Because this lagoon is a complex brew of Atlantic water and mainland runoffs, it has evolved into an environment found nowhere else on earth. It supports more than seven hundred species of fish, four of which breed in no other place. During the winter, manatees frequent the lagoon, where the water is warmer than the thrashing Atlantic. The lethargic manatees lumbering close to the surface are often scarred, and sometimes killed, by motorboat blades. For this reason the lagoon has "No Wake" zones, and law enforcement craft patrol these areas.

 South from the bridge is a small, round island that looks like something from the South Pacific. This is just one of a series of "spoil islands" created by the dredging needed to keep the lagoon navigable for the boats that use it as part of the Intracoastal Waterway that runs from Chesapeake Bay to Key West.

NASA and the National Parks

The land on the other side of the Indian River is Merritt Island, purchased in 1963 by the National Aeronautics and Space Administration (NASA) as part of its projected Cape Canaveral rocket complex. This was a protective measure to ensure there would be no civilian casualties in case of an explosion during rocket launches. But NASA leased the northern part of Merritt Island to other agencies to use during the long gaps between launches. Much of this area has become the Merritt Island National Wildlife Refuge.

A picturesque road winds through the Merritt Island National Wildlife refuge.

It is open to the public seven days a week during the daylight hours. However, it is closed three or four days before launches and on the day of the shuttle's return. To learn the closure dates call 321–867–1566.

When you come to a fork in the road, take SR 406. This will lead you to Black Point Wildlife Drive, the highlight of a visit to the refuge.

Black Point Wildlife Drive

Black Point Drive is a seven-mile journey of discovery along a road built on top of a 1950s dike. This narrow, sandy lane meanders through salt marshes, meadows, mud flats, and palm hammocks. Each of these environments has its own denizens, but foremost among the creatures who love this wet, muddy world are salt mosquitoes. Once, they thrived here year-round, but they've been roughly treated by humans, who constructed a series of dikes to eliminate the tidal ebbs and flows upon which the little insects depended to nurture their young. Some survive, however, particularly in the summer. The cool months are so relatively free of them that most visitors get out of their cars at some of the eleven observation stops to watch the wildlife or to wander along the wending road.

Birdville, USA

Bird-watching is the reason many people come to the Wildlife Refuge, for it is on the great migratory flyway used by birds from all over the eastern United States and Canada to reach their favorite winter vacation spots in the tropics. During the peak times, between late October and late March, as many as 100,000 birds of more than three hundred species may be in the refuge.

For water birds you can't beat the wide pond at stop number six. Sometimes it is almost alive with ducks, egrets, herons, wood storks, and coots—to name just the more common species. People gather on the shore with all sorts of avian identification paraphernalia. At intervals, when a strange noise or perhaps a vague sense of danger engulfs the assembly of birds, there is a sudden honking and squealing, followed by a rush of wings and a cascade of feathers. Then they rise in an awesome mass like some alien space ship that swerves and dips and flutters into the distance before looming overhead to descend with more honks and even greater turmoil onto the ruffling water. It's a thrilling scene that few persons ever forget.

You'll enjoy different experiences at other locations along the road. At stop number eight an observation tower provides a sweep of marsh extending for many miles of quiet majesty. This is a good place to spot song birds fluttering and singing amid the

Bird watchers love this lookout in the Merritt Island National Wildlife refuge. The space shuttle lands not far from here.

grass. Beside the tower is the Cruickshank Trail, a five-mile footpath that allows you to traverse a mosquito dike through the marsh and out as far as the Indian River. Incidentally, it was Allan Cruickshank who was instrumental in establishing the refuge.

Sometimes, however, it's not necessary to tramp long distances to appreciate nature. I paused on the trail one afternoon and stood still to let nature come to me. Soon a little bird strutted past my feet intently scrutinizing the ground for a tidbit to please his pallet. Next, a rabbit hip-hopped through the grass; he knew I was there but had other business on his mind. Then a parade of ducks—mamma and five little ones—came quacking down the watery ditch beside the dike. When the water cleared, I saw tiny bluish fish flitting in the shallows.

As time passed, I began to hear the subtle breathing of the marsh: the whispering of the wind, the gurgle of water, the rasping of grass, the rustle of birds' wings. From far off came the call of a mockingbird. There were other subtleties, too. Like the colors of the marsh. It wasn't just green, as it seemed at first, but shades of olive, gray, and tan with dashes of salty white and daubs of pale blue. And how the pools of open water sparkled as the wind and sun danced over them!

Out in the refuge you feel as if humans are inconsequential wayfarers of whom the true marshland citizens are scarcely aware. We pass through in our noisy machines, then are gone. The grasses grow without us; the birds mate without us; the storms frown, the sun sears, and at night the moon dusts the world with magic—all without us.

The Refuge Visitor Center

Black Point Drive, completing its lazy "U," ends back at SR 406, where by heading left you'll quickly reach a road denoted as SR 3 on older maps, but now nameless—presumably for security reasons, since it is the back door to the Kennedy Space Center. Turn right here. If it's a clear day, you'll be able to see the multi-story Vehicle Assembly Building in the bluish distance ahead. It's here that the shuttles are readied for their epic voyages. Yet despite the nearness of the Space Center, the land through which you'll be traveling is devoid of almost any other sign of human activity. That is, except for the unsightly skeletons of once graceful Australian pines, which I assume have been poisoned by avid environmentalists protecting us from these evil intruders from another continent. In three miles you'll reach the road formerly known as SR 402, but now also name-less. Ahead is the Space Center, restricted to proper personnel.

  By turning west on the road formerly known as SR 402, in a few miles you'll reach the Merritt Island Refuge Visitor Center. On your way you'll pass, to the south, the field where the space shuttles land. It was to here that *Columbia* was heading when it trag-ically disintegrated over Texas, killing its seven crew members, on February 1, 2003. You won't be able to see much of the landing area, for bushes obscure most of the view. However, you'll see more than on the actual landing days, since access to Merritt Island is closed to the public at these times.

The Visitor Center features a twenty-minute movie on animal life. It also sells videos with bird songs, as well as an amplitude of books, including a thick one called *Bird Watching for Dummies,* as if a dummy could get through all the pages. The center is open seven days a week; call 321–861–0667 for hours of operation. Admission is free.

Playalinda Beach

Now drive back east on the road formerly known as SR 402 toward the ocean. Just after you pass the road formerly known as SR 3, you'll encounter a checkpoint where armed guards search your car for weapons. Unless you're carrying a rifle or heavy artillery, it will be quick. Then you'll pay the $5 per car entry fee.

As you continue out to the beach, you'll get good views of the two space shuttle launch complexes from several turnouts, though from the distance of two miles they look like discards from a child's erector set. When the road reaches the beach, it makes a sharp turn north. You won't see the beach, for it is obscured by sand dunes. There are plenty of parking lots, although the first few are closed due to their proximity to the Space Center.

Surf-Fishing

If you park in the southernmost lot and walk over the dunes to the beach, you may find surf-casters along the shore. With their long poles they can hurl their bait more than a hundred yards to where the fish dwell along a drop-off. For bait they often use small shrimp called sand fleas that are gathered when they ride waves to shore during high tide. "I try to be nice to the pompano," one fish-erman told me. "I like to drop the shrimp almost into their mouths.

Surf fishing is popular at the Canaveral National Seashore.

It has to be easy, for they're lazy louts. The whiting and bluefish aren't so choosy."

Now that you're on Cape Canaveral you may be interested to learn that it is one of the oldest named locations in America. Although Ponce de León, exploring the coast in 1513, called this prominent point humping out into the Atlantic the Cape of Currents, Spanish mapmakers found a more descriptive name to be the Cape of Canes, or Canaveral, after the dense reed thickets that grew here.

Bare Bathing Belies Beautiful

Continuing along the road, the drive is pleasant, with rolling, Atlantic dunes on the right and the calm waters of the Mosquito Lagoon on the left.

The beach off the farthest parking lot is often used by bathers who feel that clothing of any sort is an unnecessary impediment to the fullest enjoyment of nature. But lower your expectations. This is not a parade of Miss Americas. Most bathers are middle-aged, and the sight is not always pretty.

An Actual Pristine Beach

Although the road ends here, the National Seashore continues until it meets another park road coming from New Smyrna Beach to the north. Between the two roads is a fourteen-mile stretch of sand and surf called Klondike Beach that is about as deserted as any in the civilized world. The word "pristine" is used in Florida to describe any sand that has only a few candy wrappers per square yard. So I won't use it here. But if it had meaning any longer, pristine is what Klondike would be.

Manatee Playground: the Haulover Canal

From Playalinda return via SR 402 to the road formerly known as SR 3 and drive north. In a few miles you'll come to the bridge over the Haulover Canal, so named for the original path over which prehistoric Indians hauled their boats between the Mosquito Lagoon and the Indian River. Pioneers used shovels to dig the first thin channel across the half-mile neck of land. The present broad canal was constructed as part of the Intracoastal Waterway in the 1950s. This pleased the dolphins, who love to frolic in this convenient freeway between the river and the lagoon. In the winter, manatees appreciate the canal for its warm water and lush sea grasses. To accommodate human onlookers, a viewing platform has been built on the north side of the canal.

The Vanquished Monarchs of Oak Hill

After Haulover the highway passes through uninhabited land that is part of a wildlife refuge. The now-nameless road you've been following expires when it leaves the refuge and meets US 1. Now, back on a highway that's somebody, you should continue north through the hamlet of Oak Hill. Once the land around here was ruled by proud oak trees, but they were helpless against the brigades of woodsmen who attacked them mercilessly to provide planks for the sailing ships of yore. Later, Oak Hill thrived as a fishing port on the Mosquito Lagoon. But, when Florida banned the use of commercial nets a decade ago, that enterprise sank. Today, the village is a sleepy relic of the past.

Like Oak Hill, US 1 is something of a relic. Once, it was famed as the Dixie Highway. In those days it was thronged with autos from frosty Yankeedom. Now these cars cut the balmy breezes on Interstate 95 a few miles west. But we backroaders won't weep for old Number One. The lack of cars, as well as franchise clutter, suits us just fine.

The Minorcans' Tragedy

In a few miles, upon reaching the town of Edgewater, watch for the stoplight at East Riverside Drive. By turning right here and traveling one block, you'll reach what is called North Indian River, but is actually a Mosquito Lagoon channel deepened to provide safe passage for boats on the Intracoastal Waterway. Riverside Drive bends north here to run along the river, providing a scenic entrance into New Smyrna Beach. Yet this area was anything but scenic to the 1,255 indentured men, women, and children who settled along here in 1768. Some were from Greece and some from Italy. But the vast majority were Spanish-speaking folk from the Mediterranean island of Minorca. Their indenture called for them to work for various periods of time on a plantation to be established at New Smyrna. At the end of their indenture they would receive enough land to enable them to become independent farmers.

The plantation was owned by a trio of wealthy British investors who had been awarded more than 156 square miles along the Florida coast by the king when he gained the territory from Spain in 1763. The partners had agreed to furnish the immigrants food, clothing, and shelter, which would be paid for by the plantation's exports of indigo, corn, and other products.

But the expenses were far more than the investors had surmised, and they did not meet their obligations. As a result, there was such a shortage of clothing that the settlers lived in rags. Their housing consisted of crude shanties scattered along the river for seven or eight miles. As for food, there was never enough. Even though the Indian River at their doorsteps was alive with fish and oysters, the cruel over-seers, who worked the settlers almost as slaves, insisted they labor solely in the fields and actually confiscated whatever they took from the river. Worse yet, the fields were mostly mosquito-infested marshes and the mosquitoes brought malaria. Sometimes fifteen men, women, and children died in a single day!

As you proceed along Riverside Drive, watch for Hamilton Road. Here an almost inconspicuous bridge crosses the South Canal, dug by the indentured workers, women as well as men, to try to drain the swamps to the west.

The Terrible Turnbulls

The Minorcans' plight did not bother Andrew Turnbull, who was one of the partners as well as the on-site manager of the plantation.

The stonework of what may have been an abandoned Spanish fort provided the foundation for the Turnbulls' mansion.

He lived the good life a few miles north in a mansion he constructed on the stone foundation of what probably had been an uncompleted Spanish fort. Turnbull was a Scottish doctor who had grown wealthy administering to aristocratic families in London. With Turnbull was his wife, Maria, and their seven children. Maria was the daughter of a wealthy Greek merchant. The colony was named after Smyrna, her hometown. She must have been quite a woman, for when Andrew returned temporarily to England to shore up support among influential politicians, she took over management of the plantation, which was boiling with misery and discontent.

For several years the hard-driven Minorcans produced enough for New Smyrna to show a profit. But sickness and malnutrition sapped both their strength and will to work. Finally, after nine arduous years, a delegation made the weary hike to St. Augustine seventy miles north to beg the governor to release them from their indenture. When he did so, the rest of the less than six hundred miserable and destitute survivors gratefully abandoned the hated plantation and trudged off to St. Augustine, where they began new lives. New Smyrna had been the largest colonization venture ever attempted by the British in North America, far larger than Jamestown in Virginia. But it was a horrendous failure that cost more than five hundred lives. Yet the Minorcans persisted, and today ten thousand descendants survive in and around St. Augustine.

As for Turnbull, he and his family sailed off to Charleston, South Carolina, where he resumed his medical practice, regained his prosperity, and lived happily until his death in 1792. We know of none of his descendants.

A Tyrant Lived Here

As you approach the center of town on Riverside Drive, watch for Riverfront Park, where the stone remains of Turnbull's wharf can be seen at low tide. At the north end of the park is another of Turnbull's canals, which, although it runs directly through the business section, is covered over by the town's main thoroughfare, which bears the name Canal Street. A block farther north is Old Fort Park, where you'll find the substantial stone foundation that once supported Turnbull's mansion. Within it lived the man who tyrannized the indentured families. "Well," he probably would have countered, "I was just trying to do right by my partners." You can't dispute that. It's just a matter of priorities.

New Smyrna Beach Today

With the demise of Turnbull's venture, New Smyrna virtually died. Its revival did not begin until the arrival of Henry Flagler's East Coast Railroad in 1892. Today the town is a thriving community of 21,000 persons. Many of the buildings along Canal Street have been renovated as part of the New Smyrna Main Street program.

I must inform you that many natives pronounce the town's name "SIGH myrna." Why? No one seems to know. "It just sounds better," a resident told me. Personally, I like it without the "sigh."

Since historical New Smyrna was oriented toward the water, you might want to get out on it. If so, across Riverside Drive from the Old Fort is the Fishing Cove Marina, where you can rent an eight-person pontoon boat for $200 for a full day or $150 for half a day. Call 386–428–7827 for rental hours. If you and your associates prefer deep sea fishing and have $500 to spare, you can secure a six-passenger charter boat fully equipped for four hours. (Call 386–428–6781 for more information.) But should your desires run to something not so grandiose, follow the road at the south end of the Cove's parking lot to Florida Coastal Cruise Lines where, for $15 ($12 for kids under twelve), you can take a small excursion boat for a two-hour, narrated cruise along the Indian River. The cruise line has no regular hours, but runs on a when-the-boat-gets-full-enough basis. Call 800–881–2628 for more information. While you're down on the waterfront, you can enjoy a fresh seafood meal at the Sea Harvest. It's served without frills and you'll sit at a wooden picnic table overlooking the harbor.

Over the River

Most of the action lies across the pair of high-rise causeways spanning the Indian River. The North Causeway is the more interesting, as well as the more convenient, since it begins at Old Fort Park. The original bridge was built in 1894. Constructed of wobbly palmetto logs, it gave access to the island community of Coronado Beach. The bridge had two short segments that had to be rotated to allow any ship larger than a row boat to enter the harbor. Doing the job was a burly bridge tender who lived in a former fisherman's lodge at the foot of the bridge. Over the years the bridge tender's house was enlarged and modernized, and today you'll find it still standing as the Riverview Hotel, which can be contacted at 800–945–7416. The Riverview offers comfortable rooms with private balconies. If you like peddling, bikes are complimentary and the hard-packed sandy beach three blocks east offers good riding. The Riverview also boasts a fine restaurant directly on the Indian River.

Coronado Beach

Coronado Beach was a proudly independent island community until 1946, when the need for fresh water necessitated it to become part of New Smyrna. With that, New Smyrna eagerly added "beach" to its name, a proven catchword for tourists.

Once on the island, the North Causeway becomes Flagler Avenue, old Coronado Beach's main drag. As you drive down it, you'll pass quaint little stores that reflect the humble community's glory years—such as they were. Continue on Flagler until it ends at the beach, where for $5 you can drive directly onto the sand. It's an unusual experience that will give you the opportunity to head north to where the island ends at the Ponce de Leon Inlet, connecting the Atlantic Ocean with the Indian River and the Intracoastal Waterway. The Inlet has tricky currents and shifting sandbars that have caused hundreds of boats to run aground over the years. Many have capsized and the occupants drowned.

Beach-goers can drive along the sand for many miles at New Smyrna.

To help control the currents, a pair of long jetties have been erected at the Inlet's mouth. These jetties create long, rolling waves that attract surfers. This environment also attracts herring and mullet, delicious treats for sharks.

Shark-surfing

The sharks regard surfers as bothersome intruders, for they are too bony for a good meal, and they stir up the water and obscure the good stuff. When the surf is rough, it's difficult for a shark to tell a kicking human leg from a darting bait fish. So what's a hardworking critter to do but bite and hope for the best.

To the surfers, it's the sharks who are the nuisances. Most experienced surfers don't fear them because the sharks are mostly small ones: three or four feet long. The surfers scoff that the "pup sharks" only leave small puncture wounds called "poodle bites." New Smyrna collects more such poodle bites than any place in the entire world. Even so, in an average year there are less than a dozen, and most require only a few stitches. That may be a little painful, but it's worth it just for the bragging rights. Surfers have been known to hold competitions in the midst of several dozen feeding sharks. Once, a surfer fell right onto a shark's back. He laughed as he climbed back onto his surfboard. Local shops reportedly sell T-shirts inscribed with cute sayings like "Bite Me, Baby, I'm a Bait Fish!"

Despite the joking, to swim where there may be sharks can be risky. You can't be sure when the "pups" will be joined by the "pops," such as the seven-foot bull shark that took off a boy's arm at Pensacola Beach in 2001. Nevertheless, the merriment goes on. So if you want to join New Smyrna's fun-with-sharks circus, you can rent a surfboard at one of the shops. Inlet Charley's, at 510 Flagler, charges $20 for the day. The best surfing time is when the tide is coming in. To get the tide times as well as wave height, the presence or absence of bait fish, and other pertinent information call Charley's special number: 286–427–5674.

Sand-cruising

Perhaps you feel more inclined toward recreation that doesn't include sharks. If so, drive south on the beach. Once away from Ponce de Leon Inlet, the sharks are gone, allowing New Smyrna to advertise this as "the World's Safest Bathing Beach." So why not park somewhere along the way and roll out a beach blanket? You can swim or slumber in the sun. But don't get too comfortable, for when high tide comes calling, virtually the entire beach goes for its own swim. This is a good time to watch the waves stroke the bluff from the park off the Twenty-Seventh Avenue ramp at the southern end of the beach-driving area.

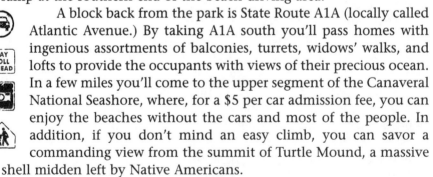

A block back from the park is State Route A1A (locally called Atlantic Avenue.) By taking A1A south you'll pass homes with ingenious assortments of balconies, turrets, widows' walks, and lofts to provide the occupants with views of their precious ocean. In a few miles you'll come to the upper segment of the Canaveral National Seashore, where, for a $5 per car admission fee, you can enjoy the beaches without the cars and most of the people. In addition, if you don't mind an easy climb, you can savor a commanding view from the summit of Turtle Mound, a massive shell midden left by Native Americans.

If instead you head north on Atlantic Avenue, you'll quickly come to a nice restaurant called Chase's overlooking the beach.

In good weather Chase's serves on an open-air deck facing the ocean.

Romantic Ruins: the Old Sugar Mill

Atlantic Avenue soon bends westward to cross the Indian

An eerie feeling surrounds New Smyrna's sugar mill ruins.

River on the South Causeway, continuing as SR 44 (Lytle Street). At this point the road closely parallels the ancient Kings Road that ran from Turnbull's wharf to St. Augustine. It followed an even earlier Spanish mission trail that the British transformed into a broad shell road. The land it traversed was good sugar-growing country that the British intended to populate with plantations like Turnbull's. After the Americans gained control of Florida in 1821, they utilized Kings Road to connect a string of sixteen of their own plantations. During the Second Seminole War in 1835, the Indians burned and destroyed most of these plantations. One of them was at New Smyrna. This ruin is now part of the Volusia County parks system. To reach it, watch for the brown directional sign at Old Mission Road about a mile after crossing US 1 on SR 44. Turn south on Old Mission and follow the signs.

Not many people visit the ruin, so it can be somewhat forbidding, what with the jungle surroundings. Many historians believe the walls were part of a holy Spanish mission. After the Americans took over, the holiness vanished as weary slaves carted freshly cut cane through the arched doorway and into the furnace room where clanging, steam-driven rollers crushed the juice from the stalks. The juice was routed to large cast-iron kettles, where fires boiled out the water. There was cussing and shouting and complaining, for everyone was hot and irritable.

Then came the Seminole attack. Amid the snap of arrows, the slaves and the overseers fled. Then the Seminoles put the mill to the torch. Soon all that was left were the charred stone walls. Today, there's an almost unearthly quiet to the place. But, perhaps if you try, you can hear the chant of the friars or the crackle of flames or the crash of massive oak roof beams falling to the floor.

Yet even with such a history, some couples find the mill ruin so irresistibly romantic that it is often used for weddings. "It's strange," a native told me. "Why get hitched at a haunted place like this? Ain't marriage scary enough without startin' out spooked?"

The Upper Atlantic Coast

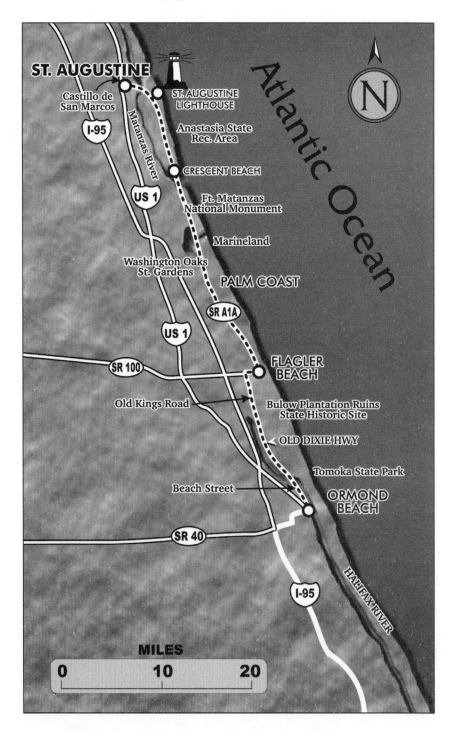

The Jungle and the Shore

New Smyrna Beach to St. Augustine • 52 Backroad Miles

The Song of the Road: Overview

This exploration begins in a subtropical forest on a road originally constructed more than two centuries ago to connect a series of sugar plantations strung out for fifty miles just inland from the coast. Although most of these plantations were demolished by the Seminoles, we'll visit one where the ruins still rise in eerie grandeur. Then we'll head east to Flagler Beach on the Atlantic for a little taste of old Florida. Turning north on A1A, we'll emerge in new Florida at Palm Coast. Here, you can rent a Carolina skiff and cruise down canals lined with yachts or motor past the dense vegetation of the Intracoastal Waterway.

Once on the road again, we'll stop at Washington Oaks State Gardens for a stroll among plants from around the world and along a beach of startlingly reddish sand. Birds in great numbers stop here during their spring and fall migrations. A short way up the highway is Marineland, long famous for its sea animal shows.

The road continues north, past dunes and through wetland swales. After crossing the Matanzas River, we'll take the launch to Fort Matanzas, to explore this abandoned outpost still keeping its lonely vigil over a bleak salt marsh. Then, we'll resume our journey north to Anastasia Island's lofty lighthouse, which we can climb for an impressive view of sea and sand.

Finally, we'll reach St. Augustine where we'll amble down pedestrians-only St. George Street, pausing, perhaps, to poke into the unique shops and restaurants. We'll also roam the massive Spanish fortress that reminds us St. Augustine is the oldest continually occupied city in the United States. As twilight gathers, we'll experience the haunting aspect of this ancient city during a ghost tour.

On the Road Again

From Interstate 95 take the Ormond Beach exit (SR 40) four miles east to Beach Street, which is just before the high-rise bridge over the Halifax River. Although our route lies on Beach Street, if you

27

want to see more of Ormond, drive over the bridge. Facing the river on your right is the Casements, former home of John D. Rockefeller, who was the world's richest man when he established his winter retirement residence here in 1918. Although the home is open to the public free of charge, it is far less imposing than you'd expect from someone of such wealth, for Rockefeller was probably one of the cheapest persons of his time. He was essentially a cold individual; his main associates were his large staff of servants. Rockefeller died here in 1937, a lonely old man of ninety-seven.

If you continue on SR 40 to the beach, you'll find yourself amidst luxurious condos and a jangle of glitzy tourist hotels.

However, our way lies along backroads. Let's not dwell on the jangle but, instead, head for the jungle. Turn north on Beach Street, which has nothing to do with a beach but runs along the Halifax River, spiked here and there with private piers and boat houses. There are old homes, too, for this residential section is designated as the Ormond Beach Historic District. Soon you'll pass a pair of weathered stone pillars that once announced to travelers coming from the North that they were entering Ormond.

The Lost Tribe: Tomoka State Park

The residential area ends abruptly as the road enters state land. Watch for Tomoka State Park where the admission fee is $3.25 per car. The park's entry road leads through a dense forest where limbs of large trees obscure the sunlight. Once, the powerful Timucuan tribe had a village here. These people lived on oysters they gathered along the Halifax River. The discarded oyster shells formed large mounds, some of which still remain. The Timucuans occupied most of northeast Florida and southeast Georgia and may have numbered 200,000. But, by the time Spain was forced to cede Florida to Great Britain in 1763, the tribe had virtually vanished.

After the British took over Florida, Richard Oswald, a wealthy West Indies planter and slave dealer, was awarded a large tract of land between the Halifax and Tomoka Rivers on the modern park grounds. Oswald's slaves converted the primeval forest and river marshes into fields for rice, sugar, and indigo. Oswald shipped these products down the Halifax River to the docks at New Smyrna, where ocean-going vessels transported them to Europe. Oswald never set foot on the humid, mosquito-ridden shore of Florida. He used rough overseers to run his plantation. Although the operation flourished, Oswald, with the rest of the British landlords

Seminole warriors once lurked in the green depths of the forest along Kings Road.

and their slaves, abandoned the area when the fortunes of war forced Great Britain to re-cede Florida to Spain in 1783.

For today's hikers, the park contains a nature trail that can be completed in fifteen minutes, although the trip may seem longer during the April-to-December mosquito season. If you have more time, you can rent a canoe for $5 per hour at the Tomoka River boat launch. Paddling up the Tomoka, you'll pass the wetlands where Oswald's slaves dug drainage canals, planted rice, and fought mosquitoes. The river's name commemorates the lost Timucuan tribe.

We know almost nothing about the Timucuans' heroes or the marvelous legends that were undoubtedly part of their folklore. Although they lived in Florida for hundreds, even thousands, of years, all that remains of their existence is the name of a stream, a few shell mounds, some sketches by French colonist Jacques Le Moyne, and a dugout canoe that, with a few other artifacts, is on display in the park museum. Otherwise all is silence.

The Old Dixie Highway

North from the state park the road crosses a pretty little bridge over the Tomoka River. The road is now called the Old Dixie Highway. When it was constructed in the late 1910s, it was surfaced with bricks and was sixteen feet wide—just wide enough to allow cars to scrape each other as they passed. During the 1920s it was alive with jalopies as Midwesterners hurried south expecting to make fortunes on Florida land. Along the way watch for the sign denoting the tomb of James Ormond, who mismanaged a large sugar plantation here and whose family gave its name to the town of Ormond Beach.

The Royal Roadway

Continuing on the tree-enclosed road, you'll soon come to a junction where Old Dixie heads due west. At this point, turn north on Old Kings Road, which faithfully follows the original British highway that ran between St. Augustine, the seat of government, and New Smyrna. This road, too, was sixteen feet wide, but instead of bricks it was composed of hard-packed shells and sand. For its time, it was an excellent highway—certainly the best in Florida. A few years after the Americans bought Florida from Spain in 1821, the U.S. military rebuilt this portion of Kings Road for use in anticipated conflict with the Seminoles. However, it was the Indians who put the road to use when they attacked and burned most of the dozen-and-a-half sugar plantations along its path.

The Genial Slave-Master of Bulow Plantation

One of the plantations the Seminoles destroyed belonged to John Bulow, a handsome, young bachelor. Although John's father, a wealthy cotton merchant, purchased the plantation in the early 1820s while John was a teenager, John spent those years in Paris. Between wine, women, and general debauchery he actually managed to pick up a decent education. When his father died, John was called on to take over the estate with its three hundred slaves. Though he was barely eighteen, he turned the plantation into one of Florida's most productive. Nonetheless, John still believed the purpose of wealth was to throw parties. The festivities he hosted were evidently wild affairs, for so much wine and ale was imbibed that he decorated his boat landing with the empty bottles. During quieter moods, he mused in his extensive library while admiring his fine furnishings and beautiful paintings. His reputation for lavish hospitality was such that John James Audubon stayed with Bulow before continuing down to the Keys. Audubon, impressed by the young man's warm manners, wrote of him as a friend.

The Seminoles, too, found Bulow to their liking and often brought him fresh meat. But when war broke out in 1835 and the local militia forced Bulow to let them use his buildings as a temporary base, the Indians' mood changed. Soon after the militia left, taking John and his slaves with them, the Seminoles set fire to everything.

John was devastated. All he had worked for was gone. He retreated to Paris, a broken man. Three months later, he died at the age of twenty-six.

Bitter Ruins

Watch for the sign directing you to the Bulow Plantation Ruins State Historic Site. The one-lane, sand-entry road is hugged by trees. After a half-mile it reaches Bulow Creek, where John's two-story mansion once stood. All that remains today are some of the foundation stones. From the landing beside his house, Bulow shipped his raw sugar and molasses down the creek and the Halifax River to the port at New Smyrna. He also had a large

The ruins of the Bulow sugar mill stand silent and lonely.

personal boat upon which he would take guests for carefree merry-making—his slaves were kept busy rowing and bottle-opening. If you'd care to paddle partway along Bulow's route, canoes can be rented at $3 an hour or $15 for the entire day.

Be sure to drive over to the sugar mill ruins. In places, you can see the soot marks of the fire that destroyed it. Plaques describe the operations that took place in the various rooms. You'll see the furnace room where steam hissed from the boiler and wood smoke roared up the tall chimney that still stands. The steam was piped to another room dominated by a large gear, which drove the noisy grinders that crushed the cane and extracted the juice. The juice, then, was channeled to evaporation kettles where steam boiled out the water, leaving thick syrup that was stored in barrels on the second floor. Over a period of time, molasses dripped out of the barrels into containers on the ground floor. What remained was raw, brown sugar. Sugar was such a rarity in Europe that it commanded an almost astronomical price.

The molasses had a saga of its own. It was shipped to New England where distillers turned it into rum. The rum was sent to Africa where it was exchanged for slaves. The slaves, in turn, were carried to New World plantations where they planted the sugar cane from which more molasses would be obtained. This molasses-for-rum-for-slaves was the nefarious Triangular Trade from whose ills we are still suffering.

Although the shacks in which his slaves spent their woeful existences were clustered barely two hundred yards west of Bulow's mansion, their misery did not concern him. He was happy to live off the fruits of their labor, and when misfortune came he paid the ultimate price.

A Seven Button Town: Flagler Beach

From Bulow's plantation continue north on Old Kings Road. Shortly, you'll reach SR 100, upon which you should turn east and pass through Flagler Beach. This ragtag community of five thousand persons grows more appealing as the years mellow its garish, hodgepodge buildings. At the end of SR 100 there's a wooden pier that has more than once been swept away by unruly waves. At last report, the structure stretched eight hundred feet into the Atlantic.

The pier is open from 6:30 a.m. until midnight. It's worth the $1 charge to walk out on it, especially during ruddy sunrises. If

The long pier at Flagler Beach is good for fishing or watching the ocean.

salt water brings out the sportsman in you, you can rent a fishing pole for $8.50 and pick up some bait for a little more. Incidentally, you don't need a fishing license. For those who'd rather eat what someone else has caught (and cleaned), there is a restaurant on the pier serving breakfast, lunch, and dinner.

If you'd prefer to keep your feet on solid land, you can grab sandwiches and drinks at one of the slap-dab establishments along Highway A1A. There are no dunes or beach plants to mar your view of the ocean, for the road was built long before environmentalists could express their horror of such a lack of beach protection. In windy weather, beach sand drifts across the pavement and, during storms, waves sometimes cover the road entirely. It's old Florida—love it or leave it.

Should you decide to linger longer, you can't do better than the vintage Topaz Inn a dozen blocks south of the pier. Accommodations begin at $55 and top out at $145. Charles Lindbergh once enjoyed the place, and chances are you will too. The Topaz also has a good restaurant with an ocean view. For information or reservations call 800–555–4735.

Before we leave Flagler Beach, I must say I didn't mean to create the impression that the town is not on the cutting edge. City hall even has a phone system with seven options. Now that's progress.

The Monster of Flagler County

Leaving Flagler Beach, A1A is routed close to the ocean. Not surprisingly, there has been some erosion of the roadbed— enough, in fact, to cause county officials to declare a state of emergency a few years back. Just north of Flagler Beach you'll come to Beverly Beach, where houses obscure the view of the ocean. Soon A1A curves away from the water to avoid a five-mile-long jumble of dunes that, in 1927, would have made road-building almost impossibly difficult and expensive. But what was true when A1A was constructed is no longer the case. Today, this half-mile-wide strip of land is being converted into three exclusive developments.

This area is part of a gigantic group of parcels assembled by International Telephone and Telegraph Company (ITT) around 1970. The core of these parcels is the town of Palm Coast.

Ever heard of Palm Coast? You have if you're a resident of Flagler County, where many residents regard this town as a voracious monster that is gobbling up the land and taking over the county. This is not far-fetched, for the population of Palm Coast now stands at almost 40,000, which accounts for more than 70% of the entire county! It's predicted that in a few years the total will top out at 80,000. Yet even this is quite a come-down from ITT's original plans, which aimed at an ultimate population of 750,000! Such a megalopolis would have been far larger than any planned community ever attempted in the entire U.S.A.

The main part of Palm Coast was to be carved out of the swampy area behind the dunes. Canals were dug and the muck piled up to form dry land. The vegetation was destroyed with such disregard for the environment that Florida's Attorney General complained that Palm Coast "had all the makings of the most frightening ecological nightmare we have ever faced in our state." Then, when environmentalists howled, the state's Pollution Control Board began an investigation. Soon the Federal Trade Commission went after ITT for unscrupulous sales practices. Under pressure, ITT considerably downsized its plans. So, although what we see today is huge for the area, it's but a shadow of the monster that might have been. ITT sold out to private concerns in 1996.

The City of Palm Coast

For a glimpse of the monster turn off A1A and on to Hammock Dunes Parkway, which will lead you across the Intracoastal

Waterway by way of a bridge with a $1 toll. At this point Hammock Dunes becomes Palm Coast Parkway, going one way. By heading west, you'll find yourself in modern suburbia with shopping centers and other amenities. In a couple of miles you'll reach Kings Road—yes, the very same one over which slave-driven sugar wagons once creaked. Immediately beyond this is Interstate 95. Palm Coast continues west of the highway, but there's no need to see more of the same.

To return to A1A you'll have to take Palm Coast Parkway East, which is a block left. But an alternative is to turn left at Club House Drive. This runs between a golf course on one side and canal homes on the other and leads to the Palm Coast Golf Resort. The resort features a 154-room hotel, five championship golf courses, and an 80-slip marina. Flagler's Restaurant overlooks the marina. Here you can pick up sandwiches for reasonable prices as well as full-course meals.

Beside the restaurant and along the Intracoastal Waterway is a large park. You'll probably see yachts cruise past—some of them from the resort's marina. There seems to be competition among boat owners. I saw an auto bumper sticker reading: "Life's too short to

This rental skiff enables visitors to explore the Intracoastal Waterway, as well as the many canals of Palm Coast.

own an ugly boat." Others might counter that life's too short to be saddled with a boat at all. If you are one of these people, you can enjoy a half-day cruise on the same forty miles of waterway and canals as the big guys by renting a four-seat skiff at the marina office for a mere $79.

Leave the resort via Palm Harbor Drive, which will get you to Hammock Dunes Parkway considerably quicker than Club House Drive.

The Crème de la Crème

As you drive over the bridge, leaving another $1 toll to help the rich pay for the bridge's upkeep, watch for the gate to the Hammock Dunes estates. Beyond the gate lie more than two thousand acres of oceanfront land complete with four golf courses, prestigious homes, and luxury condos. Sales brochures show a lush green paradise, but you won't see it. The gate denies access to all but homeowners and those who are thinking of buying, and a dense oak hammock prevents gaining much of a view from the road.

By continuing north on Hammock Dunes Parkway you'll pass through more of the land that was avoided by the A1A builders. The despised dunes have now become golf courses and sites for upscale homes. Although gates prevent public access, you can get a closer view by turning east on Sixteenth Road. On your right is a golf course and on the left, the massive twelve-story Hammock Beach Club, where condo prices begin at $300,000 and soar from there.

Now take Sixteenth Road back past Hammock Dunes Parkway to A1A. As you drive north, trees and roadside commercial buildings border the road. You'd never know what spectacular developments are changing the once-scorned land out of sight to the east.

Rich Man at the Roadside: Washington Oaks State Gardens

Just up the road from Palm Coast is Washington Oaks State Gardens. The main portion of the park is west of A1A. Admission is $3.25 per car. The entry road passes beneath a canopy of tall hickories, magnolias, and live oaks and will take you to the interpretive center on the banks of the Matanzas River. The interpretive center features exhibits relating to the park's natural history. And nature is the attraction here. Several self-guiding trails lead through the lush hammock and along the river marsh, which is usually frequented by many waterfowl. There is also a formal garden, with reflecting pools and plants from around the world.

This area once belonged to George Washington—no, not that one, but his relative. The most recent private owners, however, were Owen and Louise Young. Owen was the wealthy and talented chairman of General Electric. In his spare time, he not only founded RCA but served as a consultant to several presidents, from Wilson to Truman. Once, he was even considered as a candidate for president himself.

Famous as he was, Young never forgot his rural upbringing. In 1939, he retired from GE to his Holstein ranch in New Jersey. There, the tall, lanky man told a colleague that "it's more fun running a cow farm than it is running a corporation." A few years later, he bought the estate at Washington Oaks and promptly planted a citrus orchard. Not only that, but he picked the fruit himself, and then, in his work clothes, hawked it at a little stand he opened along A1A. Meanwhile, Louise, no longer saddled by high-society soirees, grubbed about in her formal garden.

Owen died in 1962 at the age of 87, and, two years later, Louise donated the estate to the State of Florida. The donation included her beloved formal garden, Owen's orchard, and the home where Owen and she spent much of their time during two golden decades. Their home is now the interpretive center.

The Peach Beach

The park's eastern portion runs along the Atlantic. The beach, which you can visit for $2 if you bypass the gardens, is a world unto itself. The entry road passes through a coastal scrub where none of the plants are tall, for the soil is too sandy to hold water or nutrients. The trees are mostly yaupon holly, myrtle oak, and sand live oak. Saw palmettos clump close to the ground. This area is also a stop on the Great Florida Birding Trail. Watch for gannets, sea ducks, loons, and grebes just offshore.

Even though there's no Great Boulder Trail, the rocks are worth some attention. Denoted as the Anastasia Formation, they are composed of coquina, which is a mixture of seashells and sand cemented together by lime. Although coquina underlies the barrier islands along most of Florida's east coast, to find it on the beach surface is rare. Because the ocean tides carved the rocks into a myriad of graceful grooves intermingled with miniature caverns and leaping bridges, you can see the distinct layers that were formed as the tiny shells accumulated over the centuries. The Anastasia Formation slants

These picturesque coquina rocks at Washington Oaks State Park are unusual for a Florida beach.

gently toward the land, which probably trapped the sand that formed the dunes at Palm Coast.

And there's more for you rock and dirt watchers. You'll certainly be struck by the color of the sand, which is a lush peach shade. This is caused by iron oxide embedded between the overlying coquina and the original beach. The wave action that eroded the coquina also released the red iron oxide. This beautiful peach beach extends only five or six miles along the coast. So from where did the iron oxide come? It may have been washed out of the distant Appalachian Mountains and carried all the way to Florida by meandering streams. Who says simple soil tells no tales?

The peach beach is pretty, but has its downside. The rocks that are so visually appealing are treacherous for swimmers. As with so many things, beauty is in the eye of the beholder.

A Rocky Voyage: Marineland

Just beyond Washington Oaks is Marineland, the largest, most popular attraction in all of Florida—at least for about thirty years after it was built in 1938. On opening day more than twenty thousand enthusiastic people jammed A1A to see the world's first oceanarium where sea animals cavorted in a huge tank with

The crowds have left Marineland, but revitalization is planned.

portals for underwater viewing and dolphins leaped high in the air for fish held by trainers. The park's popularity continued for three more decades. "As a kid I'd look forward to my Marineland visit more than Christmas morning itself," recalled a long-time patron.

In those days, Marineland was a place for celebrities. Ernest Hemingway toasted more than a few drinks at the bar, as did his drinking buddy, Marjorie Kinnan Rawlings, well-known author of *The Yearling*, who lived just up the road. Movie-makers loved Marineland, as it was the world's first underwater film studio. Once, Tarzan yowled from the waves and the Creature from the Black Lagoon thrashed in the depths.

But Tarzan and the Creature departed. So did the kids, who by the mid-1970s preferred Orlando's glitzy Sea World to down-home Marineland. As revenues fell, the park became old and tired. By the 1990s, the paint was peeling and the metalwork rusting. There was not enough money to advertise. The park even closed its doors and was deemed lost at sea. But volunteers have taken the place of most payroll employees, and the park gallantly sails on.

Today, Marineland focuses on eco-tourism and human-dolphin interaction. It's open every day except Tuesday between 9:30 A.M. and 4:30 P.M. For the admission fee, $14 for adults and $9 for kids, you get to watch trainers demonstrating the dolphins' intelligence and agility. There are also shows by sea lions and African penguins. In all cases the audience is encouraged to ask questions. For light meals there is the Dolphin Café.

The Bloody Bay: Matanzas

North from Marineland, the land squeezes between the sluggish Matanzas River on the left and, on the right, a wetland that ends at a dune ridge where scattered houses stand on stilts to protect them from Atlantic over-washes.

Soon A1A crosses the Matanzas Inlet on a long, low bridge leading to Anastasia Island. The area's distinctive, ruddy sand remains only as splotches, which, according to one legend, were formed by the blood of several hundred men massacred here in 1565. Here's the story.

When the Spanish first founded St. Augustine, they were not alone. Thirty miles north, the French had built Fort Caroline on the St. Johns River. The Spaniards were Catholic and the French were Huguenot Protestants; each was determined to eliminate the other.

The French, acting first, sailed down the coast with six hundred soldiers and sailors. But, while they waited for high tide before entering St. Augustine's harbor, a storm drove them south. The Spanish commander, Pedro Menéndez de Avilés, a fierce and daring warrior, believed he would have time to march against the understaffed Fort Caroline before the French fleet could reassemble. So he and four hundred soldiers made the arduous trek through swamps and hammocks. The fort was taken by surprise and every Frenchman within sword's reach was killed. Thereupon Menéndez hurried back to St. Augustine, where the skeleton garrison greeted him with the greatest relief. Then they nervously awaited the return of the French fleet.

But the fleet had been dispersed and wrecked by the monstrous waves. The survivors staggered ashore between Ormond Beach and Palm Coast without food, water, or weapons. Their only hope was to make it back to Fort Caroline, which they didn't know was now in Spanish hands. However, when they came to the wide Matanzas Inlet, they had no way to cross. At that moment, Menéndez arrived. He agreed to ferry the Frenchmen over ten at a time. But, when each group reached the other side, they were mercilessly killed. From that day forward the river was known as the Matanzas or "the Place of Slaughter."

Hell on the Matanzas

You'll be glad to know that people are no longer murdered at  the Place of Slaughter. As a matter of fact, it's so downright peaceful that it's now a national park. The highlight of a visit is the forty-five-minute motor launch trip across the river to old Fort Matanzas. The boat ride is free (as is admission to the park) and the boat leaves each hour between 9:30 A.M. and 4:30 P.M., seven days a week. To confirm launch times, call 904–471–0116.

Fort Matanzas is not large. It consists only of a rectangular tower, a gun deck, and a cylindrical sentry box. It had only a ten-man garrison, drawn from reluctant Spanish troops in St. Augustine. Although the gun deck supported just five cannons, one of them could hurl an eighteen-pound cannonball for two miles, thus effectively closing the Matanzas River to invaders who wished to attack St. Augustine from the side door. Oddly, the cannons were only fired once in anger, but their very presence deterred foreign invaders.

Because the fort was never attacked, duty here was extremely boring. There was nothing around except the languid river and miles upon miles of desolate mosquito marshes. Day after weary day, year after weary year soldiers lounged atop the walls peering across the

In the desolate marshes somewhere beyond grim Fort Matanzas, Spanish soldiers massacred several hundred French prisoners.

dismal water as they watched for an enemy that never came.

The heat was stifling and the mosquitoes almost overwhelming. The soldiers' food was often rotten. Their water, gathered from rain collected in a cistern inside the fort, was often bitter with algae and crowded with insect larvae. Yet they were forced to endure thirty long days in this miserable outpost before being relieved by a new detail of unhappy men. Their great relief in returning to St. Augustine was tempered only by the realization that, when their cycle of duty came once more, they would be back at Hell on the Matanzas.

 The park runs across A1A to the Atlantic, where a road leads down to the sand. Beach driving is permitted, but, fair warning, the sand is soft and sometimes cars get stuck.

The Talented Lady of Crescent Beach

A1A continues north on Anastasia Island, a sandy platform created by wind and waves at the close of the Ice Age. The Matanzas River parallels the road on the left, and on the right are sand dunes. After four miles you'll reach the village of Crescent Beach. At 6600 Broward Street (A1A) is the rambling home of Marjorie Kinnan Rawlings, which she purchased in 1939 with the earnings from her Pulitzer Prize-winning book, *The Yearling*. Marjorie loved to look out at the ocean, with its azure depths and tempestuous moods, but her thoughts often drifted back to her former residence, a little inland cottage. And so she sat on her salt-scented veranda and wrote a nostalgic account of her experiences in what became another Florida classic: *Cross Creek*.

Rawlings died of a heart attack here in 1953. The home continues to be privately owned and not open to the public.

Illuminating the Past: the St. Augustine Lighthouse

 At Crescent Beach this area becomes progressively more populated. A mile and a half after you pass Highway 312, watch for the sign to Anastasia State Park. One of the old Spanish quarries used to secure coquina for the forts is beside the entry road. Fortunately, it is just before the booth where a $3.25 per car beach fee is charged. Anastasia is one of the more popular parks, with swimming, surfing, and fishing. The sand is soft, having just been dredged from the inlet to St. Augustine's harbor.

Back on A1A you'll notice the black-and-white-striped cylinder of the St. Augustine Lighthouse looming ahead. Watch for the too-

You're welcome to climb to the top of this lighthouse in St. Augustine. There are only 219 steps.

small sign on the right directing you down Red Cox Drive. The light-house is only a few blocks away and well worth a visit.

It was built in 1875, when the preceding Spanish structure finally gave in to years of sea lashing. At the time that the keeper's house was added, this was an outpost amid dunes and marsh. But life out here didn't remain lonely because soon a housing development went up. Then everyone enjoyed oyster roasts on the beach and social gather-ings highlighted by clam chowder and turtle stew.

But there was the tedium too. The keeper maintained the beacon, which entailed ascending the tall tower each morning and drawing the curtains to prevent the sun from injuring the light's lens. Then, in the evening, he climbed the endless steps once more, this time carrying two gallons of kerosene for the night's operation. He also rewound the heavy spring that made the lens revolve every nine minutes.

Perhaps most tedious was the necessity of watching the kerosene lamp all night to be sure it did not go out. The beacon was an absolutely vital aid for ship captains navigating through the perilous, ever-changing sandbars called the Crazy Banks. Even with the aid of the lighthouse, nearly three hundred ships left their rotting remains in this malicious channel.

The lighthouse continues to guide ships today, although electricity has eliminated the need for an on-site attendant. The keeper's house, rebuilt after a fire, is now a nautical museum. The tower is open seven days a week between 9:00 A.M. and 6:00 P.M. to anyone who wishes to pay an admission fee ($6.50 for adults and $4 for kids) for the privilege of trudging up the 219 steps to the observation balcony. Plenty of people do, for the panorama of ocean, beaches, and the city of St. Augustine across Matanzas Bay is something to behold.

A restaurant on the grounds serves breakfast, lunch, and dinner seven days a week, but if you want something special—with a grand water vista thrown in—go to the nearby Conch House at 57 Comares Avenue. It is open from 8:00 A.M. until 9:00 P.M. (Call 800–940–6256 for more information.) Although it's a modern facility, the restaurant conveys the feeling of the 1870s, when a popular bayfront resort here catered to the wet and wild crowd.

After leaving the lighthouse, spend a few moments driving around the neighborhood. You'll find a delightful assortment of old homes, reminders of long ago when this was an isolated little community without telephones or—horrors—even e-mail!

Now, continue on A1A, which soon reaches the famous Bridge of Lions over the Matanzas River. Usually there are flags flying, and, from the arch, you get a grand view of the heart of old St. Augustine.

Fortress City: St. Augustine

St. Augustine, admittedly, is not a backroads settlement. But, since this tour segment ends here, it can hardly be ignored. Besides, St. Augustine is a tremendously interesting place. Founded by the Spanish in 1565, more than four decades before Jamestown, it is the oldest continually inhabited town in the United States. Thus, it holds a special import to Americans.

Despite its great popularity with tourists, St. Augustine is a small town of only twelve thousand inhabitants. Furthermore, St. Augustine

*The tough walls of the ancient Spanish fort at St. Augustine
defied many cannonballs.*

has never been large. Even when it was the capital of an extensive
Spanish empire that reached to the Mississippi River, St. Augustine was
a minor settlement with virtually no important exports. A major function of the town was to be a bulwark against the English to the north.
The English were so serious a threat that the Spanish eventually built
the imposing fortification called Castillo de San Marcos.

The fort, now a national monument, is beside highway A1A,
three blocks north of the Bridge of Lions. In many ways the fort
is most impressive from the exterior, which the public can
examine at no charge. The massive walls took twenty-three years to
build and were completed in 1695, just in time for the first of three
British sieges—all of which the fort withstood. Once the fort was
surrounded by a seawater moat, but the east moat has been filled in.
Now you can stroll right up to the base of the walls, which will tower
more than twenty feet above you. So skillfully was the fort planned
that wherever you stand you're exposed to the fire of defenders. So
don't act with hostility.

The walls are composed of coquina obtained from quarries on
Anastasia Island. Coquina, as was mentioned earlier, is essentially a
mixture of seashells and sand cemented together by lime. It is soft
when quarried, but hardens when exposed to the air. Coquina would
seem to be a frail substance unable to withstand the iron cannonballs

that were hurled against it during the British attacks, but in reality it simply bent before the shot. The cannonballs either bounced off or became embedded in the walls, thereby adding to their strength.

 The fort's interior is open 8:45 A.M. to 4:45 P.M. seven days a week. Admission is $4 for adults, and those persons under seventeen are free. Once inside you can roam the parade ground and visit the vaults. Troops were quartered in some vaults. Others were filled with supplies or gunpowder. You'll also want to ascend the steps to the top of the walls, where the view of the harbor is magnificent. Before you is Matanzas Bay, defined by Vilano Beach on the northeast and on the southeast by Anastasia Island, with its lighthouse as a faint smudge on the horizon. Between them is the inlet connected to the Atlantic Ocean.

Ancient Byway: St. George Street

 The fort allows only two hours for parking, so, when your time is up, move your car a block up A1A to the city lot beside the visitors center. Parking is $3, and for this fee you can come and go for two days. After picking up maps and leaflets at the visitors center, walk through the city gate onto St. George Street, the heart of old St. Augustine. Restricted to pedestrians, it is lined by old buildings, many with overhanging Spanish balconies brightened in the winter by bougainvillea in flower.

 Harriet Beecher Stowe walking down this same street around 1870, wrote, "Here you see the shovel-hats and black gowns of priests; . . . [and the] gliding figures of nuns; and in the narrow, crooked streets meet dark-browed people with great Spanish eyes and coal-black hair." The atmosphere too reflected "the indolent, dreamy stillness that characterized life in Old Spain." Today, this dreamy stillness is broken by hordes of tourists shopping in the unusual specialty stores or enjoying food in the small cafés. Nonetheless, there is still a certain indefinable atmosphere about the street that lets you imagine, perhaps only briefly, life in a different era.

After four pleasant blocks, St. George Street reaches the Cathedral of St. Augustine, distinguished by its dramatic bell tower. The parish dates back to 1565, but the current building was begun in 1793 and the interior was largely reconstructed after a fire a hundred years later. The bell tower was added at that time. Within the cathedral are several historical murals, one of which depicts the arrival of Minorcans by ox cart after the horrible experience at New Smyrna that you'll remember from the first chapter. The church is open to the public, with tours given at 1:00 P.M. and 3:00 P.M.

Flagler's Follies .

Now turn west on Cathedral Place and proceed one block to the garish structure that was the Ponce de Leon Hotel when it was constructed in 1888. At that time it was the showplace of all Florida, as well as the talk of America. The builder was business tycoon Henry Flagler, who spared no expense. He hired Louis Tiffany as his interior decorator; some of his distinctive stained glass work is still in use. The hotel awed its guests, for not only did it have that wonderful thing called electricity, but some of the rooms even had private toilets!

But despite the hoopla, the hotel was a mistake, for Mr. Flagler forgot the winter cold snaps that made St. Augustine unsuitable for pink-skinned Northerners. Nonetheless, the hotel's problems did not bother Flagler, for he was rolling in wealth from the fortune he and John D. Rockefeller had made with the Standard Oil trust. Flagler simply moved his operations 240 miles south, where he constructed new hotels in sunny Palm Beach. The once-grand Ponce de Leon was virtually abandoned to reemerge many desolate years later as Flagler College. Unfortunately, students take precedent over gawkers, and tours are given only when classes are not in session.

Across King Street was another Flagler hotel, the Alcazar. Although it was intended for slightly less affluent guests, it was, in its own way, just as spectacular as the Ponce de Leon. Today, the front portion is city hall and the southern portion is a museum displaying Otto Lightner's multitudinous Victorian-American collection. It is open daily between 9:00 A.M. and 5:00 P.M. Admission is $6 for adults and $2 for ages twelve through seventeen.

Resurrected Beauty: the Casa Monica Hotel

Immediately east of the Lightner Museum is the Casa Monica, yet another Flagler hotel. Closed during the depression of the 1930s, it reopened thirty-two years later as the St. Johns County Courthouse. Today, it has been exquisitely reconverted into a hotel. Rooms start at around $170 and top out at more than $400 a night for a suite in one of the towers. Even if you're not staying at the Casa Monica, it's worth meandering through the lobby, past the fountain, the Moorish columns, the hand-painted Spanish tiles, the colorful wooden beams, and the plush Cobalt Lounge, which hotel literature

The Casa Monica Hotel is once again one of St. Augustine's showplaces.

assures us is "an incredible culinary experience." The second floor opens onto a "magnificent" landscaped courtyard with an outdoor, heated swimming pool. For reservations call 1–888-GRAND-123.

The Heart of Old St. Augustine: the Plaza

A half block east on King Street, at the corner of St. George, is the Government House, reconstructed to appear as it did when the British ruled St. Augustine, as well as all Florida, between 1763 and 1783. Now, it houses an information center as well as a museum featuring artifacts from the city's past. It is open daily between 9:00 A.M. and 6:00 P.M. Admission is $3.50 for adults and $1.50 for kids ages six through eighteen.

Across St. George Street from the Government House and the cathedral is the Plaza de la Constitution, a park occupying two city blocks. In 1776, during the British era, effigies of John Hancock and Samuel Adams were torched here—to the acclaim of cheering loyalists. But the cheering vanished after the British lost the Revolutionary War.

At the eastern end of the plaza is the market where produce was sold and slaves were auctioned. Ralph Waldo Emerson attended a

Bible meeting nearby in 1827 during one such auction. "One ear . . . heard the glad tidings of great joy whilst the other was regaled with 'Going, gentlemen, going'!" he wrote. He was horrified at the hypocrisy of the church people. "Almost without moving from one's seat we could aid in sending the scriptures into Africa or bid for four children, without the mother, kidnapped from the same place."

The First Union Bank faces the plaza on the north. The building was completed just in time for the original bank to fall victim to the devastating depression of 1929. Today, the lobby has been skillfully restored to the awesome dignity that assured depositors in the roaring 1920s that their money was completely safe.

Along the Waterfront

Immediately beyond the market is the Matanzas River, where the city docks once were. Today, the docks have been replaced by the Bridge of Lions. The name comes from the pair of large marble statues at the bridge entrance. Despite being on the National Register of Historic Places, the bridge is highly controversial, and there has been serious talk about replacing it with a high span that does not hinder the passage of larger ships. Most citizens, however, love the obsolete structure and say it blends in well with the creaky appeal of old St. Augustine. If you have time, walk up the bridge and enjoy the unhurried view of St. Augustine that you missed when you came in by car.

From the bridge, head north on the walkway along the seawall. During the Spanish and British eras this was a beach over which unkindly storms tossed waves into the town. After the Americans took over a seawall was built, and it quickly became a favorite promenade for courting couples.

If you've become intrigued with the town, stay a while. I've barely blown a little dust off. Poke around on foot or via the cute little trolley trains that leave from 170 San Marco Avenue (A1A) every twenty minutes and cost $12 for adults and $5 for children ages six through twelve. Or take the hour-and-a-quarter bay cruise on the Victory III, which leaves from the Municipal Marina just south of the Bridge of Lions daily at 11:00 A.M., and 1:00 P.M., 2:45 P.M., 4:30 P.M., and (except in the winter) 6:15 P.M. Reservations are not required.

When night falls, you'll find the old city taking on a different aspect. Some believe an eerie spell descends on St. Augustine at this time, as the departed spirits of more than four hundred years return. Photos have even revealed strange, unearthly lights. Thus, it's not surprising that people gather at the north end of St. George Street at 8:00 P.M. for Ghost Tours. For $8 you will be taken down darkened streets and past old cemeteries, pausing to hear tales of strange happenings and spooky experiences. The tour guides insist that all their stories are taken from firsthand reports. You can make reservations by calling 904–826–4218.

The Upper Atlantic Coast

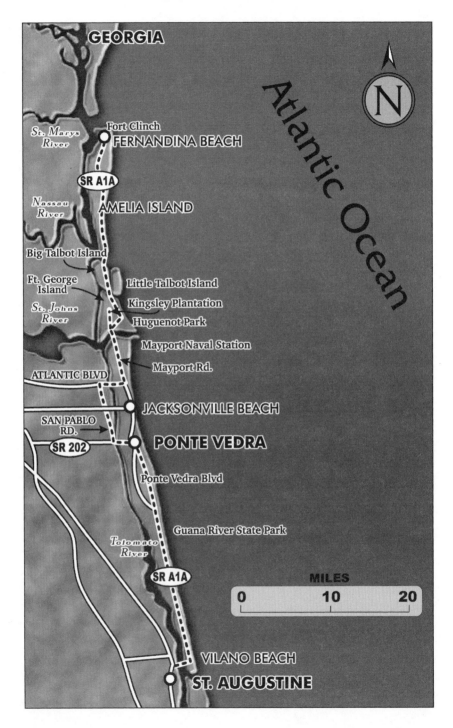

The Sandy World
St. Augustine to Fernandina Beach • 62 Backroad Miles

The Song of the Road: Overview

From St. Augustine, with its vivid Spanish mementos, we'll head north along the Atlantic coast for sixty-two sandy miles to Fernandina Beach. We'll pass Vilano Beach before stopping at Guana River State Park, named after a Spanish mission that once ministered to Timucuan worshipers in this vicinity. Boardwalks at Guana ascend some of Florida's loftiest dunes and lead to fine swimming beaches along the Atlantic. The modern world reemerges at the sparkling town of Ponte Vedra, the location of several upscale resorts.

Continuing northward, we'll reach the St. Johns River, where a car-ferry will take us to Ft. George Island. Here, we'll drive over an unpaved road that meanders beside a vast salt marsh and will take us to the Kingsley Plantation. The shells of slave cabins recall a brutal era dominated by Zephaniah Kingsley, a most unusual man, and his black wife, the mysterious Anna Jai.

Close to Ft. George Island is a narrow dune-spit where French Huguenots held the New World's first Protestant worship service. As we drive down a sand road to Huguenot Park's little-frequented Atlantic beach, armed helicopters from the powerful Mayport Naval Station across the river may rumble overhead.

Up A1A from Huguenot Park are the Talbot Islands. Along with beaches and some of the nation's best bird-watching, this area offers the opportunity to canoe through the wending island channels.

Next, we'll pass over the Nassau River to Amelia Island, which is well known for allowing horseback riding on the beach. On the island's northern tip is old Fort Clinch, whose cannons look out over the Cumberland Sound. This exploration ends at Fernandina Beach, a vintage town with Victorian charm and all the cruising, fishing, and historical rambling opportunities anyone could desire.

On the Road Again

Heading north from downtown St. Augustine on A1A, you'll be following the route of Kings Road, constructed by the British.

From the south, it began at New Smyrna, went through St. Augustine, crossed the St. Johns River at Cow Ford (now called Jacksonville), and ended in Savannah, which was, at the time of the road's construction, the capital of Georgia.

Leaving St. Augustine

Just beyond St. Augustine's old fort, which we visited in the previous chapter, A1A passes a huge stainless steel cross that marks the site of the Mission of Nombre de Dios. This was the focal point of a Franciscan religious system that, at its height in the late 1600s, encompassed thirty or more missions that extended across upper Florida, from St. Augustine to Pensacola. The missions were connected by a four-hundred-mile-long trail that we'll follow in several succeeding chapters. Although the mission is long gone, the Shrine of Nuestra Señora de la Leche provides a quiet, vine-covered retreat for people wishing to honor the devoted Franciscans who set out from here on a trail that led to danger, hardship, and, sometimes, death. The shrine is open daily between 9:00 A.M. and 5:00 P.M. Admission is free, but donations are accepted. A small museum and gift shop are nearby.

A few blocks beyond the mission is the so-called Fountain of Youth—the very fountain sought by Ponce de Léon when he landed somewhere around here in 1513, or so we are told. You can imbibe some of the magical water if you want, but, after the drink is consumed, I predict you'll only be a few minutes older, not many years younger.

A short distance beyond the fountain, A1A makes a sharp turn as it leaves Kings Road to ascend the lofty Vilano Beach Bridge. From the bridge there is a spacious view of St. Augustine on one side and, on the other, a view of the Intracoastal Waterway and the vast Tolomato marshes. If you'd care to linger, there is a walkway along the north side of the bridge.

Village of Villains

Now you're on a long barrier island that extends up the coast for thirty miles to the mouth of the St. Johns River. The word *villano*— from which Vilano got its name—has such a nice ring that it seems unfair that it's Spanish for villain. We can only guess what despicable characters once inhabited this beautiful area. Locals assure me the villains have all gone back up north.

A1A makes an abrupt turn near the Hampton Inn. (For reservations or information call 866–4VILANO.) The public beach—with a fishing pier, eateries, and charter fishing boats—is immediately east of the inn. But don't expect Miami Beach; this is a village of just 2,600. However, more people are coming: the Hampton Inn is a harbinger. A few miles north you'll pass the Reef Restaurant, which has a pleasant ocean view. Then there is Cap's-on-the-Water, a casual restaurant where you can enjoy lunch or dinner on a deck overlooking the Intracoastal Waterway. Beyond Cap's is a sprawling seashore development called the Serenata Beach Club.

You can slow down for a look at Serenata, but only members are allowed to enter. An exception is made for patrons of the Casa Monica Hotel in St. Augustine. If you are staying there, you can use the pool, the ocean-front dining room, and the other facilities that Serenata offers.

As beautiful as it is, Serenata illustrates what is happening to this portion of A1A as the natural vegetation is replaced by a wall of condos and private homes. A traveler in the 1930s wrote of the "high rounded sand dunes covered with palmettos, scrub oaks, and pines. . . . In the summer the road shoulders are carpeted with yellow partridge peas and pink horsemint, through which gilia thrusts its vivid scarlet leaves." Thankfully, the residential barricade temporarily ends when A1A enters land protected by the Guana River State Park.

Guana River State Park

The Guana River was impounded by a dam to form a long, narrow lake, and this makes up the main area of the park. Evidently, there once were trees here, for guana is Spanish for palm. One of the early Spanish missions was located on the Tolomato River, which borders the park on the west. The friars must have had fierce devotion; they braved summers in this torrid marsh where mosquitoes bred in numbers that would have dismayed even Job. But for all their ardor, nothing remains of the mission, not even the knowledge of its exact location.

Fishing is allowed, from the dam as well as from the shores of the lake and the river. There are also nine miles of trails and dirt roads leading through coastal scrub, salt marshes, and maritime hardwood hammocks. Admittedly, these are not the most inspiring of environments. Nonetheless, almost two hundred

Fishing and swimming are enjoyed at Guana River State Park. This view is from the top of the dam that formed Guana Lake. A boardwalk leads over the dunes in the background to the Atlantic beaches.

The beaches along the northern portions of State Road A1A are almost deserted.

species of birds vacation here during various parts of the year. After a vigorous hike, you can swim in the unruffled waters of Guana Lake, or, better yet, cross A1A and take the boardwalk over the dunes for a dip in the thrashing Atlantic surf.

From Guana's main entrance, A1A continues north, mostly through park territory. On the west, the flat land is covered with a bristling bayonet garden of saw palmettos. On the ocean side, the road parallels a ridge of dunes that are among the highest in the state. Homes briefly appear on non-park land along this ridge, but, for most of the next five miles, both sides of the road have a refreshingly natural look. Along the way are three more parking lots from which beach-goers can hike over the boardwalk to the sand.

Ponte Vedra Beach

In a few miles, when A1A veers left just before Mickler Landing, turn on Ponte Vedra Boulevard and continue along the coast. The change from the natural landscape of Guana to the clutter of Ponte Vedra (pronounced Pont y VEE dra) is quite startling. Gone are the rolling dunes and the fields of saw palmettos. Now you're in upper-class suburbia where each building seems to have just emerged from a beauty parlor. The grass is manicured, and not one blade dares grow out of sync with the others. Quickly, you'll reach the Sawgrass Country Club, so highbrow that, it's said, any employee who smiles is promptly fired.

Farther along the boulevard there are some modest houses built when Ponte Vedra was the home to regular people. And it was, many years ago. As a matter of fact, the site had a humble beginning as Mineral City, founded at the start of World War I by the National Lead Company. The company extracted certain minerals important in the manufacture of poison gas. The post-war years were not good times for poison gas, so National Lead built a log clubhouse and installed a nine-hole golf course. Then, in proper Florida fashion, they gave the resort community a Spanish name: Ponte Vedra, after an ocean-side city in Spain where, according to rumor, Christopher Columbus was born.

Ponte Vedra is humble no longer. The average price of a new home is just under $300,000, plus the cost of the lot. A basic place on the Intracoastal Waterway runs $1.5 million, plus or minus a negligible few hundred thousand. And a comfortable abode on the ocean can be yours for a smidgen over $4 million. Ponte Vedrans can afford these

This large fountain graces the grounds of the Ponte Vedra Inn. The condos in the background face the Atlantic.

prices; the average household income is around $100,000.

Watch for the Ponte Vedra Lodge on the beach. You can overnight here for around $250. (Call 800–243–4304 for reservations.) There are two fine restaurants on the water, but, of course, they are only for guests. Farther north, on the land side, is the Ponte Vedra Inn, under the same ownership as the Lodge. (Call 800–234–7842 for reservations.) This was the site of the original National Lead Company clubhouse, and a portion of the clubhouse is still part of the lobby. The inn boasts one of Ponte Vedra's nine golf courses. A winter room facing the ocean is only $185 per night during the week, but it shoots up to $350 during the March-through-May season. However, if you want any kind of respect, reserve a presidential suite at $500, or, better yet, the luxurious penthouse for $600 per night.

The Longcut to Mayport

Our next stop is Mayport and the ferry that will convey us across the St. Johns River. Continue on Ponte Vedra Boulevard to A1A. Here, by turning right on A1A, you'll pass through the congested resort town of Jacksonville Beach.

If, on the other hand, you believe that congestion lacks appeal, turn left on A1A and drive a few hundred yards to Butler Boulevard (SR 202). Proceed west on the elevated highway across an extensive marsh and the Intracoastal Waterway. When you come to San Pablo Road, turn north. In five miles, after passing through pines and quiet residential neighborhoods, you'll reach Atlantic Boulevard. Turn right here and go back over the Intracoastal Waterway to Mayport Road, which is our old friend A1A. Turn north on Mayport Road, toward the town of Mayport, and follow this road past the entrance to the U.S. Navy base.

The End of Nowhere: Mayport

Approaching Mayport, A1A skirts the hazy marshes of Chicopit Bay before turning to follow the St. Johns River. When the wind comes from the east, the smell of the sea permeates Mayport, which at one time was accessible only by boat. Most of the town's early inhabitants were either fishermen or bar pilots who guided ships over the treacherous reefs at the mouth of the St. Johns. Because of the reefs, the village was originally called Hazard. It became Mayport in 1839 when it gained some respectability due to the establishment of a large sawmill. The town's name commemorated the early French who called the St. Johns the River of May. A fire in 1915 devastated the town, which never really recovered.

Today, work and money are rousing this tiny fishing village from its decrepit torpor. As the fishing boats return, seafood restaurants are springing up. Another big boost to the town's economy is business from the 450-passenger La Cruise Casino ship, which has made Mayport its headquarters. The cost of the five-hour, adults-only cruise is $18, but can be considerably less at times. For those who like to gamble, the ship graciously provides all sorts of ways to lose money—including bingo for the hordes of elderly passengers. If you want to sail without the rumble of roulette wheels, you can take advantage of the ship's sun deck. For more information call 800–752–1778.

Across the River of Currents: the St. Johns Ferry

Our purpose in Mayport is to take the St. Johns Ferry to Ft. George Island. Two boats churn across the river from opposite sides each half hour between 6:00 A.M. and 10:00 P.M., seven days a week. The ride, which costs $2.75 (one way), is a

The car-ferry at Mayport transports autos and passengers across the broad St. Johns River.

pleasure, even though it's only eight minutes. If you're crossing during the tidal flow, watch the fierce current swirl around the hull. In the days of sailing ships, the flow was so dangerous that the Spanish named the St. Johns the River of Currents. In 1842, Kingsley Gibbs, owner of the Mayport Mill, took a small boat across the river during ebb tide. He was caught in the current and swept out to the Atlantic. After two-and-a-half fearful hours among circling sharks, he and his two boatmen were rescued: "thanks be to a merciful God and Father," he wrote in his journal.

Ft. George Island

Once across the river, take A1A a half mile northeast to the sign that directs you to Fort George Drive and the Kingsley Plantation. After traveling a short distance you'll reach a fork in the road. You should veer to the left and continue due north on Palmetto Avenue. Don't let the word avenue mislead you. The road quickly becomes sand, and nearly all signs of civilization vanish. Unruly oaks, cedars, and palmettos grasp at the sky overhead. On the right, the forest continues, and, on the left, where the land is lower, there is a vast savanna dominated by spartina grass and needlerush. This is part of the Timucuan Ecological and Historic Preserve, the habitat of wood storks, great blue herons, and other stilt-legged birds.

The Timucuan Indians loved the island for its extensive beds of oysters, the shells of which they deposited in large mounds. The Spanish padres found this concentration of Indians, obviously lost in sin, ripe for salvation. The padres established a mission here, and soon the mud and sapling walls of San Juan arose. The British, to the north, transferred the mission name to the river, hence the St. Johns. They also found time to destroy the mission during an unsuccessful military foray against St. Augustine in 1702. Then, thirty-four years later, James Oglethorpe, on an equally fruitless expedition against St. Augustine, built a post here. Although he named it Ft. George in honor of the king, it was almost an insult to royalty. It had but one cannon. After remaining inconsequential for a few years, the little stockade was abandoned. Today, no trace of it remains.

Jehovah On a White Horse

The island's first permanent building was a plantation home built around 1798 and into which Zephaniah Kingsley moved sixteen years later. Kingsley was born in England, but grew up in South Carolina, the son of a wealthy merchant. Short in stature, he compensated for his height by riding a spirited white steed everywhere he went. He further enhanced his presence by sporting a flamboyant Mexican poncho, a broad-brimmed hat, and shoes with bright silver buckles.

Although Kingsley disliked slavery and would eventually call for the freeing of all slaves, he was not averse to taking advantage of the system. He bought slaves in Africa and at Caribbean ports and sold them on the American mainland. With his profits, he purchased several plantations, including the one on Ft. George Island. Here, Kingsley kept more than one hundred slaves. Although they had some minimal recourse under law, the island's isolation made it all but impossible for them to question Kingsley's godly authority.

Nonetheless, Kingsley was one of the more humane plantation owners. His slaves were not driven unmercifully, but were given tasks to complete each day. When the tasks were completed, usually by mid-afternoon, the slave families were able to do as they pleased. They could tend their own gardens, fish, mend clothes, or just gab with their neighbors as they sat on benches in front of their one-room cabins.

Anna Jai: Black Queen of the Wilderness

Zephaniah did not rule alone. During one slave-buying voyage to Cuba, he purchased a thirteen-year-old girl from a royal Senegalese family. He was so taken by the statuesque beauty that he wed her on the spot in an African ceremony honoring her heritage. Although he had other black mistresses over the years, it was Anna Jai that he always considered his wife. And their four offspring, he regarded as among his heirs. After he freed Anna Jai, she remained as his help-mate, running his operations when he was gone. Eventually, she even purchased twelve slaves of her own, for the institution was an accepted practice in her African homeland.

Avenue of Ghosts

Palmetto Avenue was the main road from the slave quarters to the fields. Anna Jai and her half-white daughter, Mary, had the road lined with palmettos to provide shade for the workers. Groups of slaves moved along this stretch for six decades, with their wagons and horses, trudging wearily amid the dust and insects. Around Christmas, when they were given several days off to praise the Lord for the blessings of life, friends and relatives from outlying St. Johns River plantations would parade down the road.

As you drive along this forested way, with shadows flickering over the roadbed and leaves quivering in the forest beyond, perhaps you'll feel the spirits of the men, women, and children who passed this way before you. They have never left this island, for their bones rest here in unmarked graves. And their troubled spirits? Some feel they linger here too.

The Twenty-Three Monuments to Slavery

Palmetto Avenue ends at the slave quarters. Twenty-three of the original thirty-two shanties remain. The slave families were crammed into these tiny oyster shell shanties arranged in an arc so Kingsley could easily observe what was going on from one end to the other. All the men, women, and older children were required to work in the steamy fields. From the journal of Kingsley Gibbs, Zephaniah's white nephew, we know that eighty acres were planted in cotton, seventy in corn, and the remaining forty in sugar cane, citrus, potatoes, and peas. Mosquitoes were a plague, and the horse flies bit nearly as viciously as wasps. Fevers came out of the marshes and by September, Gibbs griped, three slaves sickened every day. Worse, someone was always dying. But that was merely an inconvenience because he or she would soon be replaced.

Today, one of the remaining slave homes has been given a new

These bleak ruins once housed slave families at the Kingsley Plantation on Fort George Island.

roof, but the rest are just weathered walls. Gone are the men with their mournful songs; gone the cry of women at childbirth; gone the questioning youngsters who knew no childhood. Only a few of their names have come down to us through Kingsley Gibbs' journal. There was Sandy, a boy who fell into the Ft. George River and whose body washed up on nearby Talbot Island. And there was Lucy, who gave birth to a nameless infant who died at the age of two months. The rest have vanished forever.

The Kingsley Plantation House

From the slave cabins, a path leads past the barn, which may also have served as the plantation jail, to the Kingsley home. The two-story building faces the Ft. George River. The river, not Palmetto Avenue, was the main route for supplies and white folks' travel. The Kingsley home is now the visitors center and is under the management of the National Park Service. It contains booklets and historical exhibits and is open daily 9:00 A.M. to 5:00 P.M. Call 904–251–3537 for more information.

When Zephaniah lived here, the home was often filled with his white relatives. Three of his nephews, including Kingsley Gibbs, lived here on a semi-regular basis. Although Zephaniah acknowledged Anna Jai as his true spouse, the mores of the time insisted that she live with her four children in the kitchen building directly behind the main home. Today, this house, too, is also open to the public.

Zephaniah died in 1843 at the age of seventy-eight. As for Anna Jai, she was merely thirty years old at the time of his death and had many good years remaining. She saw daughters Mary and Martha married to prosperous white men and her two sons become successful businessmen. This strong-willed, capable lady passed away at the home of her daughter Mary in 1870 at the age of seventy-seven.

Beaches and Choppers: Huguenot Park

Leave the Kingsley plantation by driving down Anna Jai's Avenue of Palms. Upon reaching A1A, turn left. After three-fourths of a mile, watch for the sign to the Huguenot Memorial Park. This park is on a long sand spit that, in Kingsley's time, was a shallow sandbar. Admission to the park is just $.50 per person, so it's worth a visit. The entry road runs close to the St. Johns River and offers an excellent view of the Mayport Naval Station across the water. Aircraft carriers are often tied to the docks. In years past, the public was invited to tour the carriers, but today not only is such access eliminated, but military helicopters now whir along the river and the park ready to take action against persons acting suspiciously.

It was a far different place when the French Huguenots, for whom the park was named, conducted America's first Protestant worship service here in 1562. Led by Jean Ribault, the French built Fort Caroline a few miles up the St. Johns River. When the Spanish founded St. Augustine the following year, Ribault sailed south with a war party, intending to fight the Spanish. But, after a storm wrecked his ships, the Spanish captured the French survivors at the Matanzas River and executed almost all of them. Thus, France's brief sojourn in Florida came to an unexpected and bloody termination.

The park road leads to a turnoff for a campground and a concession stand that sells pizza, hot dogs and other popular artery-clogging goodies. There is also a bath house with outdoor showers. From here, the road ambles over low dunes crested by swaying sea oats and leads to a beach. There's no pavement, and a sign warns drivers that if they get stuck in the sand, they'll also get stuck with the towing fee.

This secluded beach is at Huguenot Park.

This is a tame beach beside an ultra-calm, almost land-locked bay off the Ft. George Inlet. For this reason, many people drive east over the unpredictable sand and through a narrow gap in the coastal dunes to the Atlantic, where the waves mean business.

The Great Birding Trail: Little Talbot Island

From Huguenot Park, A1A continues north, crossing the Ft. George River on a low-level bridge. Here, beside the bridge, a sometimes-open tavern and grub house called Bootleggers presents a good view of the waterway and the vast sand flats that magically appear and disappear at the will of the tides.

During the next dozen miles, as you drive across the Talbot Islands, you'll encounter a sandscape that is as close to pristine as an environment can be and still offer a friendly face to humans. The Florida State Park System, which repeatedly wins awards, has outdone itself with the pair of parks that protect these islands.

You'll come to the Little Talbot Island State Park first. Admission is $3.25 per car. You can drive directly to the beach or hike a 2.6-mile path through the coastal hammock to the ocean, where five miles of tantalizing sandy shores await you. In the spring and fall, Little Talbot's hammock shelters a goodly array of migrating song birds, and, once on the beach, you should watch for such seabirds as skimmers, oystercatchers, sandpipers, plovers, and many others. Bird-watching is usually so good here that Little Talbot has been selected as a stop on Florida's Great Birding Trail.

The beaches also offer surf fishing. I'm told it's an exhilarating experience to stand in the sea mist, with the waves crashing against the shore, and feel your line tugged by an unknown quarry. For many, the thrill is in the test of skill, and once the fish is landed, it's released to teach its lesson to its fellows, if they'll listen.

For people who want more, the park has bikes and canoes for rent—the bikes are $2 an hour and the canoes are $4 an hour. The tidal creeks are ideal for canoeing. You may see otters, if you're lucky, but no luck is required to view plenty of wading birds in the bordering salt marshes.

It's Not as Quiet as It Seems: Big Talbot Island

Just up A1A is Big Talbot Island State Park, with a $2 per car entry fee. The highlight of the park is an area known simply as the bluffs, where rock-like outcroppings and fallen trees with weathered, often grotesque shapes give the beach a unique appeal for artists and photographers.

In the waters off the bluffs, where the currents of Nassau Sound swirl into the Atlantic, lies a pinpoint of land called Bird Island. It was among the shoals surrounding this island that forty-one pilot whales became stranded several years ago. The whales were spotted by a U.S. Navy flier from Mayport and rescuers were dispatched. Two of the whales were pushed back to sea, but the will to survive seemed to be extinguished for the others. They died in a sort of mass suicide.

While you're at the bluffs don't get carried away by the beauty of the scene and forget that this is a wild area. Recently, a lady named Tammy was playing with her small dog on the beach. She was unaware that the dog was being stalked by an eight-foot alligator. Gators are extremely fast over short distances. They also have brains the size of a thumb nail. Thus, when the gator attacked, it confused Tammy for her dog. It clamped down on her leg and threw her to the ground. But when the gator attempted to pull her into the water, it was surprised to learn it had captured a long, ungainly creature of more than a hundred pounds rather than a succulent little doggie. The chagrined gator released Tammy and stomped into the underbrush, muttering, I suspect, something to do with deceit and how tough it is to get a good meal nowadays. As for Tammy, she was left with a six-inch wound that would eventually heal and a biting memory of Big Talbot that would last a lifetime.

In case you're curious, the Talbot Islands were named after Charles Talbot, Lord High Chancellor of England, by Georgia colonists in 1735. They hoped to gain Talbot's favor, though we never hear more about him in relation to this area.

Big Talbot is bordered on the north by Nassau Sound. A new bridge spans the sound, and the old bridge is now utilized by fishermen. The Nassau River is an official Aquatic Reserve whose submerged vegetation is protected by the State of Florida.

Princess Amelia's Island

From Big Talbot, A1A crosses the Nassau River to Amelia Island, named by the British in honor of King George II's daughter—ignoring the fact that the island happened to belong to Spain at the time. Although the island is rather isolated, as it is located on Florida's extreme northeast margin, its popularity with visitors is growing. Thus, it's fortunate that Florida has preserved the island tip as a state park. The foot of the bridge is frequented by fishermen, and, for horse-lovers, there is the Kelly Seahorse Ranch, where a well-known equestrian takes tenderfeet on horseback jaunts along the seashore.

The Seahorses

Kelly's horses are not exactly the frolicsome critters that island propaganda suggests. Instead, Kelly's cowpokes lead the horses nose-to-tail at a gait slow enough to satisfy their insurance company. The horses stomp out of the old corral seven days a week, in posses of ten, at 10:00 A.M., noon, 2:00 P.M., and 4:00 P.M. You'll be slappin' leather for one hour, and it'll lighten yer wallet by forty-five bucks. Each wrangler must be thirteen years old or over. No pistol-packin' is allowed. And keep the cussin' to yerself. Make yer reservations in advance—or else!—by calling 904–491–5166.

Laid-Back on the Beach: Amelia Island Plantation

Now, continue north on A1A. After the British took over Florida in 1763, a large indigo plantation was established somewhere near here. It was this enterprise, perhaps, from which the modern Amelia Island Plantation took its name. The plantation is a highly rated, oceanside resort sprawling over more than 1,300 acres. Built as a series of low-rise condos in the early 1970s, it was the catalyst for opening the island to upscale vacationers. A multi-story hotel was added in 1998. You can spend a relatively inexpensive night in a condo with no ocean view for around $135 in the winter—or you can go for a three-bedroom luxury suite with plenty of water vista for around $1,000. (Call 800–874–68787 for more information.)

 If you want to case the joint, you should visit the Spa and Shops, where there are ten exquisite boutiques, an art gallery, and two restaurants. Or, in the evening, you can dine at the somewhat pricey Verandah Restaurant.

 Just down A1A from the Plantation is Lewis Street, which leads to American Beach. This area was set aside by the Afro-American Insurance Company in 1935 as a perk for top salesmen. Over the years, the thin strip of land became favored by blacks, who were denied most other beach locales during the long years of segregation.

Laid-Forward on the Beach: The Ritz-Carlton

 One street beyond Lewis Street is the Amelia Island Parkway, a scenic drive that leads past the Ritz-Carlton, Amelia's other premier, oceanside resort. If Amelia Island Plantation is laid-back, as it claims, then the Ritz could be considered laid-forward. When I drove up and saw the men in suits and ties at midday, I turned around posthaste. It's definitely not a backroads kind of place. Even my lovable old auto didn't feel comfortable!

Now, watch for the entry to Peter's Point Beach Front Park. Here is the same shore at which the ritzy guys-in-ties pay a fortune to loll, but the cost is zero, the dress is whatever, and anyone's car can feel comfortable. You can even drive right onto the sand.

 Continuing north on A1A (Fletcher Avenue), you'll pass under an impressive arch of utility wires before entering Fernandina Beach, population eleven thousand. At the corner, where A1A turns west on Atlantic Avenue, is the Main Beach. A few blocks up Atlantic Avenue is Fort Clinch State Park.

A Little Fakery: Fort Clinch

The three-mile road to Fort Clinch is an attraction in itself. It is shaded by large oaks and other hardwoods. Turnouts and benches provide pleasing views of the wide salt marshes along

The powerful batteries at Fort Clinch were erected to defend Amelia Island.

Egans Creek. On the far margins of this marsh is the Amelia Lighthouse, thought to be the oldest structure on the island. From the sea, its light is visible for nineteen miles. The road soon splits, with one segment continuing through sand dunes to the fort and the other leading to a beach on the Atlantic, where there is fine swimming, a pier for fishing and a pavilion for bird-watching.

The construction of Fort Clinch was begun in 1847 and work continued during the Civil War. During hostilities, Union troops occupied the fort. Today, you can climb to the top of the rampart and inspect the mean-looking cannons, which were never fired in anger. Actually, they couldn't be fired in anger because they are fake guns made of concrete! The originals were sold for scrap long ago.

The view from the top of the fort is expansive. To the south, ocean waves roll against almost deserted beaches and a mantle of trees. To the north lies Cumberland Sound, which connects with the St. Marys River. The sound is marked with buoys to guide fishing boats. In the distance is Georgia's Cumberland Island, where wild horses cavort.

The park is open from 8:00 A.M. to sunset seven days a week. You can call 904–277–7274 for more information. Admission is $3.25 per car. There is an extra $2 per person fee for entry into the fort, which is open between 9:00 A.M. and 5:00 P.M. Within the fort grounds is a small gift shop with some good literature.

Grandpa's Town: Fernandina Beach

Returning to Atlantic Avenue (A1A), drive west once more. In a very short distance you'll come to a sign for the Egans Creek Greenway at Atlantic Park. Here, a two-mile nature trail begins behind the Municipal Auditorium and follows the creek.

In a few blocks, for no apparent reason, Atlantic Avenue changes to Centre Street. Although A1A turns south when it reaches Eighth Street, by continuing on Centre Street you'll enter Fernandina's distinctive downtown. You'll feel as if you're in great grandpa's era, as, indeed, you are, for nearly all the buildings are more than a hundred years old. Perhaps the most interesting building is the Nassau County Courthouse with its weirdly Byzantine architecture.

Park your car where Centre Street ends at the Amelia River. The river, with its deep-water link with the Atlantic, provides the finest natural harbor on Florida's east coast. It was due to this harbor that the Spanish built Fort San Fernando, for which the town was subsequently named. The Spanish also constructed the mission of Santa Maria, for which the St. Marys River was named. Much later, this harbor caused David Yulee to select Fernandina as the eastern terminus of the Florida

The town of Fernandina on Amelia Island relishes its past.

Railroad, the state's first Atlantic Ocean–to–Gulf of Mexico railroad, which was completed just before the Civil War. For this reason, it's quite proper that the Chamber of Commerce is located in the old railroad station across the tracks from the parking lot. Here, you can pick up ample literature about the town, particularly the fifty-block area in the National Register of Historic Places.

One place to visit is the extensive city marina at the foot of Centre Street. Salty skippers conduct scenic nature cruises along the calm inland waterways as well as expeditions into the Atlantic for deep sea fishing. After a hard day's cruising and exploring, why not drop in at Brett's Waterway Cafe, directly on the marina. It is known for its fine servings of fish and sunsets. Call 904–261–2660 for more information.

Across Northern Florida

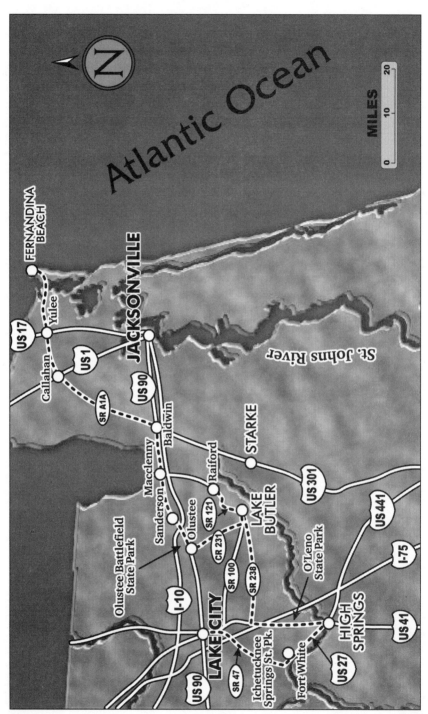

Rambling Through Old-Time Florida

Fernandina Beach to Lake City • 110 Backroad Miles

The Song of the Road: Overview

In this exploration we will leave Fernandina, in Florida's farthest northeast corner, and head westward through the pine forest. The towns are small, and the inhabitants speak with a cracker twang. Life can be a struggle in this infertile land, where a large segment of the population works for timber companies. The state has helped the local economy by building many state penal institutions here. We'll drive close to the prison at Sanderson, which is enclosed by a see-through fence of razor wire.

Just beyond the prison is Olustee Battlefield State Park. Here, Union troops marched out from Jacksonville on the same road we'll be taking. They were defeated by Confederate defenders at the largest Civil War battle ever fought in Florida. Ten thousand men were involved. A path runs through the battle front and a visitors center provides details about the battle and the events leading up to it.

From Olustee, we'll head due south to Lake Butler, where you can take a short side trip to the state prison at Raiford, the site of Florida's controversial electric chair, Old Sparky.

Then its westward to O'Leno State Park for a swim in the Santa Fe River and a hike to the sink, where the river disappears into a natural tunnel—to reemerge three miles south. Canoe enthusiasts love the Santa Fe River, and boats are for rent at the Canoe Outpost, just downstream from O'Leno. The main town hereabouts is High Springs, once an important railroad center but now filled with antiques shops and some very good restaurants.

West of High Springs is Ichetucknee Springs, a massive flow of nine springs that empties into the Santa Fe River. Tubes can be rented here for a leisurely drift down one of the most scenic streams in all Florida.

This exploration ends at Lake City, whose location at the juncture of Interstates 10 and 75 has caused a unique melding of new franchise establishments with an older town steeped in Southern traditions.

On the Road Again

Highway A1A exits Fernandina on a high-rise bridge that crosses over the Amelia River, which is more a tidewater lagoon than a true river. The bridge affords a wide-angle view of the river, which is also spanned by a CSX railroad bridge nearby. Beyond the river, you'll emerge into an extensive marsh four miles wide. A1A, which is four lanes with a center parkway, passes so easily over the marsh that it's difficult to picture this area the way vagabond John Muir saw it in 1867.

Footloose in the Wilderness: John Muir

John Muir was fresh out of college when he arrived in Florida, having hiked most of the distance down from Indiana. He was headed for Cedar Key on the Gulf of Mexico. He described his adventures and observations in a book entitled *A Thousand-Mile Walk to the Gulf*. In later life, Muir became famous as the founder of the Sierra Club, and he was instrumental in the preservation of the Grand Canyon, Yosemite Valley, and Arizona's Petrified Forest. But when he first set foot in Florida, he was just a bearded youth whose belongings consisted of a note pad, a book of poetry, a flower press, a bar of soap, a towel, and a change of underwear.

There was no road across the marsh at that time, so Muir trudged along the Florida Railroad. Now, much of its right-of-way is used by the CSX line. During his journey, on one mild day in mid-October, he became ever more entranced by the "flat, watery, reedy coast, with clumps of mangrove and forests of moss-dressed, strange trees appearing low in the distance. . . . It is impossible to write the dimmest picture of plant grandeur so redundant [and] unfathomable." He had never been in the subtropics and was as curious as a child. "Short was the measure of my walk today. A new, canelike grass, or big lily, or gorgeous flower belonging to a tree or vine, would catch my attention, and I would throw down my bag and press and splash through the coffee-brown water for specimens." Often, he'd slosh several hundred yards into the muck, unmindful of the snakes and biting insects until he retrieved his specimen or until the water's depth or entangling vines kept him from going further.

He was most fascinated by the palmetto trees, marveling as their leaf-splays reflected the sunshine like silver sparks. And he listened with wonder as their fronds rustle-talked with the wind. Each palmetto, he wrote, "has a power of expression not excelled by any plant high or low that I have met in my whole walk thus far."

With all his sloshing and gawking, Muir probably only hiked ten or so miles his first day out of Fernandina. This would put him near where the village of Yulee stands today. Here, he ate his last crust of dry bread, washed it down with brown swamp water, lay on a mound of soggy earth, and went to sleep.

Yulee

Yulee was named in honor of David Levy Yulee, the ambitious dynamo who built the Florida Railroad, the right-of-way John Muir utilized six years after its construction. Despite the town's distinguished name, it has had an undistinguished history. Today, it is mostly a gas stop for through-traffic headed to Fernandina on A1A or to Jacksonville on US 17. Yet, as Jacksonville's suburbanites locate here to experience country living, the population has spurted to nine thousand. When President Bill Clinton wanted a quiet getaway, he chose its exclusive White Oak Plantation, owned by a local timber tycoon.

Logging Country: Callahan

West from Yulee, A1A narrows to two lanes. This is pine country where logging is the main enterprise. Every so often trucks loaded with timber, headed for Fernandina mills, rumble down

Lumber is an important industry around Callahan and throughout northern Florida.

the road. In twelve miles, you'll reach the village of Callahan, which contains a cluster of churches and not much else. A1A ends here, so continue southwest on US 301. You'll be passing through a flat world that is geographically part of the Atlantic plain.

In a few miles, you'll come to the Mulch Manufacturing Company and large piles of logs resting along the highway. On the south side of the road, a sawmill converts the logs into boards. On the north side, a revolving cylinder grinds the wood into mulch. The mulch and planks are loaded onto CSX cars, which will deliver them to marketers.

Logging in this area goes way back. Near here, John Muir encountered as rough a bunch of loggers as he had ever seen. Although they begrudgingly gave him some of their pork and hominy, he was relieved when he left their camp. Later that day, he was hassled by three dogs guarding another logging camp and saved only when their masters called off the canines. The loggers were not a bad lot and presented Muir with a helping of liver pie, which may have been even less pleasant than his skirmish with the dogs.

Baldwin

Twenty miles beyond Callahan is the town of Baldwin, with a population around 1,700. Here, US 301 is joined by US 90 from Jacksonville. Baldwin is named after the builder of the Florida Atlantic and Gulf Central Railroad (commonly known as the Florida Central) that began running between Jacksonville and Lake City in 1860. Mr. Baldwin's tracks crossed Yulee's at this point, making the intersection a natural place for rail yards.

During the Civil War, the town of Baldwin became a wild place when cowboys from the southern plains arrived with their bellowing herds. The beefies destined to feed Confederate soldiers were jammed onto cattle cars and shipped west to Live Oak, where a rail line ran up to Georgia. After the Civil War, Baldwin developed into a rail center for wood products. Sometimes lines of freight cars stretched for several miles.

Although rail yards are still in operation south of town, it's quiet in Baldwin itself. Yet memories remain. Helping perpetuate them is the new County Federal Credit Union Building at the junction where US 301 turns south and US 90 heads west. The building is an enlarged version of the railroad station at Olustee, a town farther west. The credit union's overhanging roof is designed to shelter passengers waiting for a train. The grounds feature old-style light posts, each with five large globes. For people interested in old Baldwin, the credit union has a nice display of vintage photos.

The Florida Central's railroad right-of-way has been converted into the paved, fifteen-mile Jacksonville-Baldwin biking and hiking trail. The trailhead and visitors center is just off US 90 North on Center Street.

US 90: A Wonder of the Age

From Baldwin, proceed west on US 90. This road is the oldest major concrete highway in Florida—although you'll be glad to know it's been resurfaced since it was built in the early 1920s. Construction machinery was primitive in those days and Trail Ridge, hardly noticeable now, was a nightmare. Probably originating as a sand dune during a high-water, inter-glacial era, it was so unstable that the earth-moving equipment was in danger of rolling down the ridge like beach balls. But once Trail Ridge was passed, the pine-flats were so easygoing that the road crew moved rapidly ahead without even waiting for permission from the land owners.

When the highway between Jacksonville and Pensacola was completed, everyone agreed it was a wonder. Imagine being able to drive your flivver nearly four hundred miles without getting submerged in a single bottomless mud hole!

Although US 90 was once a major highway, today, with Interstate 10 so close, US 90 is half-deserted. Thus, I grant it an official backroad designation.

Mac and Lenny's Town

Continuing west on US 90, you'll quickly be out of Duval County, dominated by Jacksonville, and into Baker County, dominated, if that is the word, by Macclenny, the county seat, which has a population of five thousand. I struggled with the town's pronunciation until I imagined it being founded by two guys called Mac and Lenny. It wasn't, but the imagery helped.

Mac and Lenny's modest downtown boasts a few gas stations, a four-store shopping strip, and plenty of churches. The biggest event in memory was the opening of a huge Wal-Mart distribution center. Despite this momentous occurrence, there is a feeling of isolation about Macclenny, which doesn't even have a Chamber of Commerce to tout it. When federal writers visited the place in the 1930s, they found the folks here to be clannish and suspicious of outsiders. The menfolk frequently carried knives and guns to the dances and shindigs. "There is often as much fighting as dancing," the writers reported. Anything less than outright murder was a personal matter, affording no reason for the law to interfere.

I found no shindigs when I stopped in town for gas, so I can furnish no up-to-date comment on whatever fussin' and feudin' is going on in Mac and Lenny's town. The place looked right peaceable to me. So if you find a shindig going on, you'll just have to take your chances.

The Pride of Sanderson

Leaving Macclenny on US 90, you'll be accompanied by what was once the Florida Atlantic and Gulf Central Railroad. During the Civil War, it was the only working rail line in the entire state. In ten miles, you'll come to the hamlet of Sanderson, which an early president of the railroad probably named in his own honor. If so, he should have chosen a better namesake, for the place never prospered and even today is too small to have made the 2000 Census List.

Sanderson consists of a general store, a fire station, a brick post office, and a few trailer homes. The only reminder to villagers that they have not been forgotten by the rest of America is the formidable prison known as the Baker Correctional Institution. Within its

This guard tower at a prison near Sanderson is representative of the many correctional institutions in northeast Florida.

confines are more than a thousand of Florida's worst criminals.

You'll find this town pride beside US 90, a few miles west of town. Were it not for the watch towers, the prison wouldn't look like much. From a distance, it seems as if the long fence would not keep a cow in pasture, but the razor wire is much more effective than a traditional masonry wall, which can be scaled. Further, the wire permits the guards unobstructed observation from many angles. Pickup trucks patrol the grounds, and guards note every suspicious movement within and without.

I didn't consider my movements to be suspicious when I pulled onto the road's shoulder to take a photo. But I must have caused some stir, for a patrol truck stopped almost in my photo line. I waited for it to pass on, but it soon became clear that the guard was waiting for me to pass on. Then it occurred to me: I had made their hot list. So I took my photo, slunk back to my car, and drove off nonchalantly. But I was not nonchalant enough to prevent what I'm almost sure was an unmarked law car from following me. After he turned off to a roadside diner, I'm fairly certain other unmarked cars continued to tail me for several days—maybe they still are.

Mary Jane, We Know You're Out There

Despite the presence of John Law, the growing of marijuana is a popular occupation in Baker County. You won't see it along the highways, but up north, where the forest is thick and snoopy cops are few, a fine crop is maturing. *Florida Trend* magazine, doing a cover story on the marijuana industry, found the plant to be the state's biggest cash crop after citrus. And the bedrock of domestic pot production was in north Florida and the panhandle. According to the magazine, the sheriff of Baker County "believes that a tradition of outlaw culture that evolved during Prohibition contributed to the rise of the area as a marijuana center." But the police are diligent, and when a local outlaw farmer is caught and convicted, the road to prison is short.

From the Baker Correctional Institution, you'll quickly pass the Baker Work Camp. Immediately beyond is the Olustee Battlefield State Park.

The Civil War Comes to Florida: The Battle of Olustee

Olustee was the state's only full-blown Civil War battle. Five thousand men were involved on each side. And, when it was over, nearly three thousand of them were killed, wounded, or missing and presumed dead—making it the third bloodiest battle of the entire war.

Events leading up to the battle began on February 7, 1864, when a Union force landed at Jacksonville and easily occupied the town. Then, on February 8th, troops under General Truman Seymour marched out of Jacksonville and captured Baldwin, where they confiscated cotton, rice, guns, and other goods intended for Confederate armies in Georgia. Seymour's intention was to continue along the Florida Central Railroad for eighty miles to the bridge over the Suwannee River. By destroying this bridge, the supply of foodstuffs so important to Confederate armies would be disrupted. Furthermore, with the one rail line severed, east Florida would be detached from west Florida, enabling recruiters in this area to induce slaves to leave their masters and enlist in the Union army.

Before continuing his march, Seymour dispatched a mounted detachment under Colonel Henry to move westward along the road that paralleled the railroad. The men were to find out what sort of Confederate forces were out there. The first resistance Henry met was just beyond the site of Macclenny, where a few Southerners shot at his men from ambush. Henry easily sent them scurrying and continued. By evening, he had reached Sanderson. Here, he was greeted by flaming storehouses. News of his arrival had preceded him.

The Union horsemen rode through the night and into the next day. By late afternoon, they had covered thirty-four miles and were on the outskirts of Lake City. At this point, their way was barred by skirmishers shooting from the cover of pines. With that, the horsemen turned back, for such skirmishers would not be enough to stop a Union army. With such little opposition, the way to the Suwannee seemed open.

But Seymour hesitated. He was wary of plunging into the heart of Florida. A force his size required plenty of food, ammunition, and other supplies, and his only link with the port at Jacksonville was by way of the Florida Central Railroad. So, he paused in Baldwin while he pondered his next action.

Meanwhile, Joseph Finegan, in charge of Florida's defense, was frantically gathering up a scratch force. His appeal for reinforcements reached Georgia and South Carolina, where the defenses of Savannah and Charleston were seriously weakened in order to send men to Finegan's aid. In little more than a week Finegan amassed a force of five thousand.

Seymour knew nothing of the rapid buildup of Confederate defenders when he ordered his men to resume their march to the

Florida's largest Civil War battle occurred in this forest at Olustee. The path runs between the front lines.

Suwannee on February 20th. Many of the officers had grave misgivings, and some historians now surmise that Seymour made his decision more to advance his military career than because of any conviction of success. When the general passed through Sanderson, a defiant lady shouted at him, "You'll come back faster than yer going out!"

Finegan was ready at Olustee, a mile-wide pine barren between a swamp on the south and Ocean Pond on the north. Early in the afternoon, the two armies clashed. The fighting was vicious and deadly, for the pines were widely spaced and afforded little cover. At one point, when the Confederates ran low on ammunition, it seemed as if the Union forces would overcome their resistance. But, at the last moment, a supply train arrived, and the day was saved. By late afternoon, as Seymour saw his casualties mount, he realized he could not break the Confederate line and had no choice but retreat. The Union soldiers staggered back through Sanderson and on to Macclenny, where they made camp. Of Seymour's original force, more than a third was either dead, wounded, or missing. Finegan could not pursue, for he had suffered severely too. Two days later, Seymour's battered force limped back into Jacksonville.

Today, the road into Olustee Battlefield State Park crosses the same railroad along which the Union army marched. The park is accessible every day of the year between 8:00 A.M. and sundown. A monument commemorates the battle, and, to help visitors understand the events, an interpretive center is open Thursday through Monday 9:00 A.M. to 5 P.M.

But the highlight of the park is the footpath between the front lines. The setting is almost identical to the one in which the troops found themselves that February afternoon so long ago. The pine barren is still there. It is quiet, just as it was in the hush before battle. As you walk the path, try to imagine that on each side five thousand men nervously hold cocked rifles. Cannons are primed and ready. Then, battle cries ring out. The cannons thunder. The rifles crack. And a deluge of death snarls through the air. Soldiers charge. Men fall. There are cries of agony. Confusion. Panic. Cowardice. Heroism.

Each February, on or near the battle's anniversary, the armies reappear, but their cannons and rifles shoot blanks. And though troops fall, it's all make-believe. The blood is only washable dye. Several thousand spectators laugh and clap. What fun Olustee is!

Ocean Pond

By continuing four miles west from the battlefield on US 90, you'll come to the village of Olustee. With just a nudge, this cluster of buildings could become junky, but maybe I just missed the good stuff. A sign will point you to Olustee Beach, three-fourths of a mile north on Ocean Pond. There, you'll find a pretty park with a small, sandy area for swimming, a pier for fishing, and restrooms.

Through the Pine Barrens

Although Lake City, our ultimate destination, is only fourteen miles directly down US 90, we're not going the direct way.

Instead, we'll take some backroads that will lengthen the trip by a few miles—well, fifty if you insist on the particulars. So, at the village of Olustee, turn south on CR 231.

County Road 231 is paved but narrow. When I met a car pulling a trailer, in order for us to pass, he had to pull over so far that his right wheels dug up the turf. A road sign warned of soft shoulders, and it wasn't kidding. But trailers are unusual. So is auto traffic. How many people do you know wanting to get from Olustee to Lake Butler?

Much of CR 231's brief fourteen-mile existence is through pine barrens studded with shady fern groves. There are no advertisements, for who is there to read them? And nothing commercial, so don't count on getting gasoline. There are no homes either. Much of the way there aren't even utility poles. And when they do appear, they are skinny things supporting a pair of thin wires that try not to be intrusive. Fortunately, CR 231 country is part of Lake Butler Wildlife Area and will remain protected for years to come.

Florida's Smallest County

County Road 231 ends at SR 100. The town of Lake Butler is just a mile east, but there's no sign telling you this, since it's assumed only natives drive CR 231, and they know where they're going. On your right, as you head into town, there is a railroad embankment, but no rails. The trains around here stopped long ago.

With a population of barely two thousand, Lake Butler is well qualified to be the seat of Union County, the smallest in Florida. Originally, the county was called Bradford, and it was a respectable size. But another small town, Starke, fought Lake Butler for political predominance. The seat of government moved between them four times until Starke finally won. Thereupon, in 1921, Lake Butler seceded from Bradford County to become the proud seat of its own Lilliputian domain. The county adopted the name Union, in the hopes that it would heal the discontent among the communities that

This modest county courthouse is the centerpiece of Lake Butler.

would have preferred to remain in Bradford.

The Union County courthouse faces SR 100. It is a cute brick building that you might mistake for a grammar school. Built in 1936, it's been recently remodeled, and you'll be impressed by the neatness of the interior. But the courthouse is a needless structure, for the larger one at Starke, just fifteen miles east, could easily handle all the business in this diminutive county. And the financial support of the superfluous county government is a financial drag on a population with one of the lowest income levels in the state. Most of those who have jobs work for the timber companies, who own sixty percent of the land hereabouts, or for the prison system.

Incidentally, Lake Butler does have a lake. It is a few blocks north of the courthouse. Here, there is swimming, a boat ramp, and an open-air pavilion.

The Iron Triangle

You are now in what is known as the Iron Triangle, anchored by Lake Butler to the west, Starke to the east, and Lawtey to the north. Within this cozy area there are half a dozen major prisons. These prisons constitute almost a state welfare program for these rural communities. But the state also benefits, for the prisons are built on cheap land away from major population centers. The hamlet of Raiford, eight miles east of Lake Butler on SR 121, is the center of the Iron Triangle. Here, you'll find the notorious Florida State Prison, home of the state's electric chair, commonly known as Old Sparky.

A Baffling Mystery

The criminals at the Raiford prisons are the worst of the worst, and the guards are tougher than steel. Thus, when cop-killer Frank Valdes recently arrived at the Florida State Prison to await execution, the tension began to build. Valdes was mean, fearless, and hateful. He taunted the guards and was, in general, an unruly dude. Then one day he was found dead in his cell. He had twenty-two broken ribs, multiple skull fractures, a sternum snapped in half, and a broken collarbone. His body was covered with boot marks. The medical examiner said the only way he could have inflicted such injuries on himself was by throwing himself in front of a train. Since no train was scheduled to run through his cell, it was concluded that the guards must have been involved. But they claimed to be bewildered as to how Mr. Valdes could have received his fatal beating. The ensuing trial, held in

Starke, was postponed repeatedly, due to the difficulty of forming a jury in an area where nearly everyone either worked for the prison system or had a friend or relative who did. Finally, a jury was rounded up. They listened to the case and carefully considered the facts. Then they found the eight accused guards not guilty.

So, how Frank Valdes in his locked cell received the blows that led to his death remains a baffling mystery. Perhaps a runaway freight train is the best answer after all.

Although our route does not lead in Raiford's direction, you might take a short detour there if you want to contemplate crime and punishment from a safe distance. In the last two decades, Florida has executed more than fifty people here. Since 2000 when prisoners were allowed to choose death by lethal injection, Old Sparky is seldom used.

Lake Butler to O'Leno

From Lake Butler take SR 238 west. The land here is flat. There are some pastures, but it is mostly covered in pines planted in orderly rows for ease of harvesting. Stage coaches traveled this road when it was just sand. An important stop was the inn at Providence, ten miles beyond Lake Butler. The coaches no longer ran after a railroad was built in 1890. Then, the railroad stopped running, and today Providence consists of a Baptist church and an animal feed plant. There's little else, not even people. Nonetheless, the farms around here seem to be doing well. Beyond Providence, the flat land becomes rolling hills as you pass Olustee Creek.

Pretty in Pink

Upon reaching US 41/441, turn south. Almost immediately, you'll cross the Interstate 75 interchange, with the customary hasty-pudding of franchises. But continue south and you'll quickly be among trees and pastures. During spring and early summer the roadsides and fields here are bedecked with wild phlox, descendants of originals planted as part of the state highway beautification program begun in 1963. This phlox variety is actually native to Texas, and some environmental purists regard them as horrible exotics. Most of us, however, are delighted to see their pleasing tapestry of pinks and whites.

The Case of the Vanishing River

Three miles beyond I-75 turn into O'Leno State Park. The parking lot is beside the Santa Fe River. Ultimately, the Sante Fe flows into the Suwannee, but it has an interesting career before it comes to its end. About a mile downstream, the river disappears into what is appropriately called a sink. The sink leads the water through a tunnel in the underlying limestone. After flowing through utter blackness for three miles, the river bubbles to the surface, undoubtedly surprised to see the sunlight once more.

More than three hundred years ago, Spanish friars established the mission of Santa Fe near here. During the depression of the 1930s, the teenage boys of the Civilian Conservation Corps built a suspension footbridge over the river. The bridge will sway as you cross it, but don't worry. It has been reconstructed and is strong enough to support an elephant, so they say. On the other side of the river, a path will lead you on a twenty-minute hike to the river sink. For canoers, boats are for rent, and a paddle over the reflective water enclosed by forestry is a pleasure indeed. In addition, the park offers swimming in an area set aside for that purpose.

Here is the swimming hole at O'Leno State Park. The footbridge in the background leads to the sink where the Santa Fe River temporarily disappears underground.

It wasn't always so peaceful here. In the old days, this was the site of a gambling casino, and the settlement was called Keno, after the game of chance. Soon, a sawmill and a cotton gin began operations. Next came the ladies, and with them, a church. Then, since everyone knows that the Lord abhors gambling, not only did the keno parlor have to go, but the town changed its name to Leno. Despite the church and the new name, when the railroad bypassed Leno, everyone left. The deserted buildings became the ghost town of Old Leno. Eventually even the ghosts tired of a place where there was no one to scare. They departed, and Old Leno became O'Leno. At least that's the way I heard it.

The Stump-Knocker: The Old Bellamy Road

Now, continue south on US 41/441. Go slowly, for in less than a mile you'll come to the sign for the Bellamy Road. By turning east, you'll find yourself on the old route that was Florida's Oregon Trail.

The Bellamy Road followed a path worn by ancient Indians and the Spanish missionaries who followed them. This segment is now only a mile long and is composed of sand and gravel, but when John Bellamy and his slaves constructed it in 1826 it was two hundred miles long and ran from just south of Tallahassee to the St. Johns River, where it

It is a pleasure to drive, or stroll, along the historic Bellamy Road, built when Florida was still a territory.

connected with the road to St. Augustine. Commissioned by Florida's territorial government, it was to be twenty-five feet wide—and, in a few places, it actually was. We wouldn't have regarded the road as much today. The tree stumps were not removed, but protruded a foot off the ground—just high enough for wagons to scrape over them. But when a stump was a little too high, it slammed against the vehicles' floor boards, sometimes knocking them completely apart. Thus, Bellamy Road earned the rueful nickname Stump-Knocker. Old Stump-Knocker wormed around as it avoided swamps and water holes. The roadbed was not built up and over wet spots. Instead, logs were laid across the path in a bumpy corduroy pattern that dislocated tailbones and false teeth. Creeks were spanned by rickety things that could hardly be called bridges. But crossing the Santa Fe River here was easy since it ran underground.

Today, this intriguing segment of the Bellamy Road is graded, and the stumps have long since rotted away. Although it lacks pavement, it has plenty of memories. So drive along it slowly. Or, better yet, park and walk. Do you hear the melodic calls of Seminole hunters? The heavy stomp of DeSoto's gold-seekers? The soft tread of Franciscan missionaries? The creak of pioneer wagons? The snort of U.S. army mules? They've all passed this way.

Outpost on the Santa Fe River

Returning to US 41/441, continue south. If you want an intimate encounter with the Santa Fe River, at the sign for Canoe Outpost, just beyond the bridge, turn west. Here, you can rent a boat for an idyllic hour-and-a half paddle downstream for $12 per person with up to three in a canoe. There are longer canoe trips, too, including an all-day, down-river paddle where you can take time to swim, sunbathe, or just fool around.

The Outpost's owner is Jim Wood, a genial man who shucked his confining job in Philadelphia for the lure of the Santa Fe. Jim has many stories to tell, including ones about the night trips he conducts when the moon is full and the river shimmers like crystal. The boaters spend three hours in this magical world before returning to a big bonfire and grilled hot dogs washed down with punch or a few glasses wine. "We have a lot of fun," Jim says.

But there have been some tense times. Once, he went out late in the afternoon to pick up two high-living frat boys and they were nowhere around. Since there are phones at certain points along the

Canoe Outpost owner, Jim Wood, relaxes on the Santa Fe River near High Springs.

river, he waited for a call. None came and it was growing dark, so he called the state's Fish and Game agency. The agents sent a helicopter along the river with a brilliant searchlight. It caught the boys on the river bank passed out from too much joy juice. Roused suddenly by the horrendous noise, the frightful wind, and the unearthly light from above, they must have thought they were at the Last Judgment. As their senses returned, they staggered sheepishly to their canoe and paddled to the assigned rendezvous point, where a smiling Jim waited.

The Canoe Outpost operates seven days a week, year-round. For boat reservations call 386–454–2050.

High Springs

The town of High Springs is two miles south of the river on US 41 (US 441 cuts off on the outskirts of town). At the junction of US 41 and US 27, you'll find the century-old, two-story Opera House, now the Great Outdoors Trading Company and Café. I always enjoy eating here. The food is good and the interior has maintained the decor of yesteryear.

And yesteryear is what this little town of four thousand is all about. It's loaded with vintage buildings and antiques shops. The place to start your exploration is at the Chamber of Commerce, located in the former railroad station a block south on US 41 (Main Avenue). Be sure to pick up the Visitors Guide and the walking tour brochure. With these, you can roam at will.

The railroad meant everything to early High Springs, which thrived

The High Springs Visitors Center is in the old railroad station.

as the regional headquarters for the extensive Plant Railroad System. There was a large maintenance shop and a roundhouse with stalls for twenty-six locomotives. Commercial warehouses lined the tracks, and one of these is still occupied by the Golden Peanut Company. But the passenger trains departed a decade and a half ago and a freight train comes around only once a week.

After the railroad pulled out and the lucrative tobacco farms closed, High Springs went into a tailspin. However, today the town is in a revival because of antiquing and recreation along the Santa Fe River and the major springs west of town. Perhaps the greatest nearby attraction is Ichetucknee Springs State Park.

Up a Lazy River

To reach Ichetucknee Springs, drive west on US 27. You'll pass through countryside sculpted into gentle mounds and dells. The dells are dry sinkholes formed when the surface rocks sagged as the limestone below was dissolved by underground streams. In places, these streams well up to the surface, where they form the springs that are so common in this part of Florida.

In ten miles, you'll reach Ft. White, named for a Seminole War supply post on the Santa Fe River in use until 1842, when mosquitoes devoured the garrison. Here, you have two choices. By remaining on

Ichetucknee State Park offers canoeing and tubing on the Santa Fe River.

US 27 for four miles, you'll reach the south entrance to
Ichetucknee Springs. (The name of the springs, in Seminole,
means "pond of the beaver.") Rent a tube just outside the park
and enjoy a half-hour drift to Dampier's Landing or a full-hour
trip if you go all the way to the south take-out. You can tube
from this entrance any time of the year, but before you start out, be
aware that this water, emerging from limestone chambers, is a brisk
seventy-three degrees. Should this cool your ardor, rental canoes are
available, and there are five miles of hiking trails through the lush
deciduous forest.

If, on the other hand, you desire a full three-hour float on this beautiful stream fed by nine good-size springs, turn north at Ft. White on SR
47. When you reach CR 238, turn left and drive four miles to the north
entrance. Tubing is available here only during June, July, and August.
During this time, so many people want to tube that the number allowed
on the water is restricted. So, if you're not at the north entrance by early
morning, you'll probably be out of luck. However, at all times you can
swim in the Blue Hole Spring, where the water is such a vivid hue you'd
almost think it was dyed with the essence of sapphires.

Both entrances are open every day of the week, year around.
There is an entry fee of $3.25. For further information call
386–497–2511.

Smugglers Road

Return to SR 47 and turn north toward Lake City. During the Second Seminole War, this road was a military trail between the supply point at Ft. White and the fort at Lake City, then called Alligator. During the Civil War, Confederate blockade runners frequented the road. These men loaded their ships in England, dodged Union gunboats in the Gulf of Mexico, and traveled up the Suwannee and Santa Fe rivers to the vicinity of the old Ft. White landing. Here, they wagoned goods, such as clothing, shoes, and medical supplies, all of which were in scarce supply, to Lake City. On the return trip, the wagons carried Southern cotton for the British mills. But the Union blockade was so effective that most runners could make no more than two round trips before their brief entrepreneurial careers were terminated at gunpoint.

Today, the old Alligator Road is a tame route through a bucolic land where pastures alternate with deciduous forests. It ends at Lake City, twenty miles from Ft. White.

Welcome to Alligator: Old Lake City

In this sparsely populated portion of Florida, Lake City, with only ten thousand people, dominates Columbia County, as well as the six mostly rural counties around it. Lake City's location at the junction of Interstates 10 and 75 has become a magnet for franchise stores, restaurants, and motels. There are enough shopping centers along US 90, on the town's western outskirts, to rattle the rafters of Chambers of Commerce in cities four times its size.

But all this hustle involves the new portion of Lake City. It's far quieter in old Lake City beside US 90 at US 441 (Marion Avenue). Here, a decorative gateway welcomes everyone to Olustee Park. The park, which has been extensively remodeled, occupies a square block. Vintage commercial buildings on Marion Avenue and Madison Street face the park. The three-story Columbia County Courthouse, built in 1902, lines the park on the east. The courthouse extends to Lake De Soto, around which there is an appealing waterfront drive. Beside the courthouse, a graceful, Romanesque building, constructed during the Great Depression, serves as the federal post office.

There is a certain charm about old Lake City that speaks of what some call a kinder, gentler age. But those who claim the past was kinder and gentler either don't know the past or have a warped definition of what constitutes kinder and gentler.

Lake City's Olustee Park is a pretty oasis in the center of town.

Certainly, no one would refer to Hernando de Soto and his cruel army of avaricious freebooters who cut a swathe through here in 1539 as being kind and gentle. Neither were the early American settlers who fought for their very existence in what one visitor called "a collection of log cabins occupying a cheerless sandy clearing in the midst of pine woods." The crudest sort of frontiersmen ran the taverns of this rough hamlet. When war with the Seminoles broke out in 1835, Fort Lancaster, which faced the park on the north, became the base from which grim militiamen conducted search-and-kill missions. After two decades, the extermination of the local tribes was followed by the Civil War. The fierce Battle of Olustee was fought just fourteen miles from town. Upon the battle's conclusion, wounded soldiers from both armies were transported to the park, where they lay bleeding and groaning until places could be found for them at one of the town's makeshift hospitals.

If things got dull in this kinder, gentler era, one could attend a hog killing. At this time a hog or two was shot then butchered on the spot. After the blood and gore had been disposed of, the legs, back, and ribs were roasted. While the pig was cooking, the people enjoyed games and chitchat. Then, after the pork chops and ribs had been consumed and the sky turned to twilight, fiddlers scratched out tunes and the young set jigged, cavorted, and maybe sparked a little in the shadows. Yup, there was nothing like an old-fashioned hog killing to take one's mind off the endless drudgery of rural life.

Lake City's halcyon days took place during the mid 1920s when half the cars flooding into Florida from the North came down White Springs Road, soon to be designated US 41. Many tourists stopped for information at the Lake City Chamber of Commerce, which commenced glad-handing at six in the morning and continued until knuckles gave out around midnight. One day during the winter season, a troop of diligent Boy Scouts counted the arrival of 1,700 non-local southbound cars, or nearly three a minute. Lake City proudly proclaimed itself the Gateway to Florida. Boosters say it still is.

Across Northern Florida

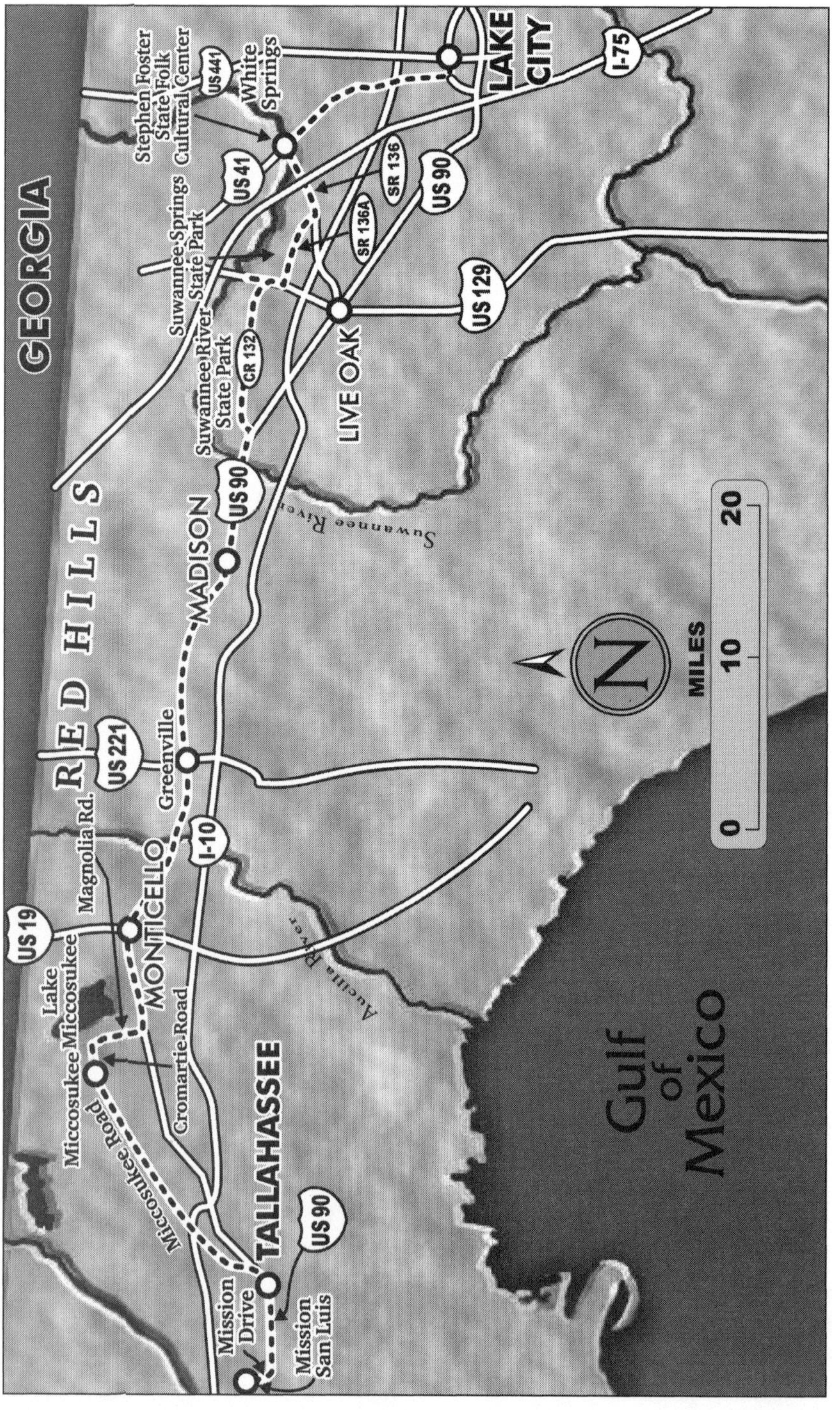

The River and the Hills

Lake City to Tallahassee • 131 Backroad Miles

The Song of the Road: Overview

This exploration begins at the juncture of Interstates 10 and 75 in Lake City. From there, we'll drive northwest to White Springs, where we'll find the storied Suwannee River and an extensive memorial to Stephen Foster. Chimes from a lofty bell tower play his songs and artisans make (and sell) handicrafts typical of Foster's era. The Suwannee River is a dominant presence for the next few stops, which will include areas known for bluegrass concerts, a sulfurous health spring, and scenic hiking trails.

Next, it's into the Red Hills region, once famed for its plantations. White cotton fields covered the hills that are, today, green with the pines that support a flourishing timber industry. The towns of Madison and Monticello are replete with mansions and memories. Then, passing into Tallahassee's Leon County, we'll mosey along some of the vaunted canopy roads, so named because of the massive live oaks that overhang them. Here, you'll encounter the Dueling Oak, which is haunted by tales of deadly encounters with pistols and knives.

In Tallahassee, we'll visit Goodwood, a lovingly refurbished mansion built during Territorial days and home to a series of planters, millionaires, politicians, and social butterflies. Next, we'll stop at the historic capitol building, a pleasing amalgam of 1846 architecture and a modern tower. From there, we'll pass the state supreme court building, which figured prominently in the disputed Bush-Gore presidential election of 2000.

We'll end at the secluded grounds of the reconstructed mission of San Luis, the largest of the twenty-five or so Spanish missions that extended across northern Florida.

On the Road Again

From Lake City, take US 41 northwest. Large numbers of Midwestern motorists traveled this route before expressways and airlines made it virtually obsolete. The land is hilly because you're skirting Florida's northern highlands. In a dozen miles, you'll cross the Suwannee River and enter the village of White Springs.

White Springs

Watch for the sparkling new Nature and Heritage Tourist Center, run by the State of Florida. It was located here because White Springs is just four miles from Florida's first major exit off Interstate 75. Center personnel will help you book hotels and arrange tours. And, if you relish free leaflets, you'll be in handout-heaven. There's stuff about every historic, cultural, and natural lure in the state. Should you want a quiet place to sort out your spoils, you can sit on the long veranda in the rear that looks out on a forested world. This veranda is much like the one at the old spring house that once made White Springs a favorite tourist and health aficionado destination.

The spring house stood across a small ravine from what is now the Tourist Center. Built in 1908, it was a four-story, hollow square around the spring. There were open halls on each interior floor from which macho showoffs took great pleasure in diving to impress the ladies. However, the springs attracted more than daredevils, for the waters were believed to cure discomforts from toe corns to toothaches—and everything in between.

Although steamboats once plied the Suwannee River, it was Stephen Foster's song that made it famous.

The Foster Fair

Today, White Springs is best known for the Stephen Foster Folk Center. Foster's famous "Swanee River" was adopted as the state song in 1935, and where better for a memorial than White Springs beside the Suwannee. The big problem was what to build here, since the song was only a ditty that could be played on a Victrola in a couple of minutes. But, because this was Florida, where most things have to have glitz, a twenty-story carillon tower was constructed. In it, the world's largest tubular bell instrument was installed. Every fifteen minutes its ninety-seven chimes propelled sound not only over the park, but down the river, into town, and out into the surrounding pine forests. And at 10:00 A.M., noon, 2:00 P.M., and 4:00 P.M. each day the world is treated to a full concert of Foster tunes. Now, that's the way to attract sightseers.

But you get much more for your $3.25 state park entry fee! At the tower's base is a spacious lobby that resembles a mausoleum. Within, Greek pillars rise from a marble floor. At the far end, a bay is inscribed with Stephen Foster's name, as if it were his tomb—although he died in New York City.

And there's more! Across a spacious meadow from the tower, a structure resembling a plantation manor was built. Inside are a series of dioramas depicting scenes from some of Foster's songs. The "Suwannee River" diorama shows black workers picking cotton while a steamboat moves across the background. "Oh Susanna" has pioneers on the Great Plains. "I Dream of Jeanie" shows a wistful woman in a flowing skirt.

And there's still more! On the other side of the carillon tower, a path leads to Craft Square. Here, there's a gift store and individual workshops where artisans demonstrate how everyday pioneer items were made.

Finally, so everyone can remember the subject of all this hoopla, a walkway on the far side of the parking lot leads to the Suwannee River. Don't be expect it to be broad like the Mississippi. Instead, you'll find that it's an ordinary stream modestly wending down a sandy channel clothed in trees and greenery. If the Suwannee had feelings, I'm sure it would blush that so much fuss is made of it. After all, it's just doing its job.

Way Down Upon the Pee Dee River

As for Stephen Foster, the folk center might have surprised him too, for, although his song made the Suwannee famous, he had no familiarity with the river and had never even been to Florida. His original lyrics related to the Pee Dee River in South Carolina. But Pee Dee lacked a certain lyrical zing. So, upon consulting an atlas, he selected the Suwannee simply for its melodious sound.

The name comes from the language of the Creek Indians, who roamed Georgia, where the river has its source. According to one interpretation, their word meant river of echoes. Today, soft rustlings still vibrate between the river's steep bluffs and down its graceful channel.

Stephen Foster the individual certainly wasn't worth the center's noble monument. He was moody and unstable. His wife, in despair, finally left him. He was completely incompetent with his personal finances, sold his songs for pittances, and lived in near poverty. At last, he turned to alcohol, dying a miserable, lonely man in 1864 at the age of thirty-seven.

Through the Wilds of Suwannee County

From White Springs take the SR 136 bridge over the Suwannee River. Although the river's ultimate destination is the Gulf of Mexico, almost due south, it flows temporarily north here following a fracture in the rocks. Now, you'll cross land that is a gently rolling mixture of pastures and pines. In four miles, you'll pass the Interstate 75 exchange, and, in two more miles, you'll come to a fork in the road. Take 136-A. This is a narrow county road that heads into a backwoods area. As you weave around the low hills, note that most of the pastures are gone and forest has reclaimed the land. After only seven carefree miles, little 136-A ends at US 129, headed toward Atlanta. Although you must travel north on this rather active federal highway, you can shake it in two miles by turning west on CR 132. If, however, you want a little surprise, continue on US 129 for a mile until you come to The Spirit of the Suwannee Music Park.

A Fiddle-Pickin' Paradise

Despite the fact that the park is basically an RV campground, there are several amenities to be had for the $5 per car admission fee. There are many miles of hiking trails along the Suwannee, and you can rent canoes to paddle on the river, which, from here, runs almost due west. The canoes cost $9 per adult for the first hour and $4 more for an additional hour. The park offers horseback riding at $25 an hour. Other amenities, such as the swimming pool, are available only for permanent guests. If you want to become one of these, a modern cabin sleeping six can be had for $65 per night, but you will probably need to reserve one at least thirty days in advance.

Some people might consider the park a cornball operation, for the clientele loves the bluegrass concerts that sometimes attract up to sixteen thousand devotees. (Tickets run from $10 to $60.) Others relish the cracker atmosphere where homegrown musicians plunk away in the pickin' room until the moonshine runs out. For more information call 386–364–1683.

Cracker Country

In case you hadn't guessed, you're in cracker country. To be known as a cracker in Florida is not insulting. The term probably originated with the old-time cowboys whose eighteen-foot-long whips could cut a cow's hide or slice off a bull's ear. But usually the crack of the whip, loud as a pistol shot, was enough to control the unruly critters. Soon the term cracker designated mostly native-born, rural people, distinguished by their fierce independence and respect for traditional values. Today's crackers dwell mainly in the double tier of counties running more than 350 miles from Pensacola to just east of Jacksonville.

So, how do you know if you're talking to a cracker? Just listen. If his voice sounds flat as an ice pond in January, that's not him, but if it twangs like a fiddle at a square dance, you're talking to a cracker.

Greetings From Hell

Continuing on US 129 for a very short distance, you'll come to the Suwannee River, which is now flowing west. Just before the bridge, on the east side of US 129, is Suwannee Springs Park. When the water here bubbles to the surface it smells as bad as last month's garbage. In fact, it smells so bad that in the late 1800s many people were convinced it had healing power. Thus, hosts of sick and silly people arrived by rail. To accommodate them, hotels were built around the springs. Today, those hopeful ladies and gentlemen have passed on to the great celestial sulfur spring and all that remains of their earthly paradise is the stone foundation of a spring house.

The land hereabouts, along the Suwannee River, belongs to the Suwannee River Water Management District, a state agency formed for flood control and to protect water quality. Because the district protects both sides of the Suwannee River for a considerable distance, the banks remain densely forested, and the shore has long, inviting stretches of clean sand. There are picnicking facilities and more than ten miles of hiking trails. Swimming is also a highlight—relax, it's in the river, not in Satan's dishwater. Admission is free, and you even get the use of a restroom.

The Old Stage Coach Road

Now, return to the CR 132 junction and head west. CR 132 is known locally as Stage Road, so named because horse-drawn coaches once rattled over this route between Jacksonville and Pensacola. In those days, this was just a rutted path through sand and pines. When automobiles came into use around 1910, travelers making the horrendous trip took an entire day just to bump and scrape between Lake City and Tallahassee, a distance of a less than 120 miles.

Suwannee County, through which you're now passing, has a population less than thirty-five thousand. Its economy is almost entirely based on agricultural products. Among the most important of these is the raising of chickens. Chicken farmers have problems we city dwellers cannot even imagine. For example, one day recently, a minor thunderstorm passed over the county. Suddenly, there was a lightning strike. In one flashing instant, eighty-five thousand chickens lay dead. It's not easy to get rid of that many poultry corpses, and they decay very rapidly in the scorching Florida sun. Within hours, a horrible stench began wafting from Suwannee's fields. "Fowl Odor Penetrates the Air," ran a local headline. It smells a whole lot better now.

Soon, pastures appear once more inside forest clearings, and, in thirteen miles, you'll reach Suwannee River State Park. Yes, the river is back. But it has found the right direction at last and is now flowing south.

Suwannee River State Park

Suwannee River State Park is not a major tourist attraction, but it is an interesting place—and admission is only $2 per car. Don't pass it by—unless you've had your fill of the Suwannee by now.

The entry road leads past a concession stand and to a picnic area overlooking the river. The opposite bank of the river is high and forested with large oaks, sweet gums, and rare cedar elms. To the right, just before the river makes a gentle bend, there is a boat ramp. To the left, at another bend, is a railroad bridge. A short stroll along the river will take you to the bridge, which is still in use.

Before the bridge was built, a ferry transported stage coaches and wagons across the river. The first bridge dates to Civil War days, when it was used by trains freighting cattle to Confederate soldiers.

Southerners, knowing that the Union troops who occupied Jacksonville might try to destroy this important bridge, built earthworks to guard it. These proved unnecessary, for the federal army was turned back at Olustee. The laborers constructing these fortifications would surely be miffed if they knew that the result of their work would be to provide future Yankee tourists with brief sightseeing thrills.

Once, a large sawmill, fed by logs floated down the Suwannee, was located here. The town of Columbus grew up around the mill, but, when the forest was transformed into stump fields, the town vanished, leaving only some badly faded tombstones in the cemetery. You can reach the graves via the Sandhills Trail, which begins at the south end of the parking lot and goes for almost a mile. Other short hiking paths lead up the Suwannee River, out to Balanced Rock, and around the Lime Sink Run ravine.

The Great Suwannee Strait

Now, drive west on US 90, which borders the park on the south. Although the highway is part of the federal system, it's not busy. Interstate 10, a few miles farther south, obligingly carries the through traffic. Almost immediately, US 90 crosses the Suwannee, but you won't see the river because the engineers have skillfully installed panels that obscure it. However, you do get a good view of the railroad bridge. Just trust me, the river is beneath it.

Once across the river, you'll be in the Twin Rivers State Forest, which is a series of smallish parcels of land along the Suwannee River and its tributary, the Withlacoochee. The segment here is only three miles wide, but it's nice while it lasts. To some geologists, this area is known as the Suwannee Strait, a massive waterway thirty miles wide coursing across Florida and Georgia to connect the Gulf of Mexico with the Atlantic Ocean. But don't be surprised that there's no water in this mighty strait—you're about forty million years too late.

The Red Hills

Soon, you'll enter the rolling countryside of Madison County. These are the Red Hills, so called because of the red color of fresh excavations. The hills are composed of runoff from the Appalachian Mountains and were originally some three hundred feet above the plain to the south. Over the eons, rainwater sculpted this flat land into the beautiful hills and valleys that we see today. These hills extend westward across Florida for 150 miles, yet they are never more than twenty-five miles wide. Pioneers found this ruddy soil, with its clay base, to be far better for growing crops, such as cotton, than the sandy soils in most of the state. So it was here that Florida's antebellum plantation system flourished.

Even before Florida became a state in 1845, the five-county Red Hill region was called Middle Florida to distinguish it from east Florida, based at St. Augustine, and west Florida, based at Pensacola. Tallahassee was Middle Florida's main city, but each county had important political and social centers. In Madison County it was the town of Madison, the county seat.

"Wish I Was in the Land of Cotton"

The entry into Madison on US 90 is impressive. The courthouse stands at the top of a hill, its clock dome rising above the trees like the helmet of some medieval baron. And, in some ways, the town was a baronial principality. It was ruled by wealthy planters and was a hotbed of secessionists. When the state quit the Union, "the streets were lighted up with bonfires," recalled a former Confederate. "Bells were rung and cannon fired; stirring speeches were made and Southern songs were sung."

The courthouse at Madison glows in the late afternoon sun.

Because Madison was where most of the county's wealthy planters resided, it was the hub of local life. Its stores provided residents with nearly all their essential goods, and the courthouse was where most legal matters were resolved. Madison's politicians were all-powerful, not only within Madison County, but even in mighty Tallahassee. Here, they and their cronies from Middle Florida controlled the legislature. This control continued for more than a century, until a hard-fought battle finally ended the rule of what had become known as the Pork Chop Gang.

Take a moment to explore Madison. The courthouse has a pressed tin ceiling, ancient chandeliers, and a court room on the second floor with lots of seasoned wood. The building has been spruced up, but it is much as it was when it was built in 1913.

Across Range Street and facing the courthouse on the west, is the Ashley Building, built in 1895 and occupied by the T. J. Beggs Company clothing store, which has been in business for more than a hundred years. A museum on the second floor has company artifacts, including proper dress for the dead—Beggs also operates a chain of funeral parlors.

Across US 90 (Base Street) is Four Freedoms Park. It was proudly known as Confederate Park until a speech by Franklin Roosevelt during World War II brought forth new patriotism. A large gazebo sits on the site of a blockhouse built around 1835 to protect frightened homesteaders from marauding Seminole warriors. The gazebo is popular for weddings, concerts, and other public functions.

The Manor House, constructed in 1904 to replace an earlier hotel, faces the park on the west. The Manor House is a bed and breakfast that offers suites from $98 to $125 a night. It also houses Miss Virginia's Café, which has courtyard seating and is open Tuesday through Saturday between 11:00 A.M. and 2:00 P.M., as well as Friday and Saturday evenings 6:00 P.M. to 9:00 P.M. (Reservations are recommended and can be made by calling 850–973–6508). Miss Virginia serves "food to die for," according to one local citizen. Unfortunately, I was not in Madison at the proper time to die at Miss Virginia's. Perhaps you'll have better luck.

Madison is loaded with fine, vintage homes, each with more history than you'd care to know. The Chamber of Commerce, beside the Manor House, offers a free walking tour booklet.

Without question, Madison's most beautiful building is the magnificent Greek revival mansion beside US 90, a few blocks west of courthouse square. It was built in 1860 for Benjamin F. Wardlaw, who dubbed it Whitehall. Four years later, the great house was utilized as a hospital for both Northern and Southern boys wounded at the Battle of Olustee. Now known as the Wardlaw-Smith-Goza Conference Center, it offers tours on Tuesdays, Wednesdays, and Thursdays between 10:00 A.M. and 2:00 P.M.

Madison's Vicious Circle

Despite the effort to present a bold face, Madison is struggling. With a population of only 3,500, the town lacks the facilities to attract businesses. For example, any new company would have to provide its own water and sewer treatment facilities. "We lack the money to update our system," a spokesperson for the Chamber of Commerce told me. "We're hoping to get help now that we're part of an Enterprise Zone," she added, referring to a state program intended to lure businesses to certain depressed areas by means of sales tax refunds, tax exemptions on electricity costs, and other incentive programs. Nonetheless, Madison seems to be in a vicious circle: new businesses won't come until there are infrastructure improvements, but these improvements can't begin without the increased tax base that only new businesses can provide. What's left? To live in the tranquility of the past, which seems pleasant enough to many Madisonians.

Plantation Country

Leaving Madison atop its gentle hill, US 90 continues west. The land here is mostly timbered now, but during the cotton era the hills were crowned with fields of white. To wealthy antebellum plantation owners, theirs seemed a way of life that would last forever. One of these owners, Reddin Parramore, owned a plantation that stretched many miles along what is now US 90. In addition to cotton, nearly four thousand cattle grazed in Parramore's rolling pastures. He had a spacious home in Madison, where he owned the western third of the present town. After he died in 1851, his young widow took over his extensive holdings.

Although the Parramores treated their slaves kindly, other plantation owners were cruel. One of the worst was a certain Judge Wilkerson, who had one slave flogged to death for taking part in a religious ceremony. Other masters forced slave women to have sex with them, anticipating light-skinned babies who would be taken from their families and brought into the manor home as house servants.

Timber trucks are frequent along northern Florida highways.

When the slaves were granted their freedom, upon conclusion of the Civil War, most of them had no place to go and remained in this area, working as sharecroppers. Many of their descendants still make their homes in Madison County, where forty-two percent of the population is black. Compare this to nearby Columbia County, which is not in the old cotton belt, where only nineteen percent of the population is black.

Timber Rules

Today, the cotton fields are gone, having provided boll weevils with many sumptuous feasts. The plantation homes, along with the slave shacks, have merged with the earth, and the pine trees that ruled before them have returned. Timber is one of Madison County's chief commercial activities. You'll probably encounter trucks hauling logs to the mills around Jacksonville, Palatka, and other locations.

Now, US 90 follows a route that for more than a hundred years was used by Spanish friars and their Timucuan converts. They called it the Camino Real, or Royal Road. Near here was the important mission of Santa Elena de Machava. To the friars, the Camino Real was a narrow cord of civilization threading past wild, New World trees that towered over the path like threatening spirits. But to the Timucuans, the shady forest corridors provided the game animals they depended on for food and clothing.

The Aucilla River

 Soon, you'll pass through Greenville, which, even though its population hardly nudges a thousand, is the second largest city in Madison County. In six miles, you'll reach the Aucilla River. During the Ice Age, Paleo-Indians hunted in this swampy area, which is more than a mile wide. Among their quarry were mammoths driven here by northern glaciers. Later, the river formed a sharp demarcation between land claimed by the Timucuan Indians to the east and the Apalachee to the west.

The two tribes were completely different. The Timucuan numbered around 200,000, but were scattered in small sub-tribal units around a vast area, reaching from Orlando into Georgia. Although the Apalachee had only a quarter of that number, their density was far greater. Furthermore, the Apalachee had an agricultural economy, superior technologically to the largely hunting-fishing economy of the Timucuans. Early European map-makers, thinking the Apalachee were a far more extensive tribe than they actually were, named one of North America's most important mountain chains in their honor: the Appalachians.

The Aucilla River still bears the designation given to it by the Spanish at the mission of San Miguel de Asyle located near here. Since missions were dedicated to a saint and then the mission's location, the asyle would have described something important to the Timucuans. But the tribe vanished before their rather musical language could be recorded.

The Spanish also had a plantation near here where honey from the tupelo trees and meadow plants was gathered and then transported by mules to St. Augustine.

Today, the river has been shorn of most of its glamour and simply divides Madison County from Jefferson County.

Walkin' Lawton

Passing the Aucilla River, watch for the small sign that pictures a pair of old boots. It's one of a series of signs dedicated to Walkin' Lawton Chiles. (His last name rhymes with miles.) When Chiles decided to run for the U.S. Senate in 1970, he realized that almost no one had ever heard of him. So, in order to gain name recognition, he

Signs along US 90 mark the route of Walkin'
Lawton Chiles.

decided to walk from the Panhandle to the Keys, talking to ordinary folks and garnering whatever publicity he could.

Chiles had many unusual experiences. One such experience concerned his underwear. "They kept creeping up on me all day," he confided in his journal. "I'd walk a couple of steps and tug them down, walk a couple [more] steps and tug them down [again]." As his plight became known, a friend presented him with two pairs of silk shorts, one bright green and the other brilliant orange. They not only cured his troubles but gave him as much publicity as anything that occurred during his thousand-mile trek.

Walkin' Lawton gained his seat in the Senate, where he served three distinguished terms. He then ran for governor, winning his second term in 1994 over the strong Republican challenger Jeb Bush. He unexpectedly died in office a few years later. As for Bush, he won in 1998 and again four years later.

Little Mountain

The rolling Red Hills continue across Jefferson County. During the antebellum era, this fertile country supported many large cotton plantations. In 1851, to handle the produce, William Bailey constructed a large mill along the dirt road that is now US 90. It was one of the earliest industrial establishments in the state, but it went bankrupt during the disruptions of the post–Civil War era.

Jefferson County's seat of government is named, appropriately, Monticello. The courthouse, just as that at Madison, rises on the crest of a hill. It was designed to resemble Thomas Jefferson's little mountain home in Virginia, but somewhere along the line an un-Jeffersonian cupola sprouted atop the roof.

Monticello was a major town in antebellum Middle Florida. The state's first elected governor was from here. And Jefferson County took a lead in secession. When the war was over, a memorial to the fallen Confederate boys was erected. It still stands before the courthouse as a single column with a cloak draped over the top.

Monticello is pungent with nostalgia. Across from the courthouse is the Perkins Block—a massive, brick monolith built in

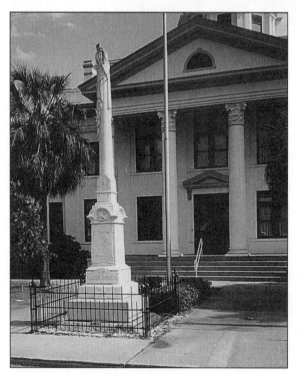

The courthouse at Monticello has an unusual memorial to the Confederacy's Lost Cause.

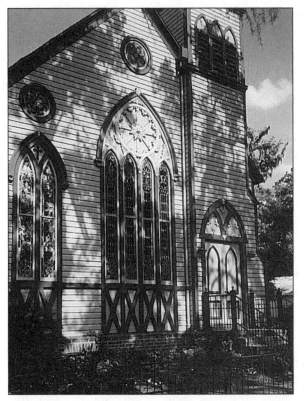

Shadows add weird Gothic designs to this graceful old church in Monticello.

1890 that was one of the largest opera buildings in the state. Visitors came to the second-floor auditorium to see vaudeville acts. Perhaps the shows got a little raunchy, since pressure from certain local churches was one reason for the opera's conversion to a movie theater in the 1920s and 1930s. But by the 1940s, the building had become an eye-sore—and remained so for fifty years until it was recently renovated. Now, the auditorium is again lively with plays and musicals— minus the raunch. There are evening performances once a month, with tickets running $10 to $12. If, however, you're just driving through and would like a quick visit to this authentic Gay Nineties entertainment hall, you can drop in any weekday between 10 A.M. and 4 P.M. There's no charge at these times.

The revival of the Opera House has helped set the pace for the rest of Monticello. The downtown has spruced up many of its old brick buildings, and north on US 19, at the corner of High Street, is the Christ Church, a timbered, Gothic gem constructed just after the Civil War. Two blocks farther north, on the northwest corner of Madison

Street, is the more-than-commodious Bailey-Eppes House, which was built by the widow of William Bailey, owner of the local cotton mill.

The Leafy Memorial

US 90, west from Monticello, continues through the rounded Red Hills. Much of the land supports deciduous trees, although there are some farms with good-size manor homes set back from the road. The road itself is something to see, for it has been landscaped with a variety of bushes and small trees, such as arbor vitae, palms, and flowering crape myrtle. The larger trees behind them are kept clipped and resemble a high hedge.

This pleasing effect continues for nearly the entire thirty miles to Tallahassee. The person responsible for this landscaping delight was Fred Mahan. During the 1920s and 1930s, Mahan's nursery beside US 90 was the largest ornamental shrubbery operation in the entire southeastern United States. Mahan dedicated himself to beautifying this highway, and his unusual legacy continues to gratify drivers today.

Welcome to the Canopy Roads

Very little commercial activity exists beside US 90. Most businesses prefer locations at the interchange of Interstate 10, which is less than four miles south of here. Soon, you'll enter the wetlands at the foot of Lake Miccosukee. Just over the bridge to Leon County is a sign displaying the well-worn shoes of Walkin' Lawton Chiles, who tramped past here in 1970. In three miles, you'll come to Magnolia Road. Turn north here to experience the pleasure of traveling on one of Leon County's vaunted canopy roads. It's a memorable five-mile drive, but don't pick an excessively rainy day, for the pavement soon gives way to a reddish mixture of clay and sand.

Magnolia Road was once used to transport cotton south, from the large plantations around Lake Miccosukee to the headwaters of the St. Marks River, from where it was shipped down to ocean-going vessels at St. Marks on the Gulf of Mexico. But Magnolia Road fell into disuse when a railroad connection was established between Tallahassee and St. Marks in the 1830s. After that, it became a local lane, which is exactly the way we like it.

The road is short, so drive slowly. Watch the interplay of leaves and branches as they drift overhead. Spanish moss swings lazily in any breeze that cares to float down the road. There are few houses or farms, just the large trees, much as when the road was laid out so long ago. In places, the road-cuts are several feet deep because the heavily laden mule wagons had trouble with inclines.

Pistols and Bowie Knives

Despite modern tranquility, violent incidents once happened along Magnolia Road. You'll soon come to Dueling Oak; you can hardly avoid it, since the tree squats directly in the middle of the road. A sign provides the name, but nothing else. We don't know what tragic dramas occurred here, but we do know that dueling was frequent in the days when Tallahassee was more a frontier town than the dignified state capital it tries to be today.

Perhaps one of the duels beneath the old oak was similar to one described by Ellen Call Long, who grew up in antebellum Tallahassee. According to Long, Oscar White and Leigh Read were bitter personal and political opponents. One of them made an insulting remark, and a challenge was issued. "The terms were severe," Ellen wrote. "They were to fire, once at ten paces, and in the event of neither falling, were to close with the use of bowie knives." The seconds counted off the paces, and the men shot. When both were still standing, they pulled out their knives and advanced on one another. "A more desperate

Dueling Oak glowers in the middle of Magnolia Road, a sandy byway near Tallahassee.

struggle was never beheld. They fell together, and the crowd looked on as if spell-bound." As some men moved to stop the fight, Read's second cocked his pistol and threatened to shoot anyone who interfered. The two adversaries stabbed one another until both were bloodied and dying. "They lingered in mortal agony a few hours, and then [both] expired."

Such is Long's account in her novel *Florida Breezes*. Although the actual fight is fictional, Ellen was personally acquainted with the dueling on Magnolia Road before law and fashion caused the custom to be abandoned.

Reeves Fish Camp

Not far beyond the dueling oak, you'll pass Cromartie Road. Then, you'll come to the road that leads to Reeves Landing. Turn right on Reeves and continue a mile or so to Lake Miccosukee where the rustic Reeves Fish Camp nestles amid shade trees. Here, you can rent a row boat for $10 a day and go out on the lake, which is surrounded by more trees. Or you can sit at one of the rustic camp store picnic tables overlooking the lake and enjoy a cool drink. Old Tom Reeves founded the camp back in 1945. Helen Reeves now owns it, and Eli Reeves operates it. A sign warns that camp regulations are enforced by Lester Reeves, who I did not have the pleasure of encountering. I did talk to Eli, who told me that the lake abounds with bass and bream, although I don't care to vouch for that assertion. He also stated that peace and solitude abound here, and that, I can say, is true.

Now, go back to Cromartie Road and follow it west. The forest that envelops Magnolia Road is on your left, and on your right are wide pastures that once were luxuriant with cotton. Ellen Long took many excursions along these country lanes, where, at harvest time, cotton whitened the hills for as far as she could see. One of the largest plantations in the vicinity belonged to Susan Blake, a relative of the road's namesake, Jack Cromartie.

Delayed Vengeance

In a mile and a half, you'll come to a crossroads not large enough to be a town or even a village. Nevertheless, it goes by the name of Miccosukee. In previous times, this was the chief settlement of the Miccosukee tribe. These industrious Indians grew corn, peas, and beans, as well as managed immense herds of cattle. The tribe's fields and pastures extended for miles. The Miccosukee nation was allied with the Seminoles; they were both adamantly opposed to the Americans just across the Georgia border. The central plaza (perhaps at this very crossroads) contained a pole hung with the blood-stained scalps of fifty Americans. Andrew Jackson and three thousand enraged frontiersmen descended on the town in 1818, burning the dwellings and killing the chief and many warriors. They also destroyed the crops, causing the remaining Indians to flee south.

After many decades of harassment, barely fifty Miccosukee Indians staggered into the Everglades. Today their descendants are gleefully exacting vengeance there from their nine-story resort and gaming casino.

Goodwood

From the hamlet of Miccosukee, turn southwest on Miccosukee Road. Before the Civil War, this road was often thronged with wagons carrying cotton to market in Tallahassee, and the plantations' mansions were often visible from the road.

One of the grandest of these mansions, Goodwood, was that built

Tallahassee's exquisitely refurbished Goodwood Plantation Mansion weaves a tale of cotton princes and society princesses.

by Hardy Croom in 1837. As his plantation prospered, Hardy decided to bring his family down from the North. But on the return voyage, Hardy, his wife, and their three children went down at sea. After Croom, the plantation had a succession of owners, most of them contributing to Goodwood's growth and refinement. During the Civil War, Confederate officers were frequently entertained at the mansion, the finest in Tallahassee. But after the war, with the slaves freed, the plantation went bankrupt. Subsequent owners used the mansion as a country estate. One owner was reputed to be the richest lady in the world, and another was a handsome state senator who hosted lavish parties for Florida's most important politicians.

You'll find Goodwood at 1600 Miccosukee Road, on the corner of Medical Drive, close to Tallahassee Memorial Hospital. Now owned by a private foundation, the mansion has been so meticulously restored that it almost glows. Much of the work was done by volunteers, including members of Tallahassee's high society.

The grounds are open, free of charge, every weekday between 9:00 A.M. and 5:00 P.M. Stop in at the office behind the manor for free descriptive literature. Then, roam the grounds, which occupy nineteen acres. Here, you'll find a dozen outbuildings, including the carriage house, stables, kitchen, and various guest accommodations, one of which carries the provocative title of Rough House. There is also a rose garden, a reflecting pool, and a beautiful grove of huge, overhanging live oaks. A forty-minute mansion tour is only $5. Tours are given Thursday and Friday between 10:00 A.M. and 3:30 P.M. For more information call 850–877–4202.

Downtown Tallahassee

Although visiting a large city's downtown would not normally be an appropriate backroads adventure, we are so close to the state capitol that I'll ignore the rules and include it. So, from Goodwood, continue on Miccosukee Road until it ends at Tennessee Street, which is our old friend US 90. Then, go three blocks west on Tennessee Street to Monroe Street. By driving a few blocks south on Monroe, you'll pass directly in front of the capitol's two buildings.

The low building in front with the Greek pillars was built in 1845 and is now used as a museum. (There is no fee for admission.) The former chambers of the state supreme court, the senate, and the house of representatives have been so meticulously restored that you'd almost expect to smell the cigar smoke and hear the squish of spit-

The old capitol building at Tallahassee recalls the tragic days of secession. The modern capitol tower rises behind it.

toons in use. It was here, a century and a half ago, that the legislators voted to secede from the Union. But the present is also noted, in an exhibit about Florida and the disputed 2000 Bush-Gore presidential election.

Behind the old building is a twenty-two-story tower, built in 1978. It is the actual seat of the legislature, which you can visit Monday through Friday 8:00 A.M. to 5:00 P.M. and Saturday 9:00 A.M. to 1:00 P.M. The legislative chambers are on the fifth floor and a splendid observation deck is on the twenty-second floor. Free self-guided tour leaflets are available in the first-floor lobby.

A Fleeting Flicker of Fame

From the capitol, drive south on Monroe Street to Madison Street. Then, proceed west two blocks to Duval Street. By going a block north on Duval, you'll be at the state's supreme court building, ground zero in the Bush-Gore election dispute. State officials often appeared on the courthouse steps to relay to the nation the latest news about the status of Florida's confusing "butterfly" ballots, the outcome of which would decide the national election.

At this time, Tallahassee was flooded with so many reporters and television crews that the city had a difficult time dealing with them. Around the supreme court building alone, an aerial photo showed forty trucks, some jammed with newspaper reporters and TV commentators, some with TV equipment, some with food and cots— and some vehicles of unknown and mysterious functions. "Well," one citizen commented. "There was enough [reporters]! Maybe at last they'll learn how to spell our name right."

When the ballots had been counted, and recounted, and disputed, and counted once more, George Bush won Florida, and thus the national election, by a mere 537 votes!

Tallahassee: Why Here?

Most people find it strange that Florida's capital is in a city that is so far removed from the rest of the state.

While Tallahassee's isolation is obvious today, when the site was chosen as the capital in 1824, this was the central location between Florida's two main cities, St. Augustine to the east and Pensacola to the west. As for peninsular Florida, it was deemed a mosquito-infested wasteland that would probably remain so for eternity. After Tallahassee became capital the region around it, called Middle Florida, soon became the center of a cotton culture that made it the state's wealthiest region.

After the Civil War, Middle Florida's prosperity vanished. Then, as the southern portion of the state became more densely settled, citizens discussed moving the capital to a more centrally located city, such as Ocala or Orlando. But the cost of such a move would have been prohibitive. So, it looks like the state is stuck with isolated Tallahassee, which suits locals just fine since a third of them have government jobs.

There's much more to see in Tallahassee, but it's not my intention to take you to popular places. If you are going to spend time in Tallahassee, get a carload of literature at the visitors center directly across from the north side of the capitol at 106 East Jefferson Street.

Now, I'll take you to a site that is properly obscure: the archeological treasure known as the Mission of San Luis.

The Mission of San Luis

Drive north on Duval Street, passing Park Avenue, which, if I were doing a city guide, I'd tell you was a street that showcases

The vanished Apalachee Indians worshipped in a temple similar to this careful reconstruction at the Mission of San Luis.

old Tallahassee. I might also tell you that after reaching Tennessee Street, if you continue four more blocks on Duval Street to Brevard Street, you'll come to the governor's mansion. But this isn't a city guide, so I won't. Turn west on Tennessee Street (US 90) and continue past Florida State University, which was begun as a women's college on good old Gallows Hill. As soon as you pass the stop light at Ocala Road, turn right on a small street called Mission Drive. Mission Drive leads through trees and along a hill to the mission parking lot. From there, a walkway continues up the hill, passing a series of display boards from which you'll learn that the Spanish mission dates back to 1656, when, at the request of certain Apalachee chiefs, Franciscan padres began the work of the Lord.

During the mission's most successful years, 1,500 devout men, women, and children honored the Christian traditions here. Gradually, the Franciscans extended Christianity through Apalachee territory until, at the height of their evangelical success, nine missions were active. Under Spanish tutelage, the province became an agricultural breadbasket. Soon, wagon caravans and mule trains transported food along the Camino Real to feed St. Augustine. Not only that, but the agricultural surpluses were such that a trade route was forged southward to the Gulf at St. Marks, where ocean shippers bought Apalachee foodstuffs for manufactured goods like blankets, hoes, axes, and cloth.

The reconstructed mission is at the top of the hill. The great church building, with its steeply pitched, palm-frond roof, once again rises more than forty feet above the original stone foundation. There had never been anything like it in Apalachee country. The church front was probably not plain, as it is today, but highlighted by an elaborate wooden facade decorated with religious figures.

Apalachee worshipers were summoned by a bell that rang over the surrounding villages like St. Peter's summons. Entering the church must have been like emerging into a strange, spiritual realm. The walls flickered unsubstantially in the light of candles, making the statues of the saints seem alive. Perhaps chanting reverberated from the walls and further enveloped the worshipers in an otherworldly sensation. The esoteric atmosphere created a mystical union between man and the awesome power that ruled the universe. That power might, at this very moment, be evaluating the Apalachee from the hovering darkness overhead. Then, from the far end of the church, the friar in his holy vestments would begin conducting the holy service in an ancient language that pleased the white men's god. Yes, there was a mighty force here that made the humble Apalachee tremble.

Across from the church is the spacious circular plaza that was the center of tribal activities. Sometimes, exciting ball games were held here. Fifty athletes at a time played with an intensity that could result in serious injury or even death. At the far side of the plaza, you'll find a pair of reconstructed buildings with tall, conical roofs. The larger building was the council house and could hold up to three thousand people during meetings and social affairs.

 The Spanish also had a fort here. Built of wooden palisades, it had a moat and eight artillery pieces. A short path leads to the site, but archaeological work is just beginning.

Unfortunately, the Apalachee tribe came to an undeserved end when one thousand British-led Creek Indians marched down from South Carolina in 1704. Once, the Apalachee could have mustered eight thousand braves to repel the invaders, but European diseases had decimated the tribe and Christian teachings of peace and good will had subdued their warlike spirit. Neither was the military garrison of much use, for the Spanish leaders had never envisioned an invasion of this magnitude and had stationed only a handful of soldiers at the fort.

So, the church and fort were burned. The invaders carried off several thousand Apalachee captives to toil as slaves. Subsequently the Spanish were forced to virtually abandon all of north Florida, except St. Augustine and Pensacola. Many years later, when the Seminoles drifted down from the north, they found the ruins of the mission and called it old town, which in their language was "tallahassee."

Mission San Luis is owned by the state. It is open Tuesday through Saturday between 10:00 A.M. and 4:00 P.M. Admission is free. While you're there, be sure to visit the former mansion of James Messer, which was built in 1938 and now houses a museum. Within, you can obtain literature about the mission and an audio wand for an in-depth tour of the site. The museum also offers a fifteen-minute orientation video and displays of artifacts found on the grounds. Those who wish to go deeper into the area's cultural heritage may purchase an excellent book with vivid color illustrations: *The Apalachee Indians and Mission San Luis* by John H. Hann and Bonnie G. McEwan. For more information call 850–487–3711.

The Panhandle Circuit

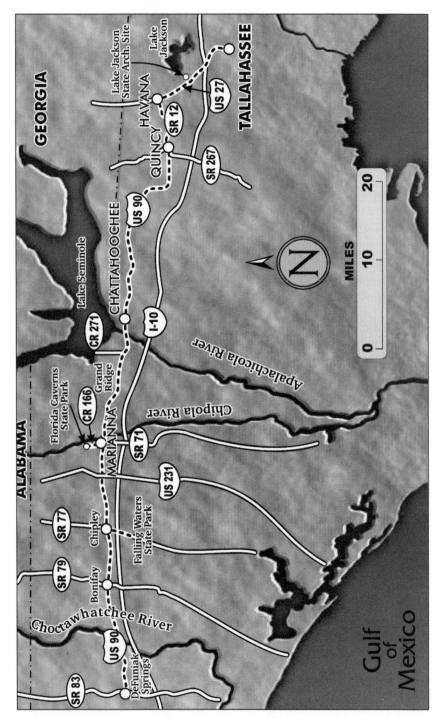

Backwoods Country
Tallahassee to DeFuniak Springs • 112 Backroad Miles

The Song of the Road: Overview

This exploration begins at the Lake Jackson Mounds, an ancient Indian religious and trading center that once thrived near Tallahassee. Then, we'll go north, through a rolling landscape, to Havana, once the center of a thriving tobacco industry. Today, the tobacco warehouses have been converted into shops locally famous for their antiques. Farther along the road is the quaint town of Quincy, highlighted by the mansions of people who became millionaires when they invested in the stock of a startup company called Coca Cola. Quincy's courthouse square is a renovated delight.

The road will then lead us through rural countryside to Chattahoochee, on the Apalachicola River. Here, a steamboat mural recalls the era when the town was an important stop for river commerce. From Chattahoochee, we enter Florida's Panhandle, a region that, in some ways, is more like Alabama, immediately north, than the rest of Florida.

Marianna is redolent with mementos of a Civil War skirmish and the turbulent days of Reconstruction. Just north of town is the Florida Caverns State Park, where fantastic caverns highlight the porous bedrock. West of Marianna, pine trees clothe the land. The CSX railroad accompanies the highway, recalling the days when the route was chopped through the wilderness by the sweating workers hired by Colonel William Chipley, who opened up this region a hundred and twenty years ago. This gruff old warrior is honored by the town of Chipley, which is also the county seat. Just eight miles farther west is Bonifay, another county seat, also named after a railroad official.

After crossing the extensive marshes of the Choctawhatchee River, we enter the town of DeFuniak Springs, the seat of yet a third county owing its birth and, for many years, its life to Colonel Chipley's railroad.

On the Road Again

Leaving downtown Tallahassee on US 27, drive northwest a mile or so past Interstate 10 to the stop light at Crowder Road.

123

By turning right on Crowder Road, you'll enter a forested area scattered with large homes. The road makes a long descent toward Lake Jackson, but before reaching the lake turn where the arrow directs you to the Lake Jackson Mounds State Archaeological Site. Admission is free.

The Mystery Mounds

From the parking lot, walk through the meadow toward the largest of the mounds. A pavilion at the edge of the meadow contains a large display board that tells about the people who once lived here. They were part of a group called the Fort Walton culture and had trade contacts with other tribes as far distant as Oklahoma.

Picture yourself in the Indian village that once occupied this site. Around you are huts with thatched roofs. It's evening, and smoke from campfires curls upward. The savory smell of cooking venison fills the air. Children laugh and play while, down at the lake, fishermen beach their dugouts and head for home. There is excitement in the air, for tomorrow the high shaman will ascend the tallest mound and communicate with the spirits.

Of course, no one knows what actually went on here eight hundred

A wooden platform at the Lake Jackson Mounds near Tallahassee permits modern visitors to stand where ancient Indian priests may once have made offering to the spirits.

years ago. But this was certainly an important centuries-old ceremonial center: the remains of a half dozen mounds attest to that. One prominent theory is that Lake Jackson was the capital town of the tribe that history knows as the Apalachee, the very people who were virtually exterminated at the mission of San Luis in the vicious campaign by British-led Creek Indians in 1704.

Ascent of the central mound is easy by way of a wooden stairway. On the summit, there was probably some sort of temple or spirit house. There's still majesty here. You can almost hear incantations to mighty beings for rain, or for relief from sickness, or for victory in battle.

As for the vista, I must report that it is disappointing, particularly if you've come to the Lake Jackson Mounds expecting to see the lake. But, if you like live oaks and hickories, you won't be disappointed.

The Disappearing Lake

After viewing the mounds, return to Crowder Road. Then, by turning right and traveling one block, you'll reach the lake—or what is the lake when the water shows up, for during frequent droughts, Lake Jackson shrinks until the water line is a considerable distance from the normal shore. But the truly strange thing about the lake is that every so often the water vanishes completely, not over a long period of time but in a matter of a few days. This unusual phenomenon is due to a pair of large sinkholes. They are usually plugged with sediment, which allows the lake to fill, but every few decades the sediment collapses into the vast caverns below. This allows the water to whirlpool into the immense underground system known as the Floridan aquifer. When this occurs, the lake's entire fish population is stranded, providing birds with a feast of utopian proportions. The last such drainings were in 1982 and 1999. The next is coming up.

It's Always Christmas Here

US 27, north from Lake Jackson, passes through land ideal for evergreens. When many people think of evergreens, they visualize Christmas trees. Although Northerners do not normally associate Florida with red-nosed reindeer and snowy roof tops, the Wilmar Christmas Tree farm may have them changing their tune. Wilmar's is where 30,000 carefully groomed evergreens unknowingly await the chopper's axe.

You'll come upon the farm with its neat rows of small, conical trees

Young Christmas trees extend over several acres near Havana.

a few miles beyond the Gadsden County sign. If you want to see more of the farm, drive through the storybook gate and down the narrow road into Wilmar's grounds. You're also invited to drive the byways that radiate far into the surrounding acres where Christmas trees of various heights create a fairy-tale landscape. Christmas ornaments and yard decorations are available at Wilmar's gift shop year-round.

Cute as it all seems, it takes a great deal of work to create a commercial Christmas tree. The trees must receive constant care during the four years it takes for them to reach a saleable height. "We clip each tree three times a year," Wil Sellars, the owner, told me. And during the summer, he sprays herbicide and insecticide at least once a month. Then, when the trees are chopped, the stumps must be pulled out using a special device Sellars has adapted for his tractor. "I don't just grow evergreens," Sellars noted with pride. "I create Christmas art."

Antiquers' Attic

Continue on US 27 through the gracefully rounded countryside. Once, this area was dotted with tobacco farms. The plants were grown under long sheets of cheesecloth that could cover several acres. Tobacco was a staple crop in this area from the time of territorial days. Eventually, the crop took on such importance that a little settlement around the railroad loading dock began to call itself Havana, after the Cuban city famous for cigars.

In four miles, you'll enter Havana, mainly a conglomeration of old brick tobacco warehouses. The demise of tobacco in the mid-twentieth century left the warehouses, along with the rest of the town, deserted and decaying.

Havana's revival began when a couple of entrepreneurs gambled that the deserted buildings could have appeal as antiques showrooms. As their little business caught on, other antiques dealers were attracted. Eventually, more than three dozen antiques stores opened up. Today, Havana attracts as many as 100,000 antiquers and other visitors annually—pretty good for a village of less than two thousand inhabitants.

For people who enjoy antiquing, Havana is like a trip to Oz. Anything old has an aura. Antiquers love the feel of Depression-era glass, of chipped cookie jars, of frayed dolls. They relish the musty fragrance of dog-eared books. They thrill to the sound of clocks that may have ticked away the years of a loved one's life. Others find simple pleasure in running a toy Hudson auto with peeling paint over a splintered table top.

Perhaps you, too, will be transported, if only for the moment, to a

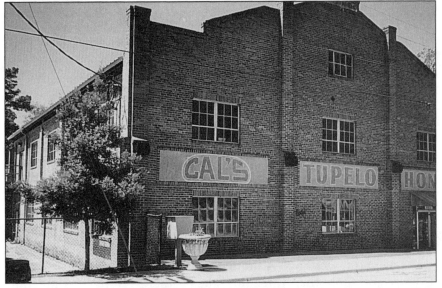

The fascinating Cannery antiques shop in Havana occupies what was once Cal's Tupelo Honey plant.

different realm—one where you'll accept that an outdated potato-masher can be worth $75; where a Teddy Roosevelt glass measuring cup can sell for $160; where a Bennington pie plate is a bargain at $1,000. There seems to be no limit to what avid collectors covet. Certain glass telephone wire insulators that date almost to the time of Samuel Morse can cost $30,000. A glass insulator, you might wonder, how many people can find a thrill in owning that? Well, for your enlightenment, the National Insulator Association has more than two thousand members.

You should mill among the antiquers. Perhaps you'll come upon enthusiasts from the Cuff Link Society talking about their last convention, which drew attendees from all fifty states. Prizes were offered for the oldest cuff link, the most unusual, the most humorous, and the one worn by the most famous person. Vendors included cuff link manufacturers, of course, but also shirt makers and authors of cuff link books.

You'll have fun just wandering the streets of this little town. Every shop sells its own particular type of antiques. The largest group of dealers is at the Cannery on Eighth Avenue, a half block east of US 27 (Main Street). This sixty-year-old brick building was originally used to can products of such rarefied appeal as collard greens and boiled green peanuts. After the cannery folded, the building became the hive of Cal's Tupelo Honey Company. Today, all that's left of Cal is his sign on the Cannery's exterior. But the building is not as decrepit as Cal's sign. Indeed, it's a thriving establishment jammed with antiques, home furnishings, and general gifts. There are more than a hundred booths in the Cannery as well as a restaurant that issues the challenge of serving "the best catfish sandwich you'll ever have."

The Cannery is open Friday and Saturday between 10:00 A.M. and 8:00 P.M. and Wednesday, Thursday, and Sunday between 10 A.M. and 6 P.M. But beware of Havana on Mondays and Tuesdays; on those days, almost the entire town is latched up as tightly as granny's corset.

The Two Faces of Quincy

From Havana, drive west on SR 12. The road is quiet because, as a partisan from Havana told me, "it doesn't go anywhere, except to Quincy." Although Quincy is the seat of Gadsden County and more than three times larger than Havana, a population of 7,400 does not exactly make Quincy a magnet city. Pine trees crowd

Quincy has many fine old mansions.

the two-lane road that will take us through wetlands along a creek with the awkward name of Attapulgus, which refers to fullers earth, an essential odor-absorbing ingredient used in kitty litter. A rather large processing plant is not too far distant.

After eleven miles, the road enters Quincy, where a quarter of the inhabitants live in poverty and the schools are among the worst in the state.

With this introduction, you may be expecting Junkville. If so, you're in for a surprise. Quincy has traditionally been the home of more per capita wealth than any small town in Florida. You'll pass some fine old residences along SR 12. One of the most impressive is the striking Greek revival structure at 306 SR 12. The owners made their fortune in tobacco and lumber. Another is at the corner of SR 12 and Madison Street. Turning south on Madison, you'll encounter more vintage buildings. At 122 Madison is a Methodist Church with stained glass windows; the middle one on the north is the work of Louis Comfort Tiffany.

In two blocks, you'll come to the courthouse square. The courthouse itself is something out of a picture book: clean, tan bricks balanced by a facade of slender Ionic pillars and a tasteful clock-cupola. The grounds are spacious, occupying an entire city block.

Refurbished commercial buildings face the courthouse on all four sides. The pride of Quincy is the sparkling Gadsden Art Center, which occupies a former hardware store at 13 North Madison Street. Nearby, at the corner of Madison and Washington Streets, is the former Quincy State Bank Building, now occupied by a clothing business. M. W. "Pat" Munroe, former bank president, was a key player in the creation of Quincy's multitude of millionaires.

In the early 1920s, Pat learned that a little Georgia company that made a bottled drink was taking its stock public. He urged his friends to buy some certificates. After all, Pat concluded, people will always be able to find a nickel for a cool drink. Many thought the idea was wacky, for who would want a cool drink in the winter? Despite the scoffers, several dozen people took Pat's advice. To nearly everyone's amazement, the stock rose, and split, then kept rising and splitting. Within two decades, simple farmers had become millionaires. The little company was Coca Cola. Today, one share of Coke stock that might have cost $40 in 1920 would be worth $4.7 million, assuming all dividends had been reinvested. It is, partially at least, from the largess of the twenty-five Coke millionaires that the downtown has been so lavishly renovated.

As you stroll around courthouse square, you may not be aware that almost two-thirds of Quincy's inhabitants are African-Americans. Their ancestors were brought here as slaves for the cotton plantations. When they were freed, most remained to work the tobacco fields. After tobacco burned out, they were stranded, lacking the money to leave and the education to find better jobs.

Education is Quincy's, and all of Gadsden County's, biggest problem. The county illiteracy rate is an astounding forty percent. The Quincy high school is dilapidated, according to a *Florida Trend* feature article. Although the whites, who apparently run the Chamber of Commerce (and whose children largely attend private schools), are actively trying to attract good-paying, high-tech companies, the labor force is at such a low educational level that these businesses shy away from the area.

The Two Faces of Gadsden County

US 90, heading west out of Quincy, is four lanes, but quickly narrows to two as it reaches deeper into Gadsden County. The low hills give way to land flattened by eons-old flooding by the Apalachicola River. The only town in this area is Gretna, which has a population of about two thousand people, nearly all black. Gretna's per capita income is one of the lowest in the entire state.

In contrast, a few miles beyond Gretna is Mt. Pleasant, location of the Robert F. Munroe private school. Here, the children, mostly white, receive a quality elementary and high school education that will enable them to go on to colleges or technical institutions.

The Cruel Forest

Forestry is the main industry hereabouts. Nearly all the pines have been planted by timber companies—you'll be able to see the rows if you view them at a certain angle. Over a million pine seedlings are planted each year.

The current trees are weak imitations of the magnificent forests that originally dominated northern Florida. Those long-ago towering trees were ideal sources of resin that was boiled and distilled into turpentine. The resin was obtained by cutting a deep, V-shaped gash into the tree about six feet above the ground. Galvanized iron gutters, hammered into the tree, channeled the resin to a clay pot hung beneath the V. The liquid was poured into barrels and hauled to the still for conversion into turpentine.

The turpentine industry seems innocent until you realize that during its heyday, from shortly after the Civil War until the First World War, the workers were mostly convicts from Florida's first state prison at Chattahoochee. The prisoners were leased to the timber companies, and the company labor camps were usually deep in the woods where brutalities could be committed without interference. Discipline was enforced by guards wielding leather whips, and misbehaving prisoners could be shoved into tiny, unventilated boxes placed in the sun where temperatures could rise to a near-baking level. At night, the men slept on boards. They were chained together, and they could hardly move.

It is a small wonder that throughout the Southern states a quarter of the leased convict laborers died during their first year of work. The convict hospital near Quincy, one of only two such hospitals in the entire state, could do little to alleviate the horrible situation. The system did not end until pressure from reformers and the beginnings of tourism demanded a change. Thereupon, prisoners were put to work building roads. One of these roads became US 90, completed in 1929.

This mural in Chattahoochee recalls the days when the town was an important steamboat landing.

The Forgotten River Port

Nineteen miles from Quincy, you'll enter Chattahoochee. This town was long known as River Junction for its location where the Chattahoochee and Flint Rivers join to form the Apalachicola, whose Indian name refers to the colored stones that brighten its riverbed.

Once, the town was an important stopover for the nearly two dozen steamboats regularly plying the three rivers. These boats transported cotton from plantations in Georgia and Florida to the port of Apalachicola on the Gulf of Mexico. Of all these steamboats only one still exists, though only on a large, outdoor mural at Heritage Park on the north side of US 90. The coming of the railroads sank the steamboats and Chattahoochee as well. Today, the town hosts the Florida State Hospital, Gadsden County's largest employer. Nonetheless, Chattahoochee seems to be continuing its long slide, and the town's current population of 3,300 is less than half of what it was just thirty years ago.

 Although Chattahoochee doesn't have much, it does have a pleasing outlook over the Apalachicola Valley and the Grand Ridge beyond. Maybe one day, somebody will think to put a park on these scenic bluffs.

The Frontier

As you drive over the Apalachicola River, you'll be passing into the Central Time Zone, so turn your watch back an hour. You are now entering the region known as the Panhandle, which many Floridians believe is actually much more than an hour behind the rest of the state. To them, the Panhandle is an unfortunate attachment. Many maps, following this line of thought, place the area as an insert in the Gulf of Mexico.

In truth, the Panhandle has always been separate. The Spanish had two political centers: St. Augustine in the east and Pensacola in the west. When the British took over in 1763, the Apalachicola River was the border between the colonies of West and East Florida. West Florida was deemed to have the most potential, for it reached all the way to the Mississippi. After the area became an American territory, East and West Florida vied for supremacy. As a compromise, the capital was an entirely new town, Tallahassee, equidistant between Pensacola and St. Augustine. No one could foresee that one day the swampy peninsula to the south, then called, with good reason, Mosquito County, would relegate West Florida to a position of near irrelevance.

Crossing the Apalachicola River

The Apalachicola River was an impressive border in the days before the first bridge was constructed in 1925. The only means of crossing was by way of a tippy ferry. The little boat could normally carry two wagons, but if you held your breath and really squeezed, it could carry three. The average trip took a full thirty minutes, what with the maneuvering and praying, but, if the water was high and turbulent, an hour of agony was more likely.

The Jim Woodruff Dam

The US 90 bridge over the Apalachicola River affords an excellent view of the Jim Woodruff Dam, completed in 1958. The dam was deemed necessary both to control downstream flooding and to furnish electricity to the impoverished nearby counties. Not only were these goals accomplished, but the impounded waters of the Flint and Chattahoochee Rivers formed Lake Seminole, now highly valued by fishermen and boaters.

For a better view of the dam and the lake, take the side road marked West Bank Overlook, just beyond the bridge. A drive of a few minutes will transport you up the slope to a scenic overlook.

The Jim Woodruff Dam at Chattahoochee forms Lake Seminole, a huge reservoir used for recreation and many other purposes.

However, if you want actual access to the lake, you should go to the Three Rivers Recreation Area, which is reached via CR 271, four miles farther west on US 90.

The Three State Water Fight

Whereas the water in the reservoir is placid, such is not the case with its allocation. If, from your viewpoint above Lake Seminole, you look directly eastward across the water, the opposite shore will not be Florida, but Georgia. And only twenty miles north is Alabama. These three states are perpetually squabbling over how much water each should get. For Florida, a good flow of fresh water is necessary to keep Apalachicola Bay from becoming too salty and thereby killing the oysters that provide the state with ninety percent of its commercial supply. But during times of drought, farmers in Georgia and Alabama resent sending their precious water floating off to Florida.

Representatives of the three states and concerned parties are valiantly trying to establish a policy agreeable to everyone. Heated negotiations have been going on for several years. "I don't know how to explain or articulate the incredible complexity of the negotiations," gasped one federal official. Ultimately, everyone may just throw up their hands and let Congress or the courts issue a decree. Then, the lawsuits will begin.

Now, back to US 90. Continuing west, the way leads through the Grand Ridge. But don't get excited. The ridge is pretty much ho-hum, despite its rather impressive appearance from the Chattahoochee bluff.

The "Mighty" Chipola

Right after you pass the junction with SR 71, you'll come to Spring Creek. This little stream has been dammed to form a wet sliver called Merritts Mill Pond. The pond runs north for four and a half miles, but is hardly ever more than six feet deep. However, don't discount it just because of its size. I am told that anglers catch largemouth bass, sunfish, and bluegills from the boat launch adjacent to the US 90 bridge.

A mile beyond Spring Creek, you'll cross the Chipola River, although you'll have a difficult time seeing the water through the mass of trees and shrubs that throngs its banks. Boosters from nearby Marianna once insisted that the Chipola was navigable for steamboats. Unfortunately, the best the gallant river could handle were rafts. Yet, in a way, the mythical, mighty Chipola still lives, for the Marianna city seal continues to feature a steamboat!

It Was Named for a Woman, But It's a Man's Town

Marianna was a relatively important market town during the pre-Civil War reign of King Cotton, but that old-time hustle is not apparent as you enter the town on US 90. Today, Marianna's main function is as the seat of Jackson County. However, that's not much, for the county contains barely 47,000 people. A somber courthouse discourages visitors, who are further intimidated by a metal detector at the doorway accompanied by a grim, uniformed guard. All in all, it's quite a change from a century and a half ago when Robert Beveridge gave the settlement a friendly name in honor of his wife, Anna Maria.

Marianna has recently improved its downtown as part of the Main Street program. These renovations were vitally needed, for, between 1980 and 1990, ten percent of the town's citizens moved to other areas. Evidently, they did not agree with Norman Crampton's inclusion of Marianna in his 1995 edition of *The 100 Best Small Towns in America*. In 2000, Jackson County was still trying to right itself. The Chamber of Commerce was urgently seeking members. "Jackson County is experiencing severe economic distress," wrote the chamber president. "We've lost lots of jobs in the last few years. . . . We desperately need your help!"

More about Marianna shortly. For now, let's leave courthouse square and head north on CR 166 for three miles to a most unusual attraction.

The Underground World

 The turnoff from CR 166 into the Florida Caverns State Park is well marked. After paying the $3.25 per vehicle entrance fee, drive to the tree-shaded parking lot and stroll up the path to the visitors center. The building is made of limestone laboriously assembled by the Depression-era youths of the Civilian Conservation Corps. The park's main attraction is, of course, the caverns, the only ones in the entire state open to the public.

A sign urges caution before you put down your fee for the forty-five-minute guided tour. (The charge is $5 for adults and $2.50 for children ages 3 to 12.) The cavern floor can be damp and slippery, and you must be careful of the overhead projections. Furthermore, a few of the tortuous passageways are barely two feet wide, so bulkier persons should be forewarned. Nevertheless, the cavern tour is quite popular. Call 850–482–9598 for departure times; then, arrive early. No advance reservations are taken.

Once inside the cavern, you'll find yourself wending along the bed

Florida Caverns State Park has stalactites in many unusual and graceful forms.

of what once was a small underground river. Although the caverns are minuscule compared to the ones like Carlsbad, these have their beauty. There are hanging stalactites shaped like stony icicles, soda straws, and rippled sea foam. There are stalagmites shaped like the towers of ancient Russian churches and wedding cakes for gnome brides. And there are rimstone pools, with water as placid as lava in lunar craters.

If you look carefully at the cavern walls, you'll discover shells of creatures that thrived here when it was an ocean, millions of years ago. Their remains hardened into the bedrock that forms the Florida platform, which underlies almost the entire state. Over time, slightly acidic ground water percolated into the bedrock and dissolved portions of the limestone; this formed the caverns and underground river channels that honeycomb subterranean Florida.

At certain places, the guide will stop to tell you vignettes about the cave. Prehistoric Indians once camped here—their tools and fire ashes revealed their presence. During the Civil War, women and children from Marianna huddled in these caverns while Union cavalry raided the countryside.

When you emerge from your cavern tour, you'll find there is even more to do in the park. You can hike along the many miles of forested trails. Or you can walk or drive a few hundred yards down the park road to the Chipola River, where there is fishing and swimming. For $10, you can rent a canoe and enjoy a half-day excursion along the unspoiled beauty of the free-flowing stream.

Now, let's return to Marianna and pause at the courthouse square.

Murders in Marianna

Marianna's most turbulent period was during the Reconstruction era. Try to imagine what it was like. The South had just lost the Civil War, and the Confederate government no longer existed. Florida was being run by Northern invaders under the Act of 1867. There was turmoil and tension, for the freed slaves believed they had been promised forty acres and a mule from plantation land that was to be divided up by the U.S. government. The whites were seething because their fields lay fallow for lack of workers and foreclosures were rampant. What resulted was a three-year outburst of violence in which 153 people were murdered in Jackson County—compared with just sixty-nine in the rest of the state!

The turmoil began when an assassin tried to kill William Purman, head of the Marianna branch of the Freedmen Bureau. Purman's black friends were so incensed that they gathered eight hundred armed men and threatened to sack Marianna in revenge. Although Purman was able to dissuade them, a day later, a white man was shot dead by unknown persons. Soon thereafter, a white farmer was killed. Retaliation came when a group of blacks on their way to a picnic was ambushed; two died. This was followed by a sniper's shot that killed Maggie McClellan, a young white girl, on the porch of a hotel in downtown Marianna. Maggie's father, who was with her and may have been the real target, thought he heard the voice of Calvin Rogers, who was black, giving the command to shoot.

The next morning, a mob of whiskey-inflamed whites surged through the square hunting for Rogers. When they couldn't find him, they satisfied their lust for vengeance by murdering one of Rogers' associates. Then, fearing an attack on Marianna by the blacks, who were largely country people, the mob looted Samuel Fleishman's store, taking all of its guns and preparing for all-out war. Fleishman, who was suspected of siding with the blacks, was run out of town. Several days later, his bloody body was found on the road to Chattahoochee. Only the arrival of federal troops from Tallahassee restored temporary order, but once the troops were gone, the violence continued. Eventually, both William Purman and Calvin Rogers had been murdered. By then, Jackson County was again dominated by the whites.

Although Jackson remained under white rule for more than a century, most blacks stayed in the area. Their homes were here, and they had no place else to go. Not until the Civil Rights Act of 1964 did African-Americans begin to integrate into the Jackson County power structure. Today, the city council consists of two blacks, two whites, and a white mayor. This is a fair representation of the city's racial composition.

The Beautiful Russ House

Leaving courthouse square, drive west on US 90 (Lafayette Street). Here, you'll pass many of Marianna's finest old homes. At a bend in the road is the Russ House, a distinctive building with a semicircular veranda and a second-floor balcony supported by six Corinthian columns. Once the residence of the prominent Russ family, today, the Chamber of Commerce proudly makes the mansion its headquarters. Visitors are invited to tour the restored building. Be

The unusual Russ House is a landmark in Marianna.

sure to ascend to the second balcony. From there, you can survey the town just the way the aristocratic Russ clan did after the prestigious structure was completed more than a hundred years ago.

A few blocks farther along Lafayette Street, at the corner of Wynn Street, is the St. Luke's Episcopal Church, a trim and appealing building. Turn right on Wynn and pull in to the church parking area.

A Wartime Incident

In early September 1864, three hundred boys and old men gathered in front of the church and hastily threw up a barricade across Lafayette Street. Word had reached the town that a column of seven hundred Union cavalry had thundered out of Pensacola intending to attack Marianna. With nearly every able-bodied white man fighting in Virginia, the young and old were the only resistance the town could offer.

Soon, the Southerners heard the rumble of men and horses approaching from the west along the dirt path that is now US 90. When the enemy was within range, they opened fire. As the astonished Union troops fell back, the elated Confederates thought the enemy had been repulsed. They didn't realize the Union commander had sent a strong detachment around the defenders. These Union soldiers easily gained control of the courthouse square, and then marched west to take the Southerners from the rear. The defenders split in disarray. A few continued the battle from within the church, but the Yankees set the building on fire. Several screaming volunteers burned to death. And when five others fled the flames, they were ruthlessly shot down.

With resistance at an end, the Union troops looted the town and terrorized the populace. Then, detachments plundered the outlying plantations, taking two hundred horses and mules and four hundred cattle and leaving the farmers helpless when spring planting came. That night, the Union force pulled out, taking six hundred freed slaves.

As a lightning raid, it had been eminently successful. As a blow to the people of Marianna, it had been devastating. As a Civil War action, it hardly made the battle reports.

The Uneasy Grave

The St. Luke's cemetery is beside the church's parking area. It's quiet here, for trees and the church building muffle the traffic sounds of Lafayette Street. Most of the stone markers show the weathering of years. In the third tier is a marker shaped like a Gothic church window inscribed with a small crown and cross over a shield. Beneath the marker are the remains of Florida's Civil War governor, John Milton.

The bones of Florida's tragic Civil War governor John Milton lie beneath this gravestone in Marianna.

Milton was a forceful man, quick-witted and a brilliant orator. He, his charming wife, and his ten children worshipped at St. Luke's. Milton possessed a two-thousand-acre plantation just north of Marianna, manned by more than three dozen slaves. He assumed the governorship of Florida in the fall of 1862 with considerable optimism, but as the war dragged on and the deaths piled up, he fell under terrible stress. By 1865, he knew defeat was inevitable.

The dread of what lay ahead was too much for the war-weary governor. On April 1, 1865, he addressed the Florida assembly for the last time. "Death," he lamented, "is preferable to defeat." Thereupon, he returned to his plantation. That evening, while his family chatted downstairs, he slowly ascended to his bedroom. Once there, he loaded his shotgun, placed it against his head, and ended his life to the cartridge's roar.

A tree overhangs Milton's grave. Sometimes the branches sigh as the wind vibrates through the leaves. Uneasy bones lie below.

Chipley: More the Story of a Man Than a Town

West from Marianna on US 90, the rolling hills give way to flatter, less fertile land where pines reign. In thirteen miles, you'll enter Washington County and, in five more, you'll be in the town of Chipley, the county seat. The rail line that parallels much of the highway predates the first through-road by forty decades. During this time, the railroad was the virtual ruler of the upper Panhandle. And the virtual ruler of the railroad was William Dudley Chipley.

Chipley was a talented yet volatile person. He joined the Confederate army when he was barely out of his teens, and, by the age of twenty-two, he had risen to lieutenant-colonel. After the war, he became an ardent foe of Reconstruction, and, at one point, he was even charged with murder, but was exonerated due to lack of evidence. Chipley combined fierce ambition with ruthlessness. One of his numerous enemies accused him of writing a political pamphlet so deceitful that even the commas reeked of falsehoods.

But Colonel Chipley, as he preferred to be called, had a great leadership ability that enabled him to attract money and followers. Soon, he acquired control of a struggling little railroad running a few miles out of Pensacola. Then, in 1881, he received a state charter to build a rail line across the Panhandle, from Pensacola to Chattahoochee. This charter granted the line alternate sections of land along six miles on either side of the right-of-way. This prize gave Chipley's projected railroad half of the best land in the upper Panhandle!

Under Chipley's leadership, the railroad was forged through the Panhandle's dense forest. When the line bridged the Apalachicola River at Chattahoochee in 1883, it linked up with other rail connections, opening the upper Panhandle for development. The town of Chipley, named in honor of the great man, not only became an outlet for numerous sawmills and turpentine distilleries but soon became known as the largest inland naval stores shipping center in the world.

That's all news from another era. Today, the boom times are long gone, and Chipley's county courthouse squats humbly beside US 90, its heavy pillars connoting weighty wishes for this town of four thousand. But there is a lot of inertia to overcome. For example, Chipley has a historical society that allows visitation at the convenience of the staff. This has resulted in the museum being open Saturday afternoons only—and, oh, that's just once a month. If you want excitement, the best Chipley can offer is a visit to the new Wal-Mart on SR 77, near Interstate 10.

The Sometimes-Waterfall

You may not find the Chipley Wal-Mart to be a major attraction. In that case, continue south on SR 77 for a couple of miles to route 77A. Then, head a mile east to Falling Waters State Recreation Area. Here is a one-hundred-foot shaft down which a pretty stream sometimes tumbles. When it's flowing, it's an honest-to-goodness waterfall. Anywhere else, it wouldn't be much, but, in a mostly flat state like Florida, it's quite a phenomenon. Unfortunately, it's impossible to guarantee that there will actually be falling water because it depends on the rainfall. It's been hit or miss the past few years— "mostly miss," a park ranger admitted.

Yet, even without the waterfall, an overlook permits an unparalleled view of the deep, dark tube leading to the vast underworld that permeates Florida's limestone basement. Beneath your feet are intertwining caves and tunnels, deep pools never pierced by sunlight, streams oozing through cracks and crannies, and rivers roaring on to destinations unknown. It's this black, alien, and largely unexplored world that is the precious aquifer that provides most of the state with its drinking water.

The park has several short paths that lead past scores of sinkholes, which are evidence of a disintegrating landscape. And, if you want a swim, there is a small lake with a sand bottom. A picnic area is nearby, but you must bring your own food, for the park does not have a sufficient number of visitors to justify a snack shop.

Yesterday in Bonifay

West from Chipley, US 90 continues along the railroad line,
now part of the CSX system. In four miles, the road passes over a
reclusive ribbon of wetness known hereabouts as Holmes Creek.
You are now in Holmes County, population 20,000. This county was
an artificial creation formed back in 1848 to give western Florida an
added seat in the state legislature and balance the growing number of
eastern Florida counties.

In four more miles, you'll come to Bonifay, the county seat—
although you may have difficulty associating a village of just three
thousand with the seat of anything. It is particularly difficult in this
case since you won't see the courthouse from US 90. It does exist,
however. To find it, turn north on SR 79 (Waukesha Street) and, after
crossing the railroad tracks, you'll come upon the modest, two-story
courthouse.

Bonifay originated in 1886 as a construction camp for the railroad.
A used boxcar was the railway station. Later, this same boxcar was
converted into the village post office. The first industry here was a pair
of sawmills furnishing lumber for the railroad. The town was named
Bonifay in honor of the railroad's assistant land commissioner—a big
man in those days.

The railroad is still active, but the CSX freights deliver just cinders
and a rush of hot air as they hurry non-stop through Bonifay. Amtrak
passenger trains also use the tracks, but they bypass Bonifay for
Chipley. Some lumbering continues in Holmes County, which is sixty
percent forest, but the county is far from prosperous, with a per capita
income among the lowest in the Panhandle.

The Choctawhatchee Challenge

US 90, heading west from Bonifay, is more like a country road
than a federal highway, since most tourists and truckers are
rumbling over Interstate 10 just two miles south. In a way, US 90 offers
the best of both worlds: it's a well-maintained federal highway, yet it's
almost as quiet as a country road. I don't even recall any billboards.
It's subtitled the Old Spanish Trail. Of course, it's not that primitive,
but it actually does approximate the path flattened by Spanish tread
several centuries ago.

In these days of easy travel, it's difficult to imagine how odious it

US 90 curves through a vast pine forest between Bonifay and DeFuniak.

was before motors and macadam. There were barriers everywhere. One of the worst was the miasmic slough around the Choctawhatchee River, which you'll encounter eight miles west of Bonifay. Before a bridge spanned this disagreeable wasteland, a traveler had to linger amid the mud and alligators until the ferryman on the opposite shore heeded his call. "I was compelled to pass the night," lamented Michael Portier in 1827, " . . . with only dirty water to drink, surrounded by all kinds of wild animals and all the insects in creation." Fortunately, a flask of rum gave him courage, and the next morning the ferry took him across the hateful morass.

Although a modern bridge leads motorists effortlessly over the mile or so of goo and glop, when Colonel Chipley's men tackled the job of bridging the river more than a century ago, it was a formidable physical barrier that took two sweaty years to conquer. More than sweat, the Choctawhatchee nurtured fevers that decimated the building crews. Despite the fevers, gators, mosquitoes, and other assorted goodies, frontiersmen turned the Choctawhatchee into a logging river that fed a large and noisy sawmill at Caryville. Today, that little settlement is mostly quiet. But there is some activity, particularly if you are in need of worms, wigglers, or crickets, which a sign proclaims are for sale here.

Beyond the Choctawhatchee US 90 continues through tall pines. These are actually tree farms, for, if you catch the pines at the right angle, you'll see that they are planted in rows awaiting harvest.

In twenty miles US 90 enters DeFuniak Springs, another of the rustic county seats that sprang to life with the advent of Colonel Chipley's railroad. The Hotel DeFuniak, at the corner of US 90 and Eighth Street, is comfortable, historic, and well managed. I describe it further in the next chapter. Newer accommodations are on US 331 at Interstate 10, a few miles south of the main part of town.

The Panhandle Circuit

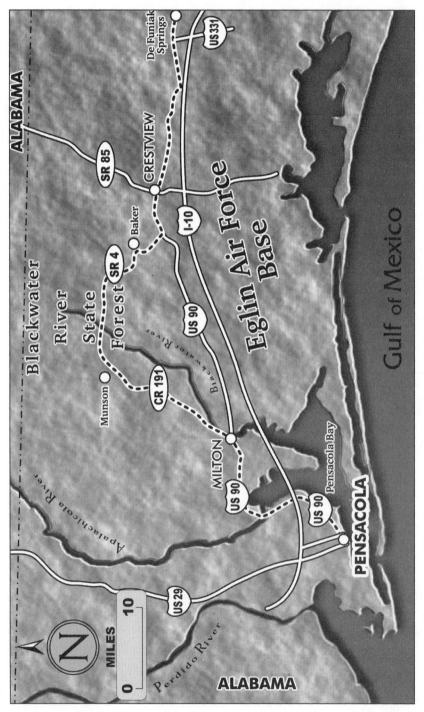

Tomorrow's Land
DeFuniak Springs to Pensacola • 97 Backroad Miles

The Song of the Road: Overview

This exploration begins at DeFuniak Springs, as pleasant a place to live or visit today as when it was the center of Florida's Chautauqua movement. The old Chautauqua building still stands in refurbished grandeur beside a lake so nearly circular that you'd think it should bear a label: Designed by Disney.

The road west from DeFuniak travels through a pine forest. At the town of Crestview, the old county courthouse has been replaced by a starkly modern structure, bespeaking the town's forward-looking aspect. Crestview's proximity to the gigantic Eglin Air Force Base has enabled it to prosper through military contracts. The fascinating Armament Museum is just outside Eglin's main gate.

Now, we'll turn northwest as our route leads through the Blackwater River State Forest, fragrant with pines. Pause at Bear Lake to enjoy hiking or fishing, or camping if you have your own gear. Then, it's on to Milton with its appealing boardwalk along the Blackwater River.

Farther west, we'll cross the wide mouth of the Escambia River, then turn south on Scenic Drive and travel along the river bluffs to Pensacola. The Plaza Ferdinand VII is dear to history buffs, for it was here that Andrew Jackson accepted the cession of Florida from a sullen Spanish commander in 1821. Finally, we'll head out to the Pensacola Naval Air Station to tour one of the world's great aircraft museums.

On the Road Again

If you're picking up this exploration from Interstate 10, exit north on US 331 and continue for two miles to US 90. Turn east here and watch for the Hotel DeFuniak. If you're arriving on US 90 from the east, you'll find Hotel DeFuniak at the corner of Eighth Street. At this point, turn south and travel one block on Baldwin Avenue, the main street of this community of five thousand.

Dream Town: DeFuniak Springs

DeFuniak Springs had its inception in 1881, when railroad surveyors thrashing through the dense pine forest were attracted by the almost circular lake. Railroad big shot William Chipley was with the surveyors as they camped beside the lake, which they named in honor of Fred DeFuniak, general manager of the railroad. "It was a beautiful star lit night," rhapsodized local historian, John McKinnon. "The moon was in its virgin glory . . . they laid themselves down on the green sward along [the lake's] gentle slopes . . . and . . . dreamed dreams and saw visions of coming prospects."

In the morning, Chipley leaped to his feet, according to McKinnon, and shouted "the railroad must come by this beautiful lake." He pictured this dream town not only furnishing water for his steam locomotives but attracting settlers who would bring commerce and profits to the railroad. So Chipley and his wealthy friends formed a company to promote and sell the land. Everything worked out better than they expected. Hardly were the rails laid, than the respected New York Chautauqua chose a site beside Lake DeFuniak for its annual, month-long winter assemblies.

Culture Comes to the Sticks

In the days before radio, television, or national newspapers, the Chautauqua center provided top-ranked speakers who lectured in subjects ranging from art and morals to history, philosophy, and the latest scientific discoveries. DeFuniak's annual sessions attracted considerable crowds, most arriving on chartered railroad cars. At first, the lectures were conducted in tents. But, in 1909, as the crowds increased, a permanent building was constructed, including the great Hall of Brotherhood, which seated four thousand.

Although the Brotherhood auditorium was destroyed by an unbrotherly hurricane many years later, the main part of the Chautauqua edifice still stands at 95 Circle Drive. Even today, it's impressive, with three columned porticoes in front and a dome worthy of a federal bureaucracy. A portion of the building now houses the Walton County Chamber of Commerce, where you can pick up informative literature about the town. The rest of the building is open only for specially arranged tours or during the annual Chautauqua Festival, held for three days in February. At this time, the building, as well as the town itself, comes alive with more than one hundred events, classes, and workshops that bring in artisans, authors, thes-

The old Chautauqua building overlooks a completely circular lake in DeFuniak.

pians, and scholars. In addition, a bevy of historic homes are open for inspection, and horse carriages offer tours of the town.

I had an unusual experience when I parked in this idyllic setting early one Sunday morning. I noticed a sheriff's squad car heading my way, but paid no attention until it came to a stop beside me. As the burly officer began unrolling his window, I searched for any possible misdemeanor I could have committed. The only one I could think of was enjoying the setting on the Sabbath. The lawman looked me in the eyes and said, "What's the way to the county jail?" Yes, he was asking me how to get to the jail! True story. It came out that he was hauling a prisoner from another jurisdiction and this area was unfamiliar to him. Well, there are always unusual experiences when you pause on the backroads. I didn't have the slightest idea where the jail was. And I intend to keep it that way.

Despite an occasional lost deputy, there's a peacefulness about the Chautauqua grounds. A profound quiet reigns. No motorboats are allowed on the water unless they run electrically. Small wonder people gathered here for almost four decades to reflect on such matters as Truth and the moral life—until the 1920s revolution in communications made such meetings almost irrelevant.

The Enchanted Circle

People still come here to walk or jog the mile-long path around the lake, just as Chautauquans did so many years ago.

Circle Drive, which likewise rounds the lake, is also a highlight. Bordering the drive on the land side are spacious homes, many featuring the bay windows, gingerbread filigree, and gracious front porches that were so popular when Queen Anne architecture was the rage, more than a hundred years ago.

At the north end of the lake, close to the railroad tracks, is the frosting-white First Presbyterian Church. Its imposing Greek revival pillars recall the days of ancient Athens. Colonel Chipley camped near here when this was a piney wilderness, and Chipley Park has a small amphitheater that offers a pleasing view of the lake. Across the street from the park is the former railroad station, once active and now used for public meetings. Part of the station is slowly being converted into a museum. Close by is the visitor's center, although you'll have to have more luck than I did to find it open.

Across the railroad tracks is this little town's business section. It's quiet and quaint. Most activity seems to be in two places: the gazebo beside the tracks, where old-timers gather to watch the trains go past, and the renovated Hotel DeFuniak.

Vagabonds' Hideaway

The Hotel DeFuniak is an award-winning conversion of what once was a pool hall and flop house. The conversion was the accomplishment of eight local partners. Although all contributed funds, most were beyond the age of physical labor. Thus, the physical burden fell on the shoulders of Bill and Barbara Kellogg and Ann Robinson. The Kelloggs are a most unusual couple. Years ago, they chucked their jobs in Michigan, bought a boat, and went off on a series of voyages that took them into the Caribbean and Mediterranean for seven carefree years. One day, they visited friends in DeFuniak. They loved the area and joined the group that had purchased the dilapidated abode of boozy transients. It was a mess. "The only thing we saved downstairs was the stairway in what is now the reception area and the hood over the stove," Barbara Kellogg told me. The entire two-story structure had to be rewired and new plumbing installed.

Although the hotel is open now, the work isn't done. Bill Kellogg is behind the desk seven days a week, unless he's on a weekend gig with his barbershop quartet. Then, Barbara takes over.

A night at the Hotel DeFuniak is an experience. The American Auto Association has awarded it a three-diamond rating, which puts it one full gem above the franchise motels beside Interstate 10. The rates run from $70 to $80 for rooms and $90 to $100 for suites. These rates include a full breakfast in the Chautauqua Dining Room. Billiard balls no longer clink in this immaculate restaurant, which serves breakfasts and lunches seven days a week and dinners every day except Sundays and Mondays. Here, large picture windows look out on US 90, where most drivers hurry by not realizing the pleasant experience they are passing up.

Too Quaint?

There is no denying that DeFuniak is quaint. But a lakeside walk, train-watching, and a night in a rehabilitated flop house are not really major draws. Of course, you can visit what is claimed to be Florida's oldest library, which is on Circle Drive. Or you can sip tiny samples of wine at the Chautauqua Vineyards beside Interstate 10. Or travel eighteen minutes north and ascend Florida's highest elevation, which turns out to be a barely perceptible hump. Then, there's the town golf course, which is only nine holes.

Small wonder, then, that the town's population actually fell between the 1990 and 2000 censuses. What DeFuniak craves are high-tech tenants for its industrial park by the airport. The town's proximity to the huge Eglin Air Force Base, which is just twenty-five miles southwest, would seem to give it an advantage in attracting aerospace firms. But competition from the towns of Ft. Walton and Crestview is severe and DeFuniak seems unable to meet the challenge. "Our economic development has never been the real boost we thought it could be," the city manager admitted to a reporter.

On the Road to Crestview

Leaving DeFuniak, head westward on US 90 once more. The country is flat, and pines comprise most of the vegetation. Every so often, you'll meet a truck hauling logs to the docks at Panama City. Usually, the bark has been stripped off for their conversion into telephone poles. The CSX tracks accompany the highway. The gleaming rails are grandsons of those laid by Colonel Chipley's crews.

When US 90 was built in the 1920s, it was denoted as State Road One. Despite its exalted title, it was just a rutted dirt pathway, two axles wide, following the mule trail left over from Spanish days. When Walton County filled the ruts with clay, motorists were elated by the improvement. Nonetheless, the road was still so narrow that scrub oak branches beat nerve-jangling tattoos on the car panels. If two cars met, a vigorous discussion ensued until one driver reluctantly pulled into the bushes and let the other pass. Because the road was hardly higher than the water table, when the Shoal River, on the eastern approach to Crestview, rose even a fraction above its banks, the road became impassable. Then, persistent travelers had to go all the way to Alabama to find a crossing!

After the route became a federal highway, it was straightened, widened, and paved. In 1970, Lawton Chiles tramped along here during the state-wide hike that brought him fame as Walkin' Lawton, as well as election to the U.S. Senate and, later, Florida's governorship. During his hike, Chiles found US 90 to be almost squirming with speeding cars and trucks. He was distressed by their windy wakes. "I can vouch for the fact that a lot of cattle and hogs are shipped through here," he wrote in his journal. "I don't know how many of these vans went by, but every time one did, it would blow my hat off and I could always tell by the smell that it contained livestock." Nearly everyone that Chiles met complained about the delay in the completion of Interstate 10. They felt the Panhandle was being left out of the main-stream, as usual. Chiles agreed and suspected there was some "finagling in the funds," as he put it.

In later years, Chiles was to call himself a he-coon to stress his vigor and his down-in-the-vegetable-patch roots. But the original claim to that salty nickname was made by Congressman Bob Sikes, whose home base was Crestview, where Chiles stopped to buy a pair of new walking boots and spend the night talking politics and massaging his swollen feet.

Den of the He-Coon

Crestview is proud of its native son, Robert L. Sikes, who rode herd on Panhandle interests from his position as U.S. Congressman for thirty-eight years. Sikes was a folksy politician—a good-ole-boy, if you will. Because he liked to compare himself to a male raccoon on the hunt, he took the nickname: He-Coon. His amazing longevity enabled him to secure the powerful chairmanship of the military construction subcommittee. Any appropriation bill that had the slightest chance of helping his district, which ran from Pensacola to just east of

Tallahassee, was fair game to the He-Coon.

Some say Sikes voted for any benefit or boondoggle onto which he could plaster his name. Thus, Crestview has the Bob Sikes Airport and the Robert Sikes Education Center. There is also the Robert Sikes Library. Pensacola has the impressive Robert Sikes Bridge. There is even a Bob Sikes Channel off of the Apalachicola River. But his special talent was for bringing military bases to his fiefdom, which he called "my far-flung counties." By the time he retired in 1979, he had obtained nine bases and three shipyards. His masterpiece was the establishment of the Eglin Air Force Base as the largest such installation in the world. To say that Sikes was a master at pork-barrel politics is an understatement.

A City on the Go

The He-Coon gave Crestview an economic impetus that it is still enjoying. Although the town has a population of only 15,000, you'll have no doubt that this is a borough on the go. The boldly modern Okaloosa County Courthouse, beside US 90, declares a defiance of stodginess. Main Street, half a block south of the courthouse, is the same. Crestview's business section runs down to the CSX rail line. (It

The modern county courthouse in Crestview is indicative of the hustling spirit of this growing town.

was the railroad that named the town Crestview because the city was the highest point on the line.)

The downtown has been landscaped and beautified as part of its Main Street program. The goal was to revitalize the shopping area without losing its small-town flavor. In this, Crestview has been eminently successful. Take the time to stroll the avenue, savoring the diverse array of specialty shops. Many restaurants maintain an old-time setting and home-style meals.

Careful planning has kept Main Street largely free of through traffic, which has been diverted to SR 85, a block east. The fast, cross-state vehicles use Interstate 10, which is two miles south. Okaloosa County's largest single employer by far is Eglin Air Force Base, located a few miles beyond Interstate 10. Eglin, concentrating on the development of high-tech military weapons, has attracted many skilled industries to the area. Furthermore, many technically skilled, former military people have chosen to settle locally, providing Crestview with an impressive labor pool that attracts more companies. Crestview currently has more than a dozen corporations with more than fifty employees, quite a feat for a town of its size.

So after you've gawked at the courthouse and driven up and down Main Street, then what? You can go to the Bob Sikes Public Library at 805 East Highway 90. While there, you might want to page through Bob Sikes' autobiography, entitled, you probably guessed, *He-Coon*. It's only around eight hundred pages. You can watch the planes come and go from the Bob Sikes Airport, just north of US 90. If you're in town the first weekend in May, you can attend the Old Spanish Trail Festival. Otherwise, the Chamber of Commerce Visitor Guide offers two suggestions. One is to drive to the Air Force Armament Museum just outside Eglin's main gate. It is eighteen miles south on SR 85, otherwise known as, what else, the Bob Sikes Highway. The museum is open between 9:30 A.M. and 4:30 P.M., seven days a week—and it's free, although the gift shop may open your wallet. For more information about the museum, call 850–882–4062. The second suggestion is to drive northwest to the Blackwater State Forest, where there is hiking, swimming, camping, fishing, picnicking, and opportunities for general frolicking. So, that's where we'll head next.

Can This Be Snow?

Back on US 90, heading west once more, I must leave you with a story about Crestview. Because the town is on the thrilling summit of

Florida's second loftiest eminence, it's natural to expect the weather to be a fraction of a degree cooler than in the lowlands. Even so, in January 2002, when it was forecast that Crestview might have a flurry of actual snow, excitement reigned. Parents woke their kids at three in the morning, bundled them in arctic wraps—or what passed for them—and together they waited.

At last it came—white, fluffy stuff floating majestically down from the sky. Children darted around trying to catch the flakes, and adults simply marveled that it was actually snowing in Crestview. More than one local motorist parked at the side of the road to gape in wonder at the intricacy of the huge flakes making beautiful designs on their windshields. Then, after one glorious hour, the snow stopped and quickly melted away. "It was like the fireworks," a child exclaimed. "I hope it comes back one day!"

The Fearsome Yellow River

In a couple of miles, you'll cross the Yellow River. It's an inconsequential stream today, but when Edward Anderson's stage coach pulled up here in 1844, the river had flooded far beyond its banks. So Anderson took the tiny pedestrian ferry through the swirling water to the other side, where someone sold him a worn-out nag. He rode through the muck for the entire night and part of the next day before reaching dry land. It was a rugged, dirty trip, not made any more pleasant when his horse stumbled, threw Anderson into the mud, then promptly fell on him. Later, Anderson stopped at an inn to dry out, but he found it "abominable and filthy." Indeed, it was so bad that Anderson felt it necessary to warn his readers of the Travelers Rest Inn. I'm relaying the warning to you as a public service. But be wary, for it might have changed its name.

Museum Town

Four miles from Crestview, you'll reach SR 4, where you should turn northwest. In a few more miles, you'll come to the settlement of Baker, defined by a convenience store and an old brick building called the Baker Block. The place was once an active lumber and turpentine center. Sawmills buzzed as they converted long leaf pines into boards and planks. When the forests were gone, cattle grazed among the stumps, and the site of the Baker Block became a cattle pen. Other stump land was turned into blueberry farms, with Baker boasting the largest in the world!

However, economic growth bypassed the town, and today it is just a crossroads hamlet. But it's not ready to die, for the Baker Block has been converted into a surprisingly well-stocked museum. I know it's well-stocked because an enthusiastic local booster insisted I admire each dusty relic, even though I had miles to go before sunset.

The Blackwater River State Forest

Continuing northwest on SR 4, you'll pass through mile after mile of second-growth trees as you enter the Blackwater River State Forest. When Choctaw Indians roamed the land, the trees were predominantly long leaf pines towering ten stories high. They were spaced widely enough for three warriors abreast to pass through easily. The ground was padded with pine needles. Sunshine lanced through the trees, brightening the forest and creating an air of majesty.

Shortly, you'll pass over the Blackwater River, although I don't recall that it was marked. The river's name refers to its dark color, which is a stain from the tannin in oak leaves. Around the turn of the last century, timber was floated down the Blackwater to the voracious sawmills at Milton. Although it may seem that the river does not have enough current to float anything heavier than a chopper's chip, the opening of upstream dams in the spring caused massive rushes of water that impelled the logs downstream.

The road through the Blackwater State Forest presents an interplay of light and shadow.

The North Woods, Florida Style

In six miles, you'll come to the sign for Red Morris Road. By turning north, you quickly reach Bear Lake. It's a placid sheet of water enclosed by oaks and pines and encircled by a four-mile hiking trail. A short pier extends into the water and beside the pier is a boat launch. Fishing is excellent, with largemouth bass almost begging to be caught. Camping is also available. With the smell of the pines, you could almost imagine you were in Minnesota's North Woods.

But this is Florida, and few things here are what they seem. The lake is artificial, made by an earthen dam across a stream. The water averages only eight feet in depth, which makes it easy to drain in order to clean out the muck. After the water is gone, rye grass is planted, for the Florida fish enjoy this tender greenery more than ordinary water plants. When the lake is refilled, bundles of hardwood brush are sunk in the water because the choosy fishies enjoy darting among the sticks. The fish themselves are not native but imported by truck. Being in Florida, the bass prefer plastic worms. Oh, and if you have come for the catfish, don't forget to bring chicken livers. They'll likely ignore you if you don't.

Camping is also done in Florida style. There is running water, showers, and restrooms. Camping with electricity costs $12, but if you really want to rough it, you can cut the electricity and save three bucks. For more information call 850–414–0871.

Returning to SR 4, drive two miles west to the junction with CR 191. The village of Munson is supposed to be here, but, if so, it must have dodged me. Turn south on CR 191. The state's forestry headquarters is a mile or so down the road. Visitors are not unwelcome, but this is a working operation where forest fires and other emergencies take precedent. You can pick up some leaflets, if you're there on a weekday—and if anyone has remembered to leave them out.

Continuing south on 191, you'll pass many miles of slash pines planted in rows close together. Although these tree-farms are on state land, Florida allows commercial harvesting. In return, the state receives a fee, which it uses to maintain the park, except for a portion it donates to Okaloosa and Santa Rosa Counties.

Canoeing Anyone?

Now, you're nearing Milton, which proclaims itself the Canoeing Capital of Florida. If you want to see why, watch for the hamlet of Spring Hill, with two modest churches and not much more. Spring Hill Road leads four miles west to Adventures Unlimited, which can be contacted at 800–239–6864. The company is located on Coldwater Creek, a branch of the Blackwater River. Here, you can rent a canoe, kayak, or tube for a float through the wilderness. There are also sand beaches ideal for creative loitering. Just be aware that Coldwater Creek was not named frivolously. The spring-fed water is a brisk sixty-eight degrees year-round. Trips cost $16 per person whether you take the two-hour drift or the all-day voyage. If you just want to check the place out, there are picnic tables. But bring your own food, unless you care to feast on pop, candy bars, and potato chips, which are sold on site.

A dozen or so miles past Spring Hill, on CR 191, you'll come to SR 87A, which goes to Whiting Field Naval Air Station. When Whiting was threatened with closure, after the conclusion of the Second World War, it was ole He-Coon Sikes who kept the taxpayers' money flowing. Whiting is a major asset in Santa Rosa County's economy. It also plays a role in its recreation, being the terminus of the Blackwater Heritage State Trail.

Blackwater Heritage State Trail is a paved pathway running about nine miles, to Milton. The route was once occupied by the railroad that supplied the air base and, before that, by an old logging line that helped denude the Blackwater Forest. The trail is rather new and, as yet, not used enough by non-county riders for local shops to provide rental bicycles.

If you imagine such a trail is easy to build, you should know it consists of twelve-foot-wide asphalt pavement over a raised limerock bed with a reinforced embankment. It's accompanied by an eight-foot-wide horse trail. It also has seven trestles and three trailheads. So how much did it cost? $314,000 per mile. Are you impressed?

Scratch Ankle, We've Arrived

Continue on CR 191 into downtown Milton, population seven thousand. Here, you'll reach US 90 (Caroline Street). Follow US 90 west to the Santa Rosa County Courthouse, a ho-hum, two-story structure that looks like a schoolhouse.

Just west of the courthouse is the Blackwater River, no longer the insignificant stream you crossed earlier. Now, it's a broad waterway offering access to the Gulf of Mexico. Because ocean-going ships could navigate only as far upriver as Milton, it was here that mills were

This mural at Milton recalls the era when sailing ships from all over the world made port here.

established for the logs floated down from upstate forests. At one time, upwards of two dozen sawmills devoured the Blackwater forests. The mills were a godsend; they let the settlement shed the prickly name of Scratch Ankle, after the briars along the river, and become the more respectable Mill Town, from which Milton is probably derived.

When the forests were depleted in the late 1920s, Milton's good times ended. Today, all that remains of the mills is a large mural across the street from the courthouse. The mural depicts the waterfront in the days when Milton was a major port. It is the first of perhaps twenty-five murals that the local Mural Society has planned to brighten up this county seat.

The Historical Society is also active. One of its achievements is the restoration of the Opera House, built in 1912 on Caroline Street across from the courthouse. On the second floor is the Imogene Theater—once more aglow with community events. The Museum of Local History on the first floor is open Wednesdays from 10:00 A.M. to 1:00 P.M. or by chance.

Now, go a block west to the river. Milton has done a commendable job of converting what was once a rundown district into the scenic Riverwalk, which consists of a wide,

The Riverwalk at Milton overlooks the Blackwater River.

wooden boardwalk and benches that overlook the water. In days past, this was an industrialized area, with a sawmill on the north end and a shipyard on the south end. In between was a long row of jerry-built structures that became ever more dilapidated over the years. It was a major beautification when this eyesore area was transformed into Riverwalk Park in 1987.

The Scenic Bluffs Drive

Leaving Milton on US 90, you'll soon come to the causeway across four miles of Escambia River wetlands. The Escambia has always been an important waterway. During the Spanish era, the dugout canoes of a tribe called the long-haired people, or Panzacola, plied the currents carrying trade goods. The river may have received its name from the Spanish *cambiar*, meaning to trade. During the nineteenth and early twentieth centuries, the Escambia was thronged with timber rafts destined for Pensacola's voracious sawmills.

When US 90 reaches the opposite side of the river and turns south toward downtown Pensacola, it becomes the Scenic Highway. However, trees and shrubs often obscure the view. For this reason, you'll be glad to know that good fortune has placed

The Boardwalk at Pensacola's Bay Bluffs Park descends through a forest to the bay shore.

a Dairy Queen-Exxon facility directly on the bluff where, because the trees have been cut away, there is a wide-angle view of Escambia Bay. Across the road, a Ramada Inn takes full advantage of the vista, if one doesn't mind peeking through Exxon paraphernalia.

The scenic drive continues southward with its accompanying veil of trees that parts only in the clearings for homes. Soon, you'll come to Chimney Park, perhaps the only public site in the state devoted solely to a ruined chimney. It's all that remains of a sawmill destroyed by the Confederates as they retreated from Pensacola during the Civil War.

Farther along this road is Bay Bluffs Park. Despite the encouraging name, there is no good view of the bay unless you take the rather steep boardwalk down through the dwarf live oaks. This is a pretty excursion with leaf-shadows making beguiling designs on the steps. The walkway ends at Escambia Bay's sandy shore, where the remains of fires indicate that you've missed some good parties. The way back is not as easy as the descent, for everyone knows there are always more steps going up than coming down.

The Million-Dollar Highway

Constructing this Scenic Highway in the late 1920s was not just a slice of corn pone. "There were alligators and snakes to deal with," recalled J. Brent Watson, who worked on the road crew as a college student. "They had wagons with donkeys pulling clay and dumping it into the swamp so we could get the road on a level basis." The way was through a virtual wilderness. It took two years to cover the eleven miles from the site of the US 90 bridge to Pensacola. The highway cost so much money that it was dubbed the Million-Dollar Road—and that was when a million would buy more than a couple of sewer lids. But when the road was completed, it was a wonder.

Young Watson would woo the gals by taking them for motorcycle escapades along the secluded highway. A favorite picnic site was the clearing where Skopelos Restaurant now offers fine views of the bay. Watson and his gal of the moment would often linger here to watch moonlight shimmer on the water. "My date would talk about the man on the moon," Watson reminisced. "But I never saw him." Perhaps he had other things on his mind. He apparently had many female friends, but the only girl who wouldn't ride on his motorcycle was the one he married.

If you want to try your own luck with the moon, or other things, Skopelos is open for dinner Tuesday through Saturday between 5:00 P.M. and 10:30 P.M. and for lunch on Fridays only. Call 850–432–6565 for more information.

 Just beyond Skopelos, US 90 makes an abrupt turn as it crosses over Bayou Texar. Turn south at Seventeenth Avenue and proceed a short distance to Bayfront Parkway, which offers an unobstructed view of Pensacola Bay as it leads westward to downtown.

Pensacola, Alabama

It might seem that Pensacola, with a population of 57,000, should be much more than an isolated appendage of Florida. Indeed, some Pensacolans feel they were not meant to be part of Florida at all; they should belong to Alabama, as geography demands. Then, they wouldn't be lying in limbo.

Back when the states were forming, it seemed as if Pensacola and the rest of the Panhandle would be included in Alabama. But when Alabama was preparing to apply for statehood, Florida still belonged to Spain. Had the impatient Alabamans waited just two years for the purchase of Florida, the Panhandle would probably have been given to them.

The Demise of Floribam

A few Pensacolans still dream of marriage with Alabama. And Alabama has persistently courted the Panhandle. As early as 1838, Alabama formally asked Florida for the transfer of the Panhandle, and the request has been made five other times, the latest being in 1963. At one point, west Floridians considered forming an entirely new state that would combine the Panhandle with southern Alabama. The new entity would be called Floribam. Alas, Floribam was stillborn and the Panhandle remains a sometimes reluctant bride of downstate Florida.

The Spanish at Pensacola

When Bayfront Parkway reaches Terragona Street, turn one block right. You'll now be in Pensacola's historic district.

The Spanish had high hopes for Pensacola, which they made the capital of West Florida, a province that extended westward to the Mississippi River and north to somewhere between Tennessee and the arctic. In 1759, they began construction of a fort in what would

A portion of the Spanish fort at Pensacola has been unearthed.

become downtown Pensacola. A small portion of this fort has now been unearthed at the corner of Terragona and Zaragoza Streets. A short boardwalk leads over the foundation of the commandant's head-quarters.

But the Spaniards' rule over Florida was weak, and they had little choice but to bow to the Americans' insulting demand that they cede the vast territory for, not cash, but U.S. assumption of $5 million in debts claimed by American citizens. Thus, in 1821, Andrew Jackson and a military contingent clattered into Pensacola to accept the formal transfer. There was a great deal of bitterness between Jackson and the Spanish governor when they met at the fort for the ceremony—so much so that after Jackson assumed power, he briefly threw the former governor in jail.

The Plaza

Today, the fort is long gone, but some of its expansive grounds are occupied by Plaza Ferdinand VII, formed by Jefferson, Zaragoza, Government, and Palafox Streets. Over the years, the plaza became seedy as some of the buildings along Zaragoza turned into a rowdy array of saloons and pool halls. Other buildings displayed red lights to attract lusty blokes from the sailing ships that jammed the harbor. Pensacola has cleaned up the old section since then and turned Plaza Ferdinand VII into a landscaped park. A pylon in the park is dedicated to former mayor and ardent railroad builder William Chipley. Across from the park is the striking T. T. Wentworth Florida State Museum, once the city hall.

 Pensacola thrives on its history. If you want to learn more, go a few blocks east on Zaragoza Street to Historic Pensacola Village, which has many restored homes and churches open to the public. For a jazzier aspect of history, try the Seville Quarter just east of the plaza on Government Street. It rocks with restaurants and night clubs.

On the Waterfront

Since sea trade was so important to Pensacola, no visit to this city is complete without touring the waterfront at the south end of Palafox Street. During its heyday, this was a forest of masts from the multitude of sailing ships that tied up along this and eighteen other piers. In a single year, four thousand ships would make port here. The docks swarmed with boisterous sailors jabbering in foreign tongues, dray men in horse wagons heaped with goods, and burly longshoremen

Pensacola diners enjoy this view of the marina.

transferring goods on and off the ships. Today, it's strangely quiet, for the port is still recovering from many bad years when it was a shabby public eyesore mired in debt.

Now, the port seems to be reviving. A new port director is working hard to attract cruise ships. In addition, big plans are in the works to replace the old auditorium with a two-story building of shops and restaurants on the first floor and condos on the second. And a major auto manufacturer is beginning to ship cars through the port. Meanwhile, the Quayside Market, with its art galleries and antiques stores, is attracting ever more patrons.

Three blocks east, at the Barracks Street dock, there is a delightful restaurant, currently called the Fish House, serving sandwiches and full meals from a terrace that overlooks the Seville Harbor Marina. It's open seven days a week from 11:00 A.M. to the wee hours. On weekends there is live entertainment. For more information call 850–470–0003.

Among Planes and Cannons

For persons with more time to spend in Pensacola, a trip to the Naval Air Museum is highly recommended. Go three blocks north on Palafox Street to Garden Street. Then, travel west on Garden Street, which becomes Navy Boulevard and leads to the base. The museum is a huge facility displaying a variety of aircraft, from a replica of a 1911 Curtiss seaplane to a squadron of actual Blue Angel jets suspended from the ceiling. The museum also features an IMAX theater and is open seven days a week between 9:00 A.M. and 5:00 P.M. Admission is free, but you may need personal photo identification, such as a driver's license. For more information call 850–452–3604.

After the museum, you should visit nearby Fort Barrancas, also on the base. The ancient walls have been restored and sport an assortment of once-deadly cannons. Barrancas means bluffs, and the fort battlements present wonderful views of the bay. During the Civil War, Confederates at Fort Barrancas engaged Union gunners at Fort Pickens across the bay in a violent artillery duel. Six thousand shots and shells were exchanged.

A Night at the Railroad Station

Should you desire to spend the night in Pensacola, why not try the railroad station at 200 East Gregory Street, at the corner of Alcaniz Street? You'll be glad to know that Mr. Chipley's engines no longer smoke up the spacious concourse, which was originally constructed in 1912 and is now the sparkling lobby of the Crowne Plaza/Grand Hotel. Although sleeping accommodations are in a modern fifteen-story tower, nostalgia is not forgotten. You can enjoy breakfast, lunch, or dinner in the former station, where perhaps you'll hear an imaginary locomotive whistle as you sip your julep. Room rates run around $135 a night for two. For reservations call 800–348–3336.

The Panhandle Circuit

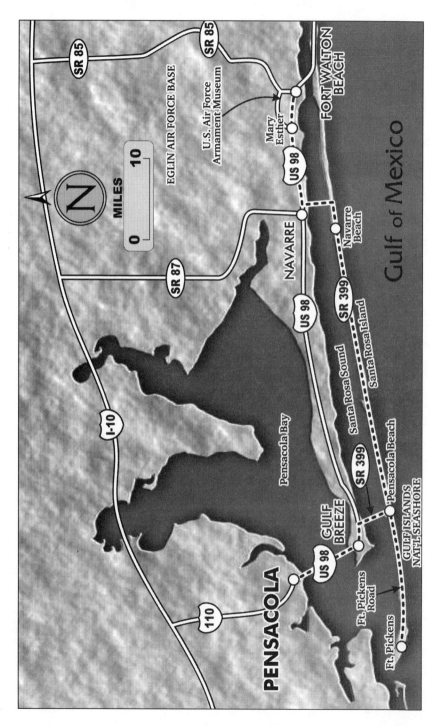

The Glorious Gulf

Pensacola to Ft. Walton • 64 Backroad Miles

The Song of the Road: Overview

This exploration will lead along the Gulf of Mexico beaches, which are famous for their white sand and emerald water. We'll begin at the community of Gulf Breeze, claimed by some to be a major base for flying saucers, floating sky balls, and assorted otherworldly oddities. From there, we'll go to Fort Pickens, where massive nineteenth-century battlements were erected to repel invaders who never came. Nearby is Pensacola Beach, with a vast array of appealing beachfront motels.

Then, we'll head east along a strip of sand called Santa Rosa Island via a highway once obliterated by Hurricane Opal. The uninhabited dunes are part of the Gulf Islands National Seashore. At Navarre Beach, the road will pass over Santa Rosa Sound and back onto the mainland. We'll skirt the great Eglin Air Force Base before ending at Ft. Walton Beach.

On the Road Again

From Pensacola, take US 98 south across the Bay Bridge over three miles of open water. When the original bridge was constructed in the early 1930s, it was an engineering wonder. Although it was only two lanes, it served the traffic adequately. But times changed and eventually the bridge became obsolete. Now, this loyal old workhorse, having given its best years to public service, enjoys peaceful retirement as a fishermen's pier.

Galactic Gateway

The causeway ends at the town of Gulf Breeze, which sits astride a slim peninsula separating Pensacola Bay from Santa Rosa Sound. The town was once a cluster of cottages and a general store that opened when the first bridge was completed. But there were hardly any residents in this isolated, windy little stub of land until the new bridge was constructed in the early 1960s. Now, the population has reached six thousand and is still climbing.

169

Many UFO phenomena have been reported from this park in Gulf Breeze.

Gulf Breeze has received a good deal of publicity due to the Unidentified Flying Objects that seem to have had a real affection for the little town between 1987 and 1998. Many of the sightings have been quite vivid: "It looked like a symmetrical ball with stars in it and a flaming tail," one observer told a reporter. "Red and yellowish lights filled it. It went up and up and up and then it just went out." Six other people at Shoreline Park around 9:30 P.M. that same mid-July night confirmed the sighting. The reporter who interviewed the eye witnesses suspected the UFOs might have been weather balloons from the nearby Pensacola Naval Air Station, but officers there told him they had none aloft at that time.

People from all over the area have reported sightings. A housewife swore she was followed home by a silver oval with rotating orange lights. Another woman saw a silver ball glimmering like a full moon—but it was mid-afternoon. One man claimed to have been illuminated by a beam of purple light from an overhead object that quickly vanished. Another insisted he saw a UFO emitting a trail of orange sparks as it streaked past the Pensacola Bay Bridge at a speed far faster than any military aircraft.

On and on the reports continued, at the rate of fifty each year, for an entire decade. Such became the town's fame that it was used to lend authenticity to some episodes on TV's fictional *X-Files* program. A book entitled *The Gulf Breeze Sightings* by local resident Ed Walters found a starry market among alien-seekers. And Pensacola's respected newspaper, the *News Journal,* did several major articles about the sightings. One article stated that "with the slow acceptance of the scientific community that the truth just might be out there, the UFO phenomenon is stronger than ever."

UFO HQ

The epicenter of the UFO action was Shoreline Park. To reach the park, watch for the Shoreline Drive stoplight a short distance after leaving the Bay Bridge. Turn west here and continue for a mile or so. Ignore the first Shoreline Park on your right; it's only a dupe to test your persistence. Shoreline Park South is just beyond, on your left. It's a large park looking out on Santa Rosa Sound. There are picnic shelters and restrooms for earthlings.

One of the most unnerving incidents during the decade of UFO sightings was observed here by at least a half dozen people around 11 P.M. on August 22, 1998. The air became still, "almost to the point of being stifling," said an eye witness. Then, a dense blackness engulfed the water near the pier. Suddenly, UFOs approached and silently descended into the water. It was as if the Santa Rosa Sound was a portal into a different universe.

For some unknown reason, this appears to have been the climax of the Gulf Breeze occurrences. Thereafter, the reports became rarer and are now quite scarce. Perhaps the aliens achieved their purpose and returned through the black water space warp off of Shoreline Park to their home galaxy. Or perhaps they were never here at all and the strange phenomena were merely group hallucinations. Or maybe they are at a base deep in Santa Rosa Sound waiting for the proper moment to return. Should this be so, you might be among the first to greet them if you watch and wait at Shoreline Park.

Colorful Causeway

At Gulf Breeze, leave US 98, which turns sharply east to follow the peninsula separating Santa Rosa Sound from Pensacola Bay. Instead, take SR 399 south across the bridge to Santa Rosa Island. There is a $1.00 toll to cross the bridge, which is named in honor of Congressman Bob Sikes who sponsored the act that kept much of Santa Rosa Island in its natural state.

Such an act was necessary, for the island became a prime candidate for development from the moment the first bridge was constructed. At this time, a large casino was built at Pensacola Beach, providing mainlanders with facilities for swimming, dancing, imbibing, and general merrymaking. Today, Pensacola Beach is still a center of merrymaking. Even the causeway from the Sikes Bridge into town is almost a carnival of restaurants and bars: most new, and many trendy, if not elegant. Almost all offer pleasing views of the sound.

Pensacola Beach

 Once in town, turn right on Fort Pickens Road and watch for the water tower. Near the foot of the tower is a 1,500-foot pier. The parking lot occupies the site of the former casino. The pier is the town's pride and is touted as the longest fishing pier on the Gulf of Mexico. It's brand new, the old one not having survived an encounter with Hurricane Opal. It costs a dollar to stroll on it. If you want to do some fishing, you can rent a pole, with bait, for $6.50. No license is needed.

The Whales' Sad Saga

Many people enjoy strolling Casino Beach beside the pier to see what strange things the waves have brought in. One of the strangest appeared one rough day in October 2001, when nine whales floundered through the surf and stranded themselves on the sand. While experts from Gulf World Marine Park in Panama City Beach were summoned, spectators poured water over the whales to keep them cool and calm. Beachings are not understood, but some experts suspect they are acts of group suicide. Although the whales were given antibiotics at Gulf World, all but one died.

Trouble in the Wind

There is considerable controversy about the direction this once-sleepy town is taking. Long-term residents—that is, anyone living here before DVDs—resent the high-rises that are beginning to give the place the aspect of Miami Beach. Despite the residents' lawsuits, buildings of more than twenty stories are going up.

Visitors can spend a night or an entire vacation at Pensacola Beach. The prime season is from May to mid-August, when the daily temperatures average in the low eighties. There are many motels and a huge assortment of condos to chose from. Prices are reasonable by Florida standards. The Best Western, for example, offers a unit on the beach for between $160 to $190 a night. (Call 800–934–3301 for more information.) You can get a list of the resorts from the Chamber of Commerce by calling 800–635–4803.

Despite the immense pleasure of owning a condo directly on the beach, the danger of hurricanes makes these very risky investments. So, in order to protect their property, the owners have successfully lobbied the state to stabilize the waterfront, using taxpayers' money of course. Thus, when Hurricane Opal flattened the natural, protective dunes in early October 1995, and Hurricane Georges a few years later wiped away the berms that had just replaced them, the state promptly allotted $3 million for a new sand berm forty-six feet wide and six feet high. Yet the new barrier was only half as strong as the one the hurricanes had laughed at. "We're still scared to death," one condo owner admitted.

Gulf Islands National Seashore

Continuing west on Fort Pickens Road, you'll pass private homes, most wisely placed on stilts. At the edge of town is Fort Pickens Park facing the Gulf of Mexico. It provides swimming, sheltered picnic tables, and restrooms. Just beyond, you'll enter the Gulf Islands National Seashore, a masterful melding of recreational use and ecological preservation.

Admission to the National Seashore is $6 per car. For that, you get a fine beach with an impressive old fort thrown in. Development ends when you enter the park. What's left are rolling dunes ornamented with scattered sand plants and a beach that won't quit. This is the way it was when Santa Rosa Island rose from the sea as a sandbar at the close of the Ice Age.

Tragedy at Langdon Beach

Watch for Langdon Beach. Its peacefulness creates the sensation of safety. Yet in the summer of 2001, eight-year-old Jessie Arbogast and some playmates were frolicking in knee-deep water when suddenly someone shouted, "Shark!" Moments later, Jessie screamed and his playmates saw the water around him turn red. "He's got me!" Jessie screamed again. "Get him off of me!" Jessie's uncle dashed into the water, where a bull shark nearly seven feet long had Jessie's arm. The uncle grabbed the shark and tried to pull it away from his nephew.

After a second violent tug, Jessie fell free, but his right arm had been bitten off.

A bystander carried Jessie to shore, while his uncle dragged the shark onto the sand by his tail. Then, a park ranger shot the shark, pried its mouth open, and retrieved the arm. Meanwhile, others phoned for medical help. Jessie lay on the beach bleeding profusely. He lost consciousness and stopped breathing. He was kept alive by cardiopulmonary resuscitation until a helicopter arrived twenty minutes later and rushed him to a hospital. There, he was given almost endless transfusions of blood. Meanwhile, emergency surgery lasting eleven hours reattached his arm. Although the boy's life was saved, his future looked bleak. The most optimistic prognosis was that someday he might be able to feed himself and perhaps even walk.

Shark attacks of such a serious nature are almost unheard of along this part of the Gulf. Sharks do not really like humans; they're too bony. Sharks prefer seals, whose blubber is a tasty treat. They attack humans when they can't see their unappetizing, angular form. This is particularly the case at dusk, when Jessie was swimming, or during times when the water is agitated after a storm. Of the millions of swimmers using Florida beaches annually, less than thirty are harassed by sharks. And almost all of these incidents are much farther south. So, enjoy the beaches secure in the knowledge that, when your time comes, it's far less likely to be in Florida waters than in your own bathtub.

Across the road from Langdon Beach, and out of sight, are several extensive camping areas. Electric sites cost $20 per night and non-electric $15. For more information call 850–934–2622.

Guns and Ghosts: Fort Pickens

The road continues westward along a neck of land composed of sand so white you'd think it had been drenched in Clorox.

On the left, the Gulf waters present a pallet of mixed blues. Listen, and you'll hear the waves doing soft-shoe dances against the shore. The land broadens toward the island's tip, where pines thrive in the wind-shadows.

Eight sandy miles from the park entrance you'll reach Fort Pickens, a rambling, hundred-year-old group of battlements constructed seemingly willy-nilly. The park's visitors center has an ample stock of literature about the fort—enough to sate even the most enthusiastic appetite for shore battlements. Although the fort was a Federal

Sand and sea oats outline the road to Fort Pickens.

stronghold during the Civil War, blood and gore buffs will be disappointed to learn that, except for one long-range bombardment from Confederates around Pensacola, it was never attacked. However, bad water and lack of fresh fruit and vegetables caused such sickness that half the barracks were turned into hospital wards. That story will have to do.

The fort is well worth exploring. So, pick up the free self-guided tour booklet at the visitors center and begin poking through the impressive maze of walls, dry moats, and shadowy passageways. The sweeping view from the tower bastion includes the Gulf and Pensacola Bay. The fort's position beside the channel, which leads to the bay, clearly shows its ability to protect Pensacola's harbor—although when occupied by the Union, it proved that it could close the harbor just as effectively. Even into the twentieth century, the fort's reinvigorated defenses aimed to prevent possible Nazi U-boats from gaining access to Pensacola shipping. But the advent of guided missiles and other military innovations made the fort obsolete. It was abandoned around 1950 and left to decay for two decades until it became part of the Gulf Island National Seashore Park.

Time rests heavily on the massive old fortifications. As you wander about the grounds, notice the geometric lines made by the bricks and masonry. If the sun is out, as it almost always is, the contrasts of light

Old Fort Pickens once guarded the entrance to Pensacola Bay.

and dark can be starkly beautiful. Arches stand out in brilliance against the cavernous blackness of the passageways, where some visitors claim to have felt the clammy presence of soldiers long since departed. The walls cast straight, unforgiving lines across the bleak parade grounds. The gleaming barrel of the formidable Rodman cannon on the tower bastion frowns upon it all, as if it's unhappy that it's not permitted to fire at least one round in anger.

Returning to Pensacola Beach, pick up SR 399 heading east. You'll pass high-rises constructed with careless optimism, given the storms and hurricanes that will challenge them. Hopefully, none of the storms will be as powerful as Opal, whose vicious surges wiped out ten miles of SR 399 along here in 1995.

Opal Was No Lady

The destruction caused by Hurricane Opal seems far distant to many people residing in the new beach-front buildings. But to those who lived through the storm, this hurricane was something they'd never forget. Opal began as a minor storm wandering slowly over the Yucatan. The National Hurricane Center watched carefully as Opal slowly gained strength and moved into the Gulf of Mexico. Once over water, it intensified into a full-fledged, category one hurricane with winds of more than seventy miles per hour. First indications were that it would hit the U.S. coast in Louisiana. So, when the center posted a hurricane watch early on Tuesday, October 3rd, people along the Panhandle coast were not overly concerned. But during the day, Opal turned eastward toward Florida. Throughout the day the center became more and more concerned as Opal grew into an extremely violent category four hurricane with winds of more than 140 miles per hour. That evening, the center issued an evacuation order for every coastal inhabitant between Pensacola Beach and Panama City.

Hardly anyone took the order seriously. They had weathered their share of storms and had no intention of packing up and trying to find a motel someplace north. They taped their windows and went to bed. But by predawn on October 4th, the wind was shrieking, loose debris was flying, and the Gulf was thrashing like an angry sea serpent. Television and radio reporters repeated the evacuation order, underlining the urgency by showing or describing unnerving pictures of the hurricane's mighty core, still out at sea.

Now there was panic as an estimated 100,000 persons attempted to flee on roads meant to accommodate a small fraction of that number. The congestion was unbelievable. People honked and raged, but the traffic barely inched northward. Some cars ran out of gas and had to be pushed from the road. Meanwhile, Opal's peripheral winds began snarling about them and the sky grew ever blacker. Water washed over the coastal roads. Some people had no choice except to return to their homes and pray. By late afternoon, Opal made landfall. "Thousands of evacuees found themselves in wind-vulnerable locations on highway evacuation routes," ran the Hurricane Center's official report. "[They parked] in service station plazas, or in whatever refuge of last resort could be found. Had Opal not weakened shortly before landfall, it is probable that winds in the core of the hurricane would have killed or injured many people."

When it was over, the damage was severe. Roads were out. Electricity was off. Sewage facilities did not work. Food supplies were delayed. And more than three-quarters of the homes in the worst-hit areas were damaged or destroyed. An estimated $1.8 billion in damages had occurred, making Hurricane Opal one of the three most devastating storms in U.S. history.

The Great Connector Battle

The evacuation problems during Hurricane Opal highlighted the woeful inadequacy of the roads leading north from this section of the coast. Even Interstate 10 was not an acceptable evacuation route, for it ran parallel to the coast. What was needed was a multilane great connector running to Interstate 65 in Alabama. It would be an expensive project, but it had to be built—everyone agreed on that. What almost no one agreed on was the location of this great connector. Pensacola wanted it. So did Santa Clara County and Ft. Walton Beach to the east. Whoever got it would receive immense economic gains. So the fight has been going on for nearly a decade, and no connector has been built. Meanwhile, the June through November hurricane seasons keep rolling around, and, with each year of relative calm, the return of another big storm grows more likely.

Opal Beach

A bike path parallels SR 399 for several miles, stopping at the boundary of a second segment of the Gulf Islands National Seashore. There is no fee if you stay on the state highway and simply drive through the park. However, it's $6 per car if you turn off at Opal Beach.

The Gulf Islands National Seashore is one of the more unusual entities in the national park system. It consists of eleven separate units stretching along the upper Gulf coast for 150 miles from Santa Rosa to

There are many beautiful beaches along the Gulf Islands National Seashore.

islands off the state of Mississippi. Most of these units are isolated and have been left in a primitive condition. Others, like Fort Pickens and the thirteen miles of Opal Beach, represent preserved bulwarks against rampant development. That such an unusual and vital system exists is due in part to the effort of J. Earle Bowden.

The Sands of All Time

Jesse Earle Bowden graduated from Florida State University in Tallahassee in 1951. Thereupon, he went to work for the *Pensacola News Journal* where he developed into a prizewinning editorialist and preeminent political cartoonist. In 1963, as chairman of Pensacola's Historical Advisory Committee, he became alarmed at the crumbling state of Fort Pickens and other historical treasures around Pensacola Bay. He made these concerns public through his columns and editorials.

As a preservation groundswell began, Bowden found Florida Congressman Bob Sikes an enthusiastic ally. Sikes was soon joined by a Mississippi congressman who had islands in his own state that he wanted to preserve. Thus, they began promoting a catch-all national park called the Gulf Islands National Seashore.

But powerful interests rose in opposition. As Bowden tells it in his book, *Gulf Islands, The Sands of All Time*, developers saw that a national park would end their dream of lining Santa Rosa with a wall of condos. There had even been talk of putting up a major amusement park.

The opposition simply could not understand Bowden's concern for what they regarded as a sandy wasteland crying to be civilized. One developer cornered Bowden at a cocktail party and grumbled, "You want a sand dune? You can build sand dunes." He said he'd put dunes in any convenient field. Local boosters wailed that a national park would prevent municipal expansion. Others had fears that a park would mean fences and toll gates that would cut the island in two. Still more warned that the park would attract hippies and campers and similar undesirables. A talk show host on Pensacola's most popular radio station saw it as another government land-grab. To some conservatives, it smelled of socialism.

The debate became so heated that the commissioners of Escambia County, which owned most of Santa Rosa Island, placed the matter up for a straw vote on the general election ballot of 1970. When the results were tallied, the voters expressed two to one approval for the transfer of large portions of Santa Rosa Island to the National Park Service. With that, Sikes' bill sailed through Congress and the Gulf

Islands National Seashore became a reality.

Many years later, Bowden wrote lovingly about the park he had helped create: "Many claim them, these sands of the global hourglass, sifting in the ebb and flow of time and timelessness; but none really own them, for the Gulf Islands—the fragile, unpredictable barriers—belong to the sea."

A Mountain Comes to Florida—Sort of

Having driven through Pensacola Beach, you can appreciate Bowden's achievement in preserving the natural beauty of this portion of Santa Rosa Island. One of the most memorable qualities of this enchanted landscape is the sand, which everyone agrees is the color of refined sugar. The sand continues into the Gulf, where its whiteness enhances the water's natural greenness so vividly that the shoreline all the way to Panama City Beach, for more than a hundred miles, is called the Emerald Coast.

Oddly, this powdery sand is not native to Florida. Whereas most Florida beaches are composed mainly of ground-up seashells, the Emerald Coast is almost pure quartz. This quartz originated as a component of the Appalachian Mountains. As the mountains eroded over millions of years, the quartz was pulverized into sand, which rushing rivers transported to the Gulf. So when you stroll the dazzling white Gulf beaches, you're actually walking on mountains. Thank you, Alabama.

Nature's Garden

This segment of Santa Rosa Island is a wonderful place to observe nature. There are actually six separate plant and animal habitats here The shore is a trove of seashells and other debris from the watery world beyond. Just inland are the primary dunes, where sea oats waltz in the salty breezes. Behind the dunes are depressions called swales. Because they have no natural outlet, they are usually wet with a mixture of rainwater and salt spray. Rosemary is common here, as is white-topped sedge. Beyond the swales, the land rises slightly. Since the sand here is drier, pines and even small, wind-shaped oaks manage to survive. As the barrier island approaches Santa Rosa Sound, there are often brackish marshes where the water level fluctuates with the tides. Here, the dark gray spikes of reeds and rough cordgrass dominate. And, finally, there is the sound, dense with aquatic plants.

Birds thrive on the island, different ones in each of the six habitats.

The park furnishes a bird checklist that contains over two hundred species, ranging from loons and pelicans to such curios as the greater scaup and the American kestrel. But even if you are a dunce at bird identification, you can still thrill to the graceful hawks gliding on invisible wind-rivers and mockingbirds chanting melodic love songs.

The Village That Shouldn't Have Been

The nationally protected seashore ends at the Santa Rosa County line, where homes and commercial buildings begin with jarring suddenness. Many of the homes in Navarre Beach are on stilts and set back from the Gulf. But along the beach, once the solitary domain of the relatively modest Holiday Inn, high-rise residential buildings and a lofty Regency Hotel thrust cement buttresses against the shoreline. This recent building splurge delights the South Santa Rosa Tourist Development Council, which recently announced that the county is the second fastest growing in the state.

In a way, the four developed miles of Navarre Beach should not even exist. The land originally belonged to Escambia County, not Santa Rosa County. In 1956, Escambia granted Santa Rosa a ninety-nine-year lease, provided they would construct a bridge to the island,

Homes supported by stilts on Santa Rosa Island are built to withstand fierce storm surges.

which they did four years later. Later, when Escambia agreed to transfer most of its portion of the island to the Gulf Islands National Seashore, Santa Rosa refused to part with Navarre Beach. So that is that—at least until 2055, when most of us won't care anyway.

At least the portion of Santa Rosa Island east of Navarre Beach is safe from development. It is part of the sprawling Eglin Air Force Base and is closed to the public. If and when the military no longer needs this seventeen miles, it will be added to the Gulf Islands National Seashore.

The Canal That Isn't—Or Is It?

The movers and shakers in mainland Navarre, which is distinct from Navarre Beach, are avid expansionists. Navarre is separated from the Gulf of Mexico by Santa Rosa Island. It would be a simple matter to dig a canal across that narrow obstruction, thereby giving Navarre access to lucrative Gulf shipping. Indeed, at one time, a canal did cross the island, having been dug in only a few months. Unfortunately, it refilled with sand even more quickly than it had been built.

Modern engineers are confident they can keep a new canal open by means of jetties that would extend seven hundred feet into the Gulf. This would prevent the westward drifting sand from blocking the canal entrance. But, since this sand is necessary for renourishment of the Gulf Islands National Seashore, dredges would constantly transfer the sand from east of the jetties to west.

Would it work? Expert coastal geologist James P. Morgan wrote that, despite the dredges, he had great fears such a canal could result in "destabilization of the beaches along the downdrift part of the island." Earle Bowden warned of "trying to alter forces of sea and shore." But the canal is a tantalizing dream that won't die. If it worked, it would bring an economic bonanza to Navarre. If it failed, it might wreck Santa Rosa Island. It's a continuing story, so stay tuned.

🚗   Now, follow SR 399 as it bends north and crosses Santa Rosa Sound to Navarre. Here, you should turn east on US 98 and head toward Ft. Walton.

Tar Trap

Today, a drive down US 98 is nothing to get excited about. But in the mid-1930s, when the road was built, an excursion on this highway was a big-time thrill—right up there with popcorn and bubble gum. It connected Pensacola with Tallahassee, utilizing a series of spanking-new bridges, including the three-mile-long Pensacola Bay Bridge and a marvelous one across the extensive, hitherto almost impassable marshes at Apalachicola. The road did have a few drawbacks, for the road-builders had gotten their tar mix from Northern sources, not realizing they needed a far more viscous substance to bear up under the fierce Florida sun. "Beware of oiled road shoulders," cautioned the 1939 WPA Guide, "which look safe but are almost as liquid as quicksilver." Despite the alert, oily autos and cussing drivers were common along old US 98.

Military Might

After entering Okaloosa County, you'll pass a sign warning about low-flying planes. Hurlburt Field is immediately left of the highway, and farther north is the main portion of the Eglin Air Force Base. Eglin concentrates on developing military hardware, such as the smart bombs used in Afghanistan and Iraq. The importance of Eglin and Hurlburt to Okaloosa County is difficult to overestimate. Not only do they generate seventy percent of the county's jobs, but they have encouraged more than two hundred high-tech civilian research plants to locate in the vicinity.

Eglin has a museum on aircraft weaponry just outside the base gates on SR 85. It's open seven days a week from 9:30 A.M. to 4:30 P.M. Admission is free, except for what you spend at the gift shop. Call 850–882–4062 for more information.

Just beyond Hurlburt, you'll see a sign announcing that Mary Esther welcomes you. But, if you hope to encounter a friendly young lady, you'll be disappointed. For she's long dead—or I should say they, for Mary and Esther Newton were daughters of the town's founder.

Upon entering Ft. Walton Beach, the road travels close by Santa Rosa Sound, which is bordered by marinas and seafood restaurants.

The Panhandle Circuit

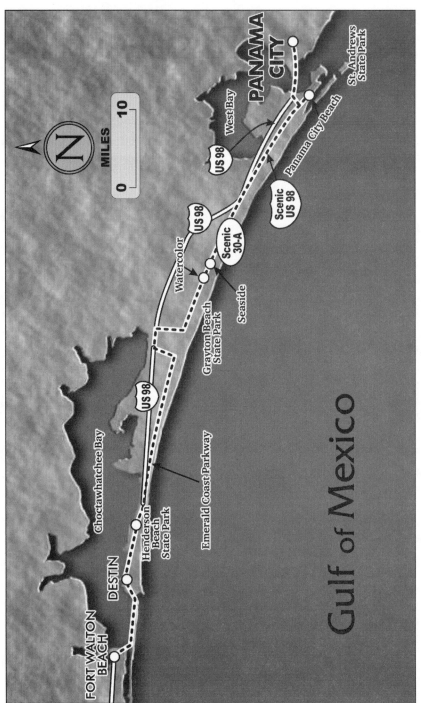

White Sands and Emerald Waters

Ft. Walton to Panama City • 63 Backroad Miles

The Song of the Road: Overview

We'll start out in Ft. Walton Beach and take an easy stroll up Temple Mound. Here, you can examine a reconstructed, ancient Indian temple and learn about this people's elaborate burial ceremonies. Another part of Ft. Walton Beach lies on Okaloosa Island, where vacation getaways face the Gulf.

Destin, Ft. Walton's sister city, lies on the other side of East Pass, and is home to more sparkling units on the beach. Destin boasts the largest fleet of charter fishing craft in Florida. Henderson State Park offers swimming and other recreational opportunities. East from Henderson along the Emerald Coast Parkway lie other public beaches, as well as restaurants with scenic vistas.

By turning onto County Road 30-A we'll enjoy a unique excursion along the Gulf. First comes Grayton Beach State Park, whose picturesque dunes and self-guided nature trail have long made it one of the world's top seashore attractions. A hiking-biking trail begins near Grayton and continues through the backwoods and hidden lakes behind CR 30-A.

There are some unusual settlements along here. One is called WaterColor, an upscale, planned community being built by the St. Joe Company, which has recently emerged as a major force in the revitalization of this part of Florida. Another interesting settlement is the village of Seaside. This town's architectural style and concept of town planning have become models for the New Urbanization movement.

Next, we'll visit Panama City Beach. Although it has been called the Redneck Riviera, the St. Joe Company has a major beach-front project that should upgrade the community. There are some exceedingly beautiful resorts here, and at the tip of the peninsula is St. Andrews State Park, with public beaches, nature trails, a fishing pier, and launches to primitive Shell Island, where you can roam the beach in search of shells or snorkel through a strange world of sea grasses.

Finally, our route will lead us across the bridge into Panama City, highlighted by Old St. Andrews, a once-decayed fishing port now known for its unique seafood restaurants, quaint shops, and rebuilt marina.

Wooden Indians

Ft. Walton Beach's main street is called Miracle Strip Parkway, more prosaically known as US 98. The town originated as a temporary Confederate encampment during the Civil War. In their spare time, the soldiers dug around the nearby Indian mound, pulling out the skeletons and stringing them up as decorations. Ironically, the camp has vanished but the mound has become a city landmark.

I'm not going to overplay the mound. Although the climb to the summit is easy—it's only twelve feet high—the display at the top is somewhat hokey. No, more than somewhat. It consists of a slightly slap-dab timber structure that is called a temple. Inside are plywood sheets cut in life-size shapes of Indian men, women, and children. On the ground lies another piece of plywood representing a dead tribal leader called Tattooed Serpent.

But when you're done smirking, take a moment to reassess the

An ancient Indian burial scene is depicted by these rather crude, but authentically dressed, life-sized figures atop Ft. Walton's Temple Mound.

scene. Although the figures are crude, their clothing and hair styles are based on Jacques Le Moyne's three-hundred-year-old on-the-spot drawings of actual Timucuan Indians. And there was a leader called Tattooed Serpent whose burial ceremony was described by eye-witness Europeans in 1725. Furthermore, this very mound was used for burial ceremonies. We know this because Confederate soldiers found skeletons that were lying on their backs with their hands crossed.

So loosen your imagination. Let the Indians come alive. Perhaps you'll hear them chanting for the spirit of their dead chief. Perhaps you'll hear the priest's rhythmic rattles. Perhaps you'll feel the sadness of the mourners. You don't need a full stage and elaborate scenery to convey emotions. Shakespeare would have understood.

If you want to learn more, pay the $2 admission fee to the first-class, little museum at the foot of the mound. It's open during the summer Monday through Saturday, 9:00 A.M. to 4:30 P.M., and Sunday, 12:30 P.M. to 4:00 P.M. During the winter, it's open Monday through Saturday, 11:00 A.M. to 4:00 P.M., and closed on Sunday. Some of the artifacts in the museum, such as the bowls and cups used in family suppers, are quite personal. The museum even has a display of the remains of what must have been someone's pet dog that was given a formal burial around 500 A.D. Some of the exhibits rouse your imagination, such as the urn in the form of a grotesque being. Did this grumpy fellow dwell in the urn? Or was he simply a caricature to make the children laugh? Then there are coins left there by Spaniards, who probably also left some of their European diseases.

It's something of a shock to leave the tree-enclosed temple compound and remerge on Miracle Strip Parkway. Although a street with such a name seems to promise great things, you can't expect too many miracles from a town of just 20,000 inhabitants. It's enough of a miracle that the shopping area is still alive, given the age and condition of many of its buildings.

Okaloosa Island

Several blocks beyond SR 85, Miracle Strip Parkway passes over Santa Rosa Sound onto Okaloosa Island, known farther east as Santa Rosa Island. Just over the bridge is a fine public beach, with a boardwalk and some restaurants. Nearby is the Gulfarium, which features the world's oldest continuously operating marine aquarium. It managed to survive a hit by Hurricane Opal, but just barely. Shows featuring either dolphins or sea lions run continuously seven days a week from 10:00 A.M. until 5:15 P.M., with a later closing time of 7:15 P.M. in the summer. But the $16 admission might induce you to pass it by. It did me.

As if this portion of the island is not sufficiently packed with condos, homes, businesses, and marinas, the Emerald Coast Conference Center is under construction on fifty-four acres, which were formerly occupied by a roller coaster and a mini-racetrack. With 70,000 square feet, it's not only twice as spacious as that of its rival in Pensacola but is the largest conference center in all of north Florida, not including Jacksonville. If you're looking for a place to stay, you'll be glad for a motel like the Holiday Inn, directly on the beach. At the height of the mid-May to mid-August season, a room with a balcony facing the Gulf costs $179, although a lesser view can be had for $149. In the winter, the same rooms drop to $89 and $79. For reservations call 800–238–8686.

The Return of a Friend: The Gulf Islands National Seashore

As US 98 reaches the island's eastern tip, the buildings end. Suddenly, you're among low, knobby sand dunes. You could almost imagine you've returned to Timucuan times were it not for the multilane highway thronged with cars and perfumed with exhaust. Nonetheless, it's nice to have the original island back, thanks to the Gulf Islands National Seashore.

This slim line of dunes was ground-zero during Hurricane Opal in 1995. As the wind roared up to 144 miles per hour, massive wave surges taller than two-story buildings crashed ashore, flattening the dunes and obliterating four miles of the road. Since then, this portion of US 98 has been rebuilt and the dunes are slowly reforming. Soon, they will be their old selves—that is, until the day Opal's boisterous brother comes calling.

Sand or Cement: Destin's Dilemma

As the road ascends the bridge over the East Pass, you get a fleeting view, on the right, of the Emerald Coast's beautiful greenish-blue waters. On the left is the more somber Choctawhatchee Bay. Then, descend into Destin, where high-rise monoliths enclose the world in cement. Even Destin's mayor admitted the town was out of control: "I think it's going to continue to grow up to the point where we're built out and the sand is covered with asphalt and the only trees are in the parking lots," he told a reporter.

One of Destin's most popular draws is its charter fishing fleet, which, with more than a hundred vessels, is Florida's largest. Certainly such a number would astonish humble Leonard Destin who came here in 1845 to enjoy the pristine seashore and whatever he could hook from his rocking scow. The town promotes itself as the "World's Luckiest Fishing Village," which is a bold assertion, since most fishermen insist it's their skill, not their luck, that enables them to snare the big ones. Much of the fleet is docked near the foot of the bridge. Also, there are some good restaurants with fine views of the harbor.

A rowboat could get through Destin faster than a car. So stay cool. You might want to take a brief excursion on Gulf Shore Drive to Holiday Isle and view the spectacular array of condo towers up close. Almost all have units for rent, most are directly on the beach. The Sandpiper Cove, for example, consists of nearly six hundred condominiums on forty-three landscaped acres. For more information call 800–874–0448.

Destin's year-round population is only 12,000, so eventually you'll reach the outskirts where signs along US 98 point to the Gulf beaches. A short turn south takes you to the Emerald Coast Parkway and Henderson State Park.

The Beaches

Henderson State Park has more than a mile of seashore ideal for swimming. Surf fishing is also popular, as is the walking trail. Admission is just $2 per car.

More beaches are farther east along the parkway, including James Lee Park. Here, there is not as much beach as at Henderson, but there is no admission fee. Roadside parking is free, if you can find a place. I was there on a warm day in May and had no problem. It would probably be different during the height of the summer season. The park has playgrounds, restrooms with showers, and a casual eatery called the Crab Trap, which offers a savory selection of seafood, sandwiches, salads, and such.

Is the Sand Always Sugar White?

The sand along this stretch of road is the brilliant quartz typical of the Emerald Coast. Sugar white is used so often to describe it that the word has become almost a cliché. As I sat on the beach at James Lee Park, I wondered if there weren't other adjectives that could be used.

The beach is wide at Destin's James Lee Park

Why not call the sand salt white? Milk is white, too. So is vanilla ice cream. And how about coconut? Or soda cracker? Or almond? Or eggshell? Then there's tooth paste white and flour white. Moving away from food, the sand could be described as the color of surf or foam or clouds or desert wind, to get poetic. And there's ivory or alabaster or porcelain. Bone white is descriptive. So is tusk white. Milkweed fuzz is white, so are magnolia petals and Easter lilies. To connote coolness there is frost, icicle, snowflake, glacier, fog, and mist. Egrets are white; and they're good Florida birds. Stars are white. And couldn't the beaches be compared to powdered moonlight or comet dust? There's also . . . well, you get the idea.

The Fabled Destin Dome

After solving the puzzle of how to describe the sand, I began to consider renaming the emerald water. But it was so beautiful that I let my thoughts wander farther out, twenty miles to be exact. That's where the underwater Destin Dome begins. Although you may never have heard of it, it's on the minds of many people along this part of the Gulf. For within the Destin Dome lies one of the richest untapped reservoirs of natural gas, and probably petroleum, on the American continent. The problem is that the Dome lies so close to the tourist beaches.

When the Bush administration considered granting leases to oil companies to drill in the Destin Dome, a howl went up not only from the usual environmentalist groups, but also from tourist agencies, motel and hotel owners, chambers of commerce, individual home and condo owners, and almost anyone else who could find an audience. The outcry was quickly taken up by political leaders, including Florida's Republican governor, who happened to be George Bush's brother, Jeb. Newspaper editorials bewailed the danger of oil spills turning the white sand into a black, gooey mess. There was also the specter of oil rigs ten stories high puncturing the skyline. And the smell!

Administration officials retorted that the danger of oil spills and odors was nonexistent, for the drilling would be for natural gas, which would be piped directly to refineries in Mobile, Alabama. As for seeing the rigs, they would be far beneath the horizon. Even so, the uproar continued. Eventually, President Bush agreed to exempt the Destin Dome from the leases that he granted. These leases kept the drilling to one hundred miles off shore. But drilling may happen later, as the only commitment to the contrary was an agreement between the Bush brothers to withhold a leasing decision until 2007. Then the dome is up for grabs.

Spreading Sprawl

From James Lee Park, continue east on the Emerald Coast Parkway, also known as Scenic US 98. For the next few miles, the Gulf is nearly always in view and, even though handsome residences line the way, there are lots of palms and greenery. Every so often, you'll pass a restaurant overlooking the water. At Miramar Beach, there is public parking directly on the Gulf. A leaflet states that Miramar is the home of several award-winning restaurants, but I am not an award-winning gourmet, so I did not hunt them down.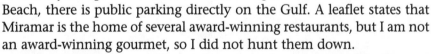

Beyond Miramar, you'll pass homes built to hang recklessly over the low bluffs. Signs indicate more such homes are on the way. When the final build-out is completed, alas, they will effectively block many water views for motorists.

Shortly, the Emerald Coast Parkway merges into US 98, which has finally shaken free of Destin's commercial conglomeration and now leads through semi-forested land. But the roadside is slated for development and scattered construction has already started.

In three miles, you'll come to Scenic 30-A, upon which you should turn right. There are more homes, whose staggered and stilted heights make them rather picturesque. Most have balconies looking toward the beach, which is out of sight for travelers. The land is composed of knobby dunes covered with vegetation. Then, the road wanders through backwater marshes, where mirror-calm water is dotted with lilies.

Suddenly, you'll come to a sign for Grayton Beach State Park. Be sure to turn into the main entrance and not the cabin road.

Resurrection is Slow

Grayton Beach State Park is not one of Florida's largest, but it is one of its prettiest. Admission is $3.25 per car, and it is open seven days a week between 8:00 A.M. and sunset. For many years, Grayton consistently won recognition as the best beach in all of North America. But Hurricane Opal tossed Grayton's vaunted dunes over Alabama and Georgia, and, although nature is gradually rebuilding them, Grayton has yet to reappear on the best beach list.

Nonetheless, being a shadow of its former self is nothing to scoff at. The baby Grayton dunes have a wild look that makes them especially appealing. A forty-five-minute-long nature trail begins at the parking lot on Western Lake and leads through a series of landscapes: dunes, hammocks, oak thickets, pine flatwoods, and salt marshes. You may spot such wildflowers as golden asters, purple lupines, tread-softly plants with their small

Dunes create a wild landscape at Grayton Beach State Park.

white blossoms, and gaillardia boasting showy red flowers with yellow fringes. In the swales are sea oats. The bright green plants capping many dunes are dwarf live oaks, whose growth has been stunted by lack of nutrients in the sandy soil and by shearing from the relentless winds. Beyond the dunes is a mile-long beach for swimming. The park restrooms can be used for changing. Surf fishing is also available, but you'll have to bring your own gear.

A Titan Strides the Great Northwest

Immediately east of Grayton Beach, Scenic 30-A passes through the new village of WaterColor, which has over a thousand residences. Designed to be a virtually self-contained community, WaterColor has 100,000 square feet of commercial establishments around a town center embellished by a clock tower that looks like it could have tolled the hours in Renaissance Italy. An artificial little channel between the lake and the Gulf runs through Cerulean Park, a large green space in the heart of the development. On Western Lake, canoes, kayaks, and sailboats may be rented.

If you want to purchase a residence in WaterColor, the prices generally run between $300,000 and $1.5 million. However, just to try it out, you can rent for a single night. The least expensive unit is in the town center, where you'll pay around $400 for one bedroom in the summer and $325 in the winter. For more information call 866–426–2656.

WaterColor is a showcase development of the St. Joe Company. Although, in terms of revenue, St. Joe barely makes the top fifty Florida companies, the company has a massive presence in the Panhandle. St. Joe was begun in the 1920s as a paper company and, as such, accumulated vast forest lands to supply the huge mill it constructed at the Panhandle town of Port St. Joe. When the company left the paper business for the development of its real estate in the late 1990s, it quickly realized that the Panhandle itself had to be reinvigorated before the company's holdings could be marketed effectively. So St. Joe became the catalyst in the formation of Florida's Great Northwest, Inc., an organization of business and civic leaders from across a twelve-county region. We'll examine this exciting company in greater detail when we visit Port St. Joe in the next chapter.

Pastel Paradise

WaterColor was inspired by and modeled loosely after neighboring

The town of Seaside is setting a new style of neighbor-friendly living.

Seaside, which originated in the early 1980s. Seaside was a radical concept that envisioned a community where the inhabitants could actually know their neighbors! To facilitate this interaction, Seaside built its homes close together, with old-time front porches from which folks could chat across property lines. The architecture was in yester-year's style, which gave the community a bond with the past. The town was designed to be small to allow its inhabitants to walk where they needed to go. Every street led someplace. None ended in a forbidden cul-de-sac. The streets were narrow so residents could be aware of what was going on around them. This would be particularly appealing to parents, whose kids, it was thought, would stroll down-town for ice cream cones. Walking was so encouraged that one store sold tee shirts picturing a pair of shoes with the caption "The Seaside Transit Authority."

The town is mostly built-out now. The downtown consists of fifty stores, most trying to be quaint. There are around 250 cottages crowding a dozen and a half tree-lined streets. As you stroll these streets, you'll notice that nearly every house has a designation, some whimsical, like *EcstaSea* and *Sisters Three By the Sea*. Often the resi-dents' names are displayed on a street-side board. Every person is supposed to be one's neighbor here.

 A restaurant directly on the beach provides the setting for

leisurely contemplation of the Gulf, although, at times, the place can be lively enough to short-circuit casual musings. There are other activities at Seaside. If you enjoy cycling, you can rent a bike. If you like kayaks, they are available for river trips. And charter boats can be had for deep-sea fishing. Call Go Fish Outfitters at 850–231–1717.

A Pricey Paradise

Seaside has so captured the public fancy that prices have shot up to almost unbelievable heights. Although rentals by the bushel are available, a typical two-bedroom cottage, for a single night, costs around $350 in the winter and $570 in the summer. A week's rental is $2,300 to $3,300. Outright ownership of a slice of paradise is likewise pricey: a half million dollars will only get you a one-bedroom abode.

Despite its apparent success, Seaside has not turned out as its developer envisioned. Instead of a permanent citizenry, nearly every resident is here on vacation. Few kids walk merrily to the corner ice cream shop. Indeed, children are so lacking that a vast majority of the town's charter school pupils are bussed in from surrounding areas. The vaunted front porches are now so effectively enclosed by overgrown shrubs that if a visitor wants to talk to his neighbor he'd better have a megaphone handy. Cars are not obsolete, but jam the crowded streets. The town has almost become a sort of theme park and is often thronged with curiosity-seekers.

Perhaps Seaside's greatest contribution has been its example of New Urbanism. Other similar communities are springing up using Seaside's ground-breaking concepts. One of the largest such communities is Walt Disney's town of Celebration just outside Orlando. With the long-term goal of 20,000 inhabitants, Celebration will be the ultimate test of neighborliness and front porches vs. privacy and autos. I'm betting on autos.

A Nice Little Road: Scenic 30-A

From Seaside, Scenic 30-A continues east, often accompanied by a friendly bike path. Walton County is justly proud of this path, which skirts small lakes, secluded woodlands, and beach areas as it extends from Grayton Beach to the eastern end of 30-A. And, speaking of bike paths, there are several more biking-hiking trails a short distance back from the coast. They range in length from 3.5 to ten miles. This area is part of the Florida state forest system, and the trail head is about five miles north of Seaside on SR 395.

Continuing on SR 30-A, you'll soon pass Camp Creek, another St. Joe development. Then come other developments, usually hidden from the road, including Rosemary Beach, done by the architect of Seaside. One of its attractions is Eternity Pool, which may be a little unnerving for persons not yet ready for the Everlasting.

After a pleasant drive of eighteen miles, route 30-A merges with US 98. Despite a few gainsayers, most of us will admit that it was a nice road brimming with energy and surprises. It told us it would be scenic and did its best to live up to that promise. SR 30-A: we're sorry to leave you.

A New Definition of Scenic

So we're back on rumbling US 98. For a brief moment, it beguiles us with an agreeable landscape as it passes over Powell Lake. Then US 98 splits. The left branch makes no claims, but the right calls itself Scenic US 98. An accompanying sign proclaims that this road will deliver us to "Panama City Beach: the World's Most Beautiful." Wow. We've seen some gorgeous sands since leaving Pensacola, so this must be something truly memorable.

Memorable it is, but not in the expected manner. The words scenic and beautiful apparently have whole new meanings in Panama City Beach. Scenic indicates to most of us a pretty, even inspiring scene. But, when local boosters tacked scenic onto this highway, they must have meant simply something to see. If this was their definition, they were right. Seldom will you see such an uncomely conglomeration of tourist ticklers and gaudy gewgaws. There's the Original Goofy Golf set amid plaster dinosaurs so old they might actually date to the Jurassic. Then comes the Magic Mountain store in a pathetically artificial cavern. Beyond is NASCART Park, where go-cart drivers make believe they are whizzing by at speeds that would humble Daytona's pros. The Palace gives tattoos in a three-story, all glass building. One business heralds its stock of five thousand swim suits, although, as far as I know, no outsider has verified that number by actual count. And don't miss Bungee Manic. The goodies just go on and on. Such is the character of this rollicking strip that it has earned Panama City Beach the unchallenged title of Redneck Riviera.

The strip may be rollicking during tourist season, but that is nothing when it's descended on by up to 500,000 college students during spring break. It's just their style—at least according to those

students who remain clear-headed enough to recall the festivities.
Popular motels include Days Inn, which can be reached at
800–633–0266, and Quality Inn, which can be reached at
800–874–7101.

Truly, Panama City Beach is different, to be kind, from any other
place on the Emerald Coast. It even has its own sand. A few years back,
the town decided to replenish its beach and pumped in a thick layer
of sand. Surprise! This sand was a dingy tan, not the expected brilliant
white. Although the engineers assured the town that it would bleach
into the desired color, that hasn't happened yet, nor will it ever. For
the sand is stained with iron oxide, commonly called rust. And rust
does not bleach.

But Panama City Beach is changing for the better. The St. Joe
Company is bringing a degree of refinement to the town—after all, the
well-healed residents of WaterColor are accustomed to entertainment
that is a little more chic than Goofy Golf. St. Joe's project is Pier Park,
which involves turning 270 acres of Gulf beach front into a huge
entertainment and retail complex.

After twelve miles of wonders, Scenic US 98 veers left toward
the bridge over St. Andrews Bay. But continue west on Thomas
Drive, which leads through the classier part of town. Among the large
motels and condos is the Dunes of Panama with 1,500 feet of private
beach and three swimming pools. A one-bedroom unit runs between
$90 and $145 depending on the season. For more information call
800–874–2412.

Swim with the Dolphins

When Thomas turns abruptly north, stay on the shoreline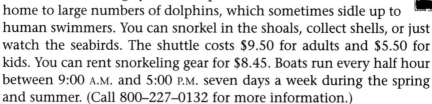
road to St. Andrews State Park. (For park information call
850–233–5140.) Here, amid almost unspoiled dunes, you can
stroll along a nature trail through a series of plant communities.
Swimming is also available, as is surf fishing or pier fishing. Be
sure to take the shuttle boat across a manmade channel to Shell
Island, which is largely undeveloped. The waters hereabouts are
home to large numbers of dolphins, which sometimes sidle up to
human swimmers. You can snorkel in the shoals, collect shells, or just
watch the seabirds. The shuttle costs $9.50 for adults and $5.50 for
kids. You can rent snorkeling gear for $8.45. Boats run every half hour
between 9:00 A.M. and 5:00 P.M. seven days a week during the spring
and summer. (Call 800–227–0132 for more information.)

Returning to Thomas Drive, follow it north over the Grand Lagoon. Here, the Marriott Golf and Yacht Club (which can be reached at 800–874–7105) overlooks a 1,100-acre nature preserve and award-winning, thirty-six-hole golf course. When Thomas meets US 98 in a few blocks, turn right on US 98 and cross St. Andrews Bay into Panama City.

The Other Panama

Panama City is often confused with Panama City Beach, its flamboyant namesake. But they are radically different. Whereas P.C. Beach was a virtual wilderness until the 1970s, when the inhospitable dog flies were muzzled, P.C. Beachless dates back to pirate days, when the customary treasure was buried on the shore. P.C. Beach is a visitor-dependent strip of sand with less than eight thousand permanent residents. But Beachless has a real harbor, which has enabled it to develop into a well-rounded city of nearly 40,000. Their only similarity is that both are becoming more and more beholden to the ubiquitous St. Joe Company—P.C. Beach for the Pier and P. C. Beachless for the spacious new airport planned on land donated by St. Joe.

Originally, there were three separate villages here: Panama City, Millville, and St. Andrews. For many years, St. Andrews was the most important. Even before the Civil War, it was a thriving fishing port, with a hotel, a post office, and a tavern—the real indication that a place had arrived.

Although the three towns merged many years ago, St. Andrews kept a distinctive identity. To reach St. Andrews, follow US 98 to where Business 98 splits off to join Beck Avenue, then turn south on Beck Avenue. As it passes Twelfth Street, it enters the heart of old St. Andrews. The two-block downtown is in the process of revival. A good example is Le Shack Restaurant at the corner of Beck Avenue and Tenth Street.

"Le Shack dates back to around 1930," Linda Janikowski, the owner, told me. "In those days it was a Pure Oil station on the main road between Panama City and Pensacola." We sat alone in the restaurant early in the morning. The old wooden walls were quiet, yet somehow alive with chatter and laughter. There is hardly a square inch of the restaurant's wall space not hung with baskets or dolls or memorabilia—among them signed photos by such celebrity diners as Vic Damone and Diahann Carroll. The Dalai Lama and his entourage have also enjoyed Le Shack's hospitality. Shelf after shelf is heavy with wine bottles, most signed and dated by customers. One couple has

In Panama City's old St. Andrews section, once-decrepit buildings are being converted for other uses. This former gas station is now Le Shack Restaurant.

This tree sculpture has become a landmark beside St. Andrews' harbor.

been "coming to the restaurant to celebrate their wedding anniversary for nearly three decades," Linda said with pride.

Linda has a tender feeling for St. Andrews. "There's big changes going on here," she said enthusiastically. "Beck Avenue is going to be landscaped and the whole community brought back."

On the opposite corner from Le Shack is the former bank, which opened in 1907 with capital of just $15,000. It was so short of quarters and nickels that any person coming to town was urged to bring his own. Now, it's a police substation. A block west of Le Shack is the marina, revived after a $2 million dollar dredging. From the dock, you get an excellent view of the spacious harbor fronting St. Andrews Bay. To the south is the Gulf of Mexico, from which early fishermen brought the catches that gave the town its start. Spanish explorers even named the locale after St. Andrew, the patron saint of fishermen. In Civil War times, a fleet of Union warships descended on St. Andrews, a major source of salt and salt fish for the Confederacy, to bombard the town and leave it a smoking ruin.

 A boardwalk running along the waterfront passes a tree sculpture that adds an air of artificial authenticity to the area where great pines thirty stories tall once hummed in the Gulf breezes. At the far end, Uncle Ernie's Bayfront Grill and Brewhouse stands where, a hundred years earlier, a large railroad pier jutted into the bay. Trains from Alabama deposited tourists here, where they boarded launches for a frolicsome sail around the bay.

At the other end of the waterfront you'll find the St. Andrews Bay Seafood Restaurant and the Ramada Inn. (For hotel reservations call 800–272–6232.) This was the site of Ware's Dock, where a casino was constructed in 1912. From its popular dance hall, music and beer fumes wafted over the waterfront.

After St. Andrews merged with Panama City in 1926, the commerce moved to Panama City's better port facilities a few miles east. Then, St. Andrews settled down to peaceful decay. Little did it expect that decay would become quaint, and today the once-sleepy district is evolving into a tourist attraction.

St. Andrews is a good place to end this trip. So why not enjoy a fresh seafood dinner at one of the restaurants and settle in for a quiet slumber at the Ramada.

The Panhandle Circuit

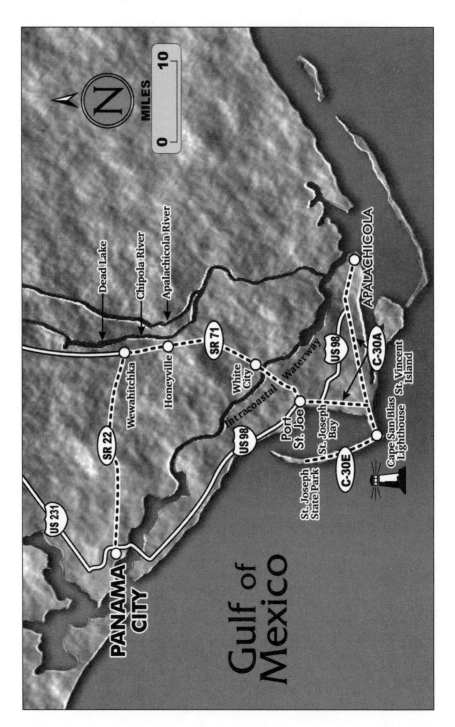

Beaches and Honey Bees

Panama City to Apalachicola • 102 Backroad Miles

The Song of the Road: Overview

Leaving Panama City, we'll pass through an immense pine forest to Wewahitchka, almost lost amid the trees. The village is famous among certain gourmets for its tupelo honey. We can stop for a while at the rustic residence where the honey is refined and sold. Then, we'll continue down a country road to the Dead Lake, which presents an exotic panorama of cypresses killed by a flood many years ago.

From there, the way leads south through the pines once more to Port St. Joe, where the imposing mill that belonged to the St. Joe Company once stood. Port St. Joe boasts a modern marina with a restaurant that offers a view in addition to food. Next, we'll travel along the St. Joseph Bay, rich with scallops that can be gathered by hand during the summer season. The bay is partially enclosed by the St. Joe Peninsula, which also goes by the name of Cape San Blas. You can drive almost to the tip of the cape, where a state park provides unexcelled swimming from beaches that stretch for ten miles along the Gulf of Mexico.

This exploration ends at Apalachicola, a quaint river town replete with a waterfront where shrimp boats glide past restaurants serving seafood delicacies.

On the Road Again

Heading east on SR 22 from Panama City, you'll find yourself in a vast pine forest that belongs to the St. Joe Company. The company owns an astonishing eighty percent of Gulf County, as well as massive tracts in nine other counties in the Panhandle and north Florida. At first, you may not be aware that these trees are planted in rows, just as corn or any other cash crop. But when you view the trees from the right angle, you'll see the long files.

The company originally bought this land to furnish timber for its huge paper mill at Port St. Joe. But that mill was sold when the company left the paper business to develop its land holdings. So the

203

Timber roads cut straight routes into the vast forests belonging to the St. Joe Company.

land here is in limbo while company bigwigs debate creative ways to utilize it.

Tupelo Town

The road continues through St. Joe land for twenty-three miles to Wewahitchka, a quiet little community of around 1,800. Tiny as the village is, a Chamber of Commerce leaflet proclaims "We've Got It All." The challenge is to discover just what can be included in this all.

They certainly have a name that is among the most awkward in Florida. Perhaps Wewahitchka sounded better when the Indians pronounced it, for to them it meant the place of the water eyes, referring to the pair of perfectly round lakes that SR 22 squeezes by as it enters town. Modern inhabitants call their town Wewa, wisely leaving tourists to struggle with the long version.

Wewahitchka's is also the home of the county's major employer, the Gulf Correctional Institution. While corrections is not a prestige industry, at least it provides employment for several hundred people. Nor is life in prison always dull. One inmate, using the public phone only a few minutes daily for six years, managed to swipe the identities of enough people to enable his girlfriend and her accomplices to steal up to $3 million in clothing, jewelry, furniture, and other goods from unsuspecting creditors. Who says prison is not fun?

But having it "all" must surely refer to Wewa's beloved honey bees. Sure, they're just insects, but they work hard for the glory of Wewa. Their field of endeavor is in the swamps along the Apalachicola and Chipola Rivers just east of town. And the objects of their endeavors are the flowers of the tupelo trees, which are in bloom for only a few weeks each spring. The result is tupelo honey, the lightest, sweetest, and generally most delectable honey in Mother Nature's pantry. Wewa claims it's the only place on earth where tupelo honey is produced commercially. So where in Wewa do you buy tupelo honey? That's easy: from L. L. Lanier & Son, who have been in the business for nigh over a hundred years. And where do you find the Laniers? Well, follow me.

Honeyville

The center of Wewahitchka is at SR 22 and SR 71. From this junction, turn a half block south on SR 71 to Lake Grove Road and head east. After a block or so you'll approach the water tower, where there's an old country home with a smallish sign for tupelo honey. Turn up the driveway, which seems to end in a junk yard with four old vehicles in various stages of repair and five sheds overloaded with useless discards.

My first time, I persisted in looking for a sales booth until I had driven completely through the back yard and onto a side street. The second time around, I noticed that there was a back porch protruding into the junkyard, and there, on the steps, was Glynnis Lanier, smiling at me. She had experienced many first timer drive-throughs. Glynnis was a pretty young woman with long hair the color of forest shadows. Her face had a friendly glow that I could sense would remain even if I didn't purchase anything. Fortunately, I was not there during the honey-gathering spring season, so she had time to take me around the grounds.

We walked across the backyard to a one-story, cement block building that she called the honey house but looked more like someone's abandoned garage. On the way, we passed within a few feet of several active bee hives. "Don't mind them," she said casually, as bees flitted around our heads. Some of them escorted us into the honey house, where Glynnis completely ignored them. But I didn't.

At the height of the season, six people prepare the honey here.

Glynnis Lanier draws tupelo honey from this large drum.

Today, there was only one. The process is actually very simple. During the season, wooden frames are removed from the hives and brought here. These frames are sixteen inches long and only an inch thick. They are filled with more than a thousand small honey comb chambers. The frames are placed on a conveyor belt where small rotating blades cut off the waxy comb cap, thereby exposing the thick liquid within. The frames are then placed in a centrifuge that spins the honey out and into large drums where it is drained into commercial bottles as needed.

But this is the easy part.

Raised in a Beehive

This is where Glynnis' husband, Ben, comes in. During the brief spring season, he and five other stalwarts transport a thousand of their hives from other locations to the nearby tupelo swamps along the Apalachicola and Chipola Rivers. Here, the hives, which weigh around ninety pounds each, are lifted onto mounds as high as ten feet to protect them from flooding. The work is made even tougher by the bugs and the humidity that clings like hot beeswax.

The tupelo trees bloom only for a few weeks, and then the bees begin searching out other flowers whose honey is not of the same quality. In order to have pure tupelo honey, the bees must be briefly smoked out of their hives and the honey-filled frames removed at the precise moment tupelo production ends. So how does Ben Lanier know when it's time to act? He just knows—-it's an ability learned over many years. "I grew up in a beehive," Ben's father once told a reporter, and that's true for Ben, too.

When tupelo time is over, the men must move all one thousand hives to new locations, where the bees diligently gather nectar from other flowers.

What is so special about tupelo honey? It was best expressed by father Lanier himself: "Its the only honey I know that when you taste it you see the tupelo trees blooming, you see the moonlight shimmering on the Apalachicola River, and you can hear the bees buzzing away." That pretty much says it.

Ulee's Gold

Once in a while the Laniers get to know their patrons intimately. This was the case with one persistent buyer who kept asking so many questions that they thought he might be from the IRS. But, as it happened, he was a movie director researching a script entitled *Ulee's Gold* about a honey-maker who runs into trouble with some bank robbers. After the Laniers agreed that he could use their facilities as the setting, a year-long adventure with sixty or seventy actors and production people began.

The film crews crowded into the Laniers' bathrooms and kitchen. They ate late meals on Laniers' porch. During lulls, they sat around chatting with the family. The star of the film was Peter Fonda, who later won an Oscar nomination for his role. Daddy Lanier described Fonda as "just one of the crowd, a friendly man who didn't demand anything special." Glynnis Lanier agreed. "The movie people were real good," she told me. "We were the film consultants, and Ben read the script carefully. They filmed in our bee yards, but had to stage their own honey house because they were shooting during the honey flow. You can't have a bunch of people in our honey house with clatter and bright lights without some serious stinging."

It was a heady experience for the Laniers. "We went to Park City, Utah, with them," Glynnis continued, "where *Ulee's Gold* was the centerpiece of the Sundance Festival that year." The Laniers also flew to New York City "where [the crew] put us up on Park Avenue. We did mostly radio and print interviews. The stars did the big TV shows. But stories about us came out everywhere, even Canada and overseas."

By now, you probably have a craving for tupelo honey. If so, the Laniers sell it from their back porch. A five-pound jar costs $11. If you get back home and wish you had more, the Laniers will mail you a five-pound plastic jar for around $22, depending on the postage to your area. You can contact them at 850–639–2371.

The Eerie Waters

A mile north of Wewahitchka is the Dead Lake, which is actually a ten-mile flooded section of the Chipola River. It's worth the short drive on Lake Grove Road from the Lanier's to the dam.

At one time the Apalachicola River, into which the Chipola flows, created a sandbar that dammed the Chipola. The resulting high water killed the cypress trees. Over time their trunks rotted away, leaving only stumps and cypress knees remaining above the water. Today, many of the cypress are sending fresh growth upward once more. With the reflective water intermingling images of the gray stumps and the emerging greenery with the sky and clouds, Dead Lake presents one of the most weirdly beautiful landscapes in Florida.

The Laniers have bee yards on the south side of the bridge, for, although the cypress trees seem to be everywhere, tupelos are mixed in. They are tall, ungainly trees as crooked as river ripples. But they're

The Dead Lake near Wewahitchka presents an almost other-worldly landscape.

mighty sweet creations when they bloom.

On the far side of the bridge is a country store going under the grandiloquent title of the Dead Lake Sportsman's Lodge. When I asked the clerk about rental fishing boats, she said they had a couple of motorless motor boats. When I asked how the sportsmen ran these boats, she said they either brought their own paddles or bought some at the store. Cabins can be rented for $45 to $55 a night. If this is too expensive, the clerk added quickly, you can get a cheaper room for $35.

But Hiltons are in short supply on backroads, and the setting is most pleasing. Fishing is very good, even from the shore, and the general store—er, lodge—sells everything a fisherman needs to hook the big ones, especially beer. Sportsman's can be reached at 850–639–5051.

There is also a Dead Lakes State Recreation Area off of SR 71, one mile north of Wewahitchka. Although it's a minimal facility, there is a launching area for boats (bring your own), some picnic tables, and a short nature trail leading around a couple of former fish hatching ponds. Admission is $2 per car and camping is $8 a night, no reservations needed. A bathhouse contains hot showers. For more information, call 850–639–2702.

South from Wewahitchka

Driving south from Wewahitchka on SR 71, you re-enter the St. Joe Company pinelands. The company is still mulling over how to develop this land. One idea is to sell ten- to forty-acre tracts to people who have the urge to retreat periodically to a cabin in the woods. Perhaps "cabin" is an understatement, for many of the homes would have swimming pools resembling natural springs. The grubby chores would be done by company groundskeepers. Owners would have the use of a luxurious lodge, and the kids could play in large tree houses. There would be facilities to stable horses—since surely a gentleman's retreat is unthinkable without them. Although such a plan is still in the maybe phase, under St. Joe's leadership changes are in the wind all over this part of the Panhandle.

At White City, the road passes over the Intracoastal Waterway. The original canal was cut so that steamboats on the Apalachicola River could sail to Port St. Joe, thereby diverting them from the town of Apalachicola. There is a marina and a small park where you can picnic or just watch the occasional pleasure craft cruise past. The Eastern

Time Zone begins at White City, for here the demarcation line runs in a crazy northwestern direction. Scuttlebutt has it that it was a result of St. Joe's influence on the Florida legislature, for executives at the company's paper mill, six miles down the road, wanted to operate in the same time zone as their East Coast customers.

Meltdown Town

As you enter Port St. Joe, population four thousand, the trees give way to small homes. During territorial days, the town was known as St. Joseph. It was one of Florida's major settlements, due to the protected harbor. St. Joseph was confident it would soon displace Apalachicola, twenty-one miles east, as Middle Florida's most active port. The town's prospects were such that it was selected to host the state constitutional convention in 1838. It lost being named the state capital by just one vote.

But then, a pair of tragedies struck. First, a ship brought yellow fever, which killed more than half the town. Then, a fierce hurricane and tidal wave ripped the buildings apart. When it was over, St. Joseph was finished for most of a century.

Things began to change in the 1920s and 1930s when Alfred duPont, from one of America's wealthiest families, began buying up north Florida's forests. As duPont saw it, these trees would be rich sources of pulp for the paper plant he envisioned. Shortly, the huge mill of the St. Joe Paper Company rose on the waterfront of a new town called Port St. Joe. Prosperity reigned for six decades.

But the golden days ended abruptly when the plant closed in 1998. The effect was catastrophic, for the company was the only major employer in Gulf County. With the closing, city and county services were slashed, since mill taxes had accounted for an important portion of their budgets. It was what *Florida Trend* magazine called a complete meltdown. "Now," a discouraged former worker told a *Trend* reporter in 1999, "it's almost like the last one left needs to turn out the lights."

Driving Through Town

One block before SR 71 ends at US 98, you'll come to Reid Avenue, where you should turn right and head north. Although Reid Avenue is Port St. Joe's business center and has recently undergone a face-lift, it's sadly quiet, for people are hardly shopping any more. Reid ends at the A. N. Railroad Company headquarters on First Street. The A. N. stands for Apalachicola Northern, though many people say "absolutely nothing" is more descriptive. Once, the yards throbbed with hooting steam engines drawing platform cars heaped with timber to feed the hungry mill immediately west, but today the trains are gone and the freight yard is quiet.

Now, turn one block left on First Street to US 98. You can get a good view of the land where the mill complex once stood from the US 98 bridge over the A. N. tracks.

The Death of a Dream

It wasn't supposed to be like this. When Alfred duPont came to Florida in 1926, he dreamed of putting his share of the family fortune into a business that would not only prove profitable, but would benefit the state. Although duPont died nine years later, under his brother-in-law, Edward Ball, the dream became the St. Joe Paper Company in 1936. Two years later the company's huge paper mill opened at Port St. Joe and the ancient town was reborn. The town enjoyed a modest prosperity until 1996, when the St. Joe Company, dropping "paper" from its name, decided to sell the plant and concentrate on developing the company's extensive land holdings. Under new owners the antiquated mill did not turn a profit, so they closed it a year and a half later and subsequently tore it down.

With that, hard times once more descended on Port St. Joe

Up From the Ashes?

Local boosters insist all is not lost. The town, they claim, is in the midst of a metamorphosis. Recreation, not industry, is the main thrust. A promising start has been made with the opening of a two-hundred-boat marina, which you'll find at the foot of First Street. If you're so inclined, stop at the marina's Dockside Café. Its food is excellent, or so I'm told by the Chamber of Commerce, who, of course, never fibs. The marina is leased to and run by the St. Joe Company. Most of the users seem to be residents of St. Joe's upscale community, WindMark, a few miles up the coast on US 98. Nearby, at the corner of First Street and US 98, a modest shopping center has just been built. Its completion was epochal, for it's the first shopping center in all of Gulf County, which has a population of barely 14,000! Furthermore, the center features a genuine Piggly Wiggly grocery store, and you don't find many of those these days.

Scalloping

Now, back to our tour of Port St. Joe. A few blocks south of the Piggly Wiggly, you'll come to SR 71, the road you arrived on. At the foot of SR 71 is a park directly on St. Joseph Bay. The view is mildly impressive, with a sheet of water extending westward for six miles to the pencil-thin ridge that separates the bay from the Gulf of Mexico. The park offers tennis courts, a boat launch, a picnic pavilion, and restrooms. What it doesn't offer is good swimming, since the bay is fringed with dense seagrasses. For real fun in the water, you'll have to follow me out to that pencil-thin ridge, which is actually the luscious, dune-fringed beach of the St. Joseph Peninsula State Park. But don't demote the seagrasses just because they might interfere with your recreation. St. Joseph Bay, being one of the very few embayments not receiving fresh inflows from a river, depends on the seagrasses to help maintain water quality and clarity. The grasses also provide habitat and protection for shrimps, crabs, and scallops.

Scallops, in particular, find St. Joseph Bay to their liking. For people who think scallops are created neatly breaded and deep-fried, it may be astonishing to learn that they are shelled sea animals that live quiet and contented lives until humans put them into fryers. Everyone is invited to go scalloping between July 1st and September 10th. All you have to do is wade into the shallows, where the scallops can be harvested by hand. The limit is two gallons, unshucked. Port St. Joe has an annual Scallop Festival that lasts for several days around September 1st. There's entertainment, artisans, and, as you'd expect, plenty of seafood. To get the exact dates, call the Chamber of Commerce at 850–227–1223.

Now, head south on US 98. In a few blocks, you'll pass the renovated St. Joe Motel. Just beyond the motel is the colonnaded mansion that once belonged to Alfred duPont's wife, Jessie, who was involved in local philanthropic activities until her death in 1970. The duPont Foundation continues her work. The mansion is currently occupied by Arvida, the St. Joe Company's real estate arm.

The Iowa Connection

Back on the road, watch for Allen Memorial Way, an appealing residential street flanked by a park with columns of cabbage palms and tall pines. At the end of the park is the Constitution Convention State Museum. The museum is dedicated to the men who spent five weeks here in 1838–1839 crafting the state's first constitu-

The constitution monument in Port St. Joe.

tion. Ironically, there was no need to rush, for Congress refused to permit Florida to become a state until Iowa was also ready, since the nation was so delicately balanced that a slave state would not be admitted to the Union until it could be matched with a free state. The big event occurred in 1845. Sixteen years later, Florida quit the Union it had been so eager to join and entered the ill-fated Confederacy.

The constitution was a relatively insignificant event, for it was thrown out after the Union victory in 1865. Nonetheless, later politicians saw it as a major opportunity for self-promotion. Thus, in 1922, they scrounged up the funds to erect an ornate granite monument. Upon it they inscribed their own illustrious names—yet, oddly, neglected to include most signers of the constitution. A museum came along almost as an afterthought three decades later. It's open Thursday through Monday and has a nominal entry fee. Behind the museum there is an old steam locomotive that once hauled timber for the St. Joe Company.

A Sandy Outpost

Just beyond this hallowed memorial, US 98 turns east. But you should continue south on route C-30A. Some of the best scal- loping is along here for as far as Simmons Bayou. In six miles, the road comes to another fork. Take C-30E, on the right, which leads onto a neck of land. Because this neck protrudes into the Gulf of Mexico, it is often exposed to shoreline currents and contrary winds, making it highly subject to erosion. This is particularly true of the area called Cape San Blas, where a lighthouse warns ships of dangerous shoals. Lighthouse-lovers can visit the structure, but don't get excited, for it's merely a beacon on unenclosed scaffolding. Picturesque it's not. However, it has been active since the days of the Model T. That's better than most of us can say.

At this point, the road turns north onto the main part of the peninsula. Because this locale, known as Stump Hole, was hit particularly hard by Hurricane Opal in 1995, limestone chunks have been installed to thwart future storms' efforts to sever the peninsula.

Bowls and Boxes

As you continue along route C-30E, you'll pass the Dome House, a strange, bowl-shaped structure elevated by several dozen sturdy supports. It looks like some kind of bizarre sea critter stranded here at high tide. But it's built to withstand the forces of wind and surf from any future hurricane. However, this architectural style, while quite appropriate for the environment, has found no acceptance on the peninsula. Instead, almost all the homes are box-shaped. Many are two stories, with large windows presenting inspiring vistas of the beach and the Gulf. Wrap-around balconies give residents a shady

The unusual Dome House on Cape San Blas is built to withstand hurricane winds and wave surges.

retreat when the weather is a trifle tepid and a sunny deck when they'd like to tint their tans. But, with flat surfaces subject to the full force of frontal winds, these structures seem likely candidates for journeys to Oz.

If you have fallen in love with this sandy getaway, it's probably best to try a rental. Nearly the entire cape is for rent, judging from the thick booklet I received from a local realtor. A house on the beach that sleeps six people can be had for $950 per week during the choice mid-May through early September weeks and for several hundred dollars less at other times. A seven-day stay is the minimum.

Flirting with Lady Luck

Although run-of-the-mill tropical storms pay regular visits to the Gulf coast, the damage they cause is minimal. While the odds of being lambasted by a full-blown hurricane during the June through November season are not high, they are real. When severe storm warnings are received, evacuation of Cape San Blas, as natives call the entire St. Joe Peninsula, begins. It's not a pleasant task. "When we got the warning at 10:00 A.M., we immediately reserved a motel at Tallahassee, then threw together our overnight duds and hit the road," one resident told me. "SR 71 going north was a nightmare. It was jammed with cars, especially when we got above Wewahitchka, where cars from Panama City flooded onto the two-lane highway. It took almost six hours to complete a trip that ordinarily takes just an hour and a half. Next time, I'm going to remain on the cape. I don't care what the authorities say. They can't make us leave."

But remaining here can be very dangerous. Over the past hundred years, thirty hurricanes have pounded the Panhandle. Most have been categories one and two, with winds between seventy-four and 110 miles per hour creating storm surges of five to eight feet. This is enough to sometimes breach the dunes and sweep over parts of the island. Theoretically, most homes could withstand such surges, although the wind damage could be significant.

However, category three hurricanes carry winds up to 130 miles an hour, whipping up storm surges twelve feet high. Few buildings on the peninsula could escape unscathed from such a lashing. Hurricane Opal in 1995 was this kind of storm, but it only brushed the cape. Even so, it took out nineteen homes and completely isolated the area when it washed out the road at Stump Hole. A category four would be worse. And category fives, the grand daddies of ferocity, with winds

above 155 miles per hour and surges above eighteen feet, could oblit-
erate the entire peninsula. Hurricanes Hugo in 1989 and Andrew in
1992 were category fours. Hurricane Camille in 1969 and an unnamed
hurricane in the Keys in 1935 were category fives. Although each of
these storms lashed Florida, none blasted the St. Joe Peninsula directly.
But Lady Luck will not dance with the cape indefinitely, for she is a
fickle partner.

America's Most Beautiful Beach

PAY
TOLL
AHEAD
    The peninsula's northern ten miles have been set aside as the
St. Joseph Peninsula State Park. It's worth the $3.25 per vehicle
entry fee to reach the beaches of which you've always dreamed.
Here is clean white sand fringed with surf that seems to reach forever.
People are few and the birds are many.

At Eagle Harbor, there are picnic facilities. The harbor, which faces
St. Joseph's Bay, is a semicircular indention marking where the peninsula was formerly divided by a water passage. During Hurricane Opal,
the dunes were breached at this point and Gulf water thundered into
the bay, dividing the peninsula once more.

Access to the Gulf of Mexico is provided by a boardwalk over a
frontal dune. You're prohibited from walking on the dune itself in
order to preserve the sea oats that form a scalp lock along its crest. Sea

*The beach at St. Joseph Peninsula State Park has been declared the most beautiful in
America.*

oats are one of the few plants that can grow in sand. Their roots, some twenty-five feet long, reach far down to get to water. In doing so, they anchor the dunes and thus are vital to the dunes' preservation.

Once on the beach, you'll see why Stephen Leatherman, affectionately known hereabouts as Dr. Beach, has named this stretch of sand as the best in continental America. It's not a frivolous choice, for Leatherman is a respected coastal geologist who uses fifty criteria to rank the beaches, including sand size, water temperature, number of sunny days, and wildlife. It's just a coincidence that he teaches at a Florida university.

Perhaps, as you sit on the beach, you'll watch the wind playing on the sand around your feet. It moves the sand silently, but steadily, building up miniature hills whose rounded tops grow to crests that drop sharply on their lee side. Then, look at a full-scale dune. It formed the same way. And it, too, is moving with the air flow. Actually, everything on this sand spit is in motion. Nothing is even exactly as it was when you came over the boardwalk.

Should you want to explore the bay, you can rent a canoe at Eagle Harbor for $3 an hour. That is, if you're fortunate enough to find one—the park only has two. A concessionaire just outside the park entrance is better stocked.

From Eagle Harbor, the road follows a swale behind the frontal dunes. In a few hundred feet, it divides. Follow the right fork another few hundred feet to a parking area. Here, you can take a forty-minute hike along the bay. If this is not enough to satisfy you, continue on the road a short distance to where it ends near some rental cabins. From here, a primitive trail meanders through a preserve for seven wilderness miles to the peninsula's end. You'll pass through several plant communities, including scrub, marsh, pine flatwoods, and dunes. If you are gong to hike this trail, a good supply of bug repellent during the warm months will save you a lot of swatting and swearing. You'll also need a permit, which you can pick up for no charge at the park entry booth.

Incidentally, the cabins here rent for around $70 a night between March 1 and September 15, less in the off-season. They can accommodate up to seven people. They're not bad and even have central air conditioning, although purists don't turn it on. For reservations call 850–227–1327.

Through the Wilderness

Leaving the St. Joseph Peninsula on C-30E, you'll come once more to the junction with C-30A. Take the right fork, which heads through a mostly uninhabited forest. Be sure not to turn on C-30B, for you'll dead end on the Indian Peninsula. C-30A gets narrower and wilder the farther you travel. Every so often, it runs close to the St. Vincent Sound. Just when you think you'll never return to civilization, the road emerges at US 98. When it's over, it may be difficult to believe that the total trip on C-30A was only twelve miles.

By turning right on US 98, you'll approach Apalachicola as you travel down an impressive aisle of stately pines. The aisle would be even more impressive if the stately pines were sufficiently dense to hide the acres of less-than-stately new-growth pines behind them.

Seesaw Town

Although Apalachicola has only about 2,500 people, the town seems much larger. Certainly its setting and history would call for it to be so. The Apalachicola River forms a natural harbor, and as early as 1840, while Florida was still a territory, the Apalachicola Land Company laid out the town streets and sold lots. Soon, up to two dozen or so steamboats were transporting cotton down from plantations as far distant as Alabama and Georgia to the town's forty-three warehouses. From here, ocean-going ships carried the cotton to textile mills in New England and Great Britain. But the Civil War disrupted the plantation system and Apalachicola's cotton trade never recovered.

Timber soon took cotton's place. Apalachicola's Cypress Lumber Company, the largest in the entire South, converted cypress and pines into boards by the millions. But by 1920, the cypress was depleted and the town's seesaw descended once again.

Then, the seafood industry rose to prominence as more than a hundred oyster boats worked the extensive beds in the Apalachicola River estuary. Oyster shucking houses lined Apalachicola's water front. Special trains expressed oysters packed in ice to restaurants in Atlanta. And a group of canneries prepared oysters, as well as shrimp, for shipment as far north as Boston. But today, the oyster industry is suffering, so now Apalachicola is in the process of reinventing itself once more. Tourism is the current thrust, for the town's remoteness and isolation from the fast life of mainstream cities have made it appealing. As has its history.

One Cool Physician

Most tourists visit the John Gorrie State Museum in the small, brick building at Sixth Street and Avenue D, just off of US 98. Doctor Gorrie migrated to Apalachicola in 1833, arriving just in time to be confronted by a yellow fever epidemic. He believed that the sickness was caused by hot, muggy air. Accordingly, he invented a device that cooled the patients' rooms. It was the world's first air-conditioning machine. But it was not a success, for his patients went on dying just the same. Nonetheless, Gorrie was enthusiastic about the possibilities of his air conditioner. He even received a U.S. patent for it. But he was unable to get financial backing to mass produce his cumbersome, steam-driven machine. His main success was helping a friend win a bet by serving chilled champagne in the summer.

Gorrie never made a penny on his revolutionary invention. Not until a more economical, electrical air conditioner was designed in 1911 by Willis Carrier did air conditioning achieve widespread use. Nonetheless, the State of Florida honors Gorrie as the father of air conditioning and has even included a statue of him as one of its two allotted representatives in Congress' National Statuary Hall.

The Gorrie museum is open Thursday through Sunday from 9:00 A.M. to 5:00 P.M. The entry fee is only $1.00, so why not pay a visit? You'll see a replica of Gorrie's machine, as the original is in the Smithsonian Institute.

Despite his setbacks, Dr. Gorrie did not have an entirely frustrating career. Before something called nervous collapse abruptly ended his life at the age of fifty-two, he served as Apalachicola's mayor and a director of the town's bank.

Gorrie was also a founder of the Trinity Episcopal Church, which is across the quiet traffic circle from the museum. This compact Greek revival building is certainly a jewel among churches. It was constructed in New York, then disassembled, loaded on a schooner, and shipped to Apalachicola. Here, in 1837, it was put together with wooden pegs to become one of Florida's first prefabricated buildings. Members had their own family pews, purchased with donations to the church. Slaves took side stairs to the balcony, where they must have listened to sermons about the brotherhood of man with considerable skepticism.

The Heart of Apalachicola

Back on US 98 (Avenue E), continue east. You'll pass some of

Apalachicola's finer old homes. A few were constructed of wood from buildings at old St. Joseph that were torn down when the town was abandoned after the yellow fever epidemics of the 1840s and 1850s.

Stay on 98 as it makes a sharp turn onto Market Street, Apalachicola's two-block business section. The Chamber of Commerce, at Avenue E and Market Street, is located in the State Bank Building and has excellent literature, including a walking tour leaflet no visitor should be without. Farther along Market Street, you'll discover the Gibson Inn, a long, three-story wooden building dating back to 1907. Although it was renovated several years ago, it retains the flavor of the past. The first-floor veranda and second-floor balcony give overnighters an excellent view of the comings and goings along Market Street and the modest Franklin County Courthouse across the way. The lobby is made of the building's original wood. The restaurant is reputedly very good, although I make no claims. Room rates are between $90 and $135. You can get more information by calling 850–653–2191.

From the Gibson Inn, drive east on Avenue C. Past the courthouse two blocks is Water Street. At 123 Water Street is Caroline's Restaurant, directly on the water. From Caroline's, you can watch

The refurbished Gibson Inn is a good place to stay in the heart of old Apalachicola.

the movements of fishing boats while dining on the seafood they hauled in hours earlier. The town is famous for its oysters, harvested mainly from Apalachicola Bay and St. George Sound just down river. In recent years, oyster sales have suffered from foreign imports as well as evidence that a bacterium in uncooked oysters occasionally causes death to elderly persons and persons with bad livers, with diabetes, or who are undergoing chemotherapy. Although the government has the authority to shut down harvesting, such an action would utterly devastate Apalachicola's economy. Currently, the emphasis of the prevention program is on educating the public. Restaurants serving oysters put notices on their menus warning people who might be at risk about eating oysters raw. (Though cooking kills the bacterium and renders the oysters safe to eat.) Avid oyster-lovers seem to enjoy them as fully as always, and just recently a thirty-one-year-old Briton swallowed his way into the record books by shucking and gulping down ninety-seven raw oysters in three minutes. How did he feel after this championship display of gluttony? "Full," he gasped.

The Apalachicola River Inn and Marina adjoins the Caroline's Restaurant. Rates for regular rooms run between $80 and $100. But people who want to frolic take the Jacuzzi suite for around $150. For more information call 850–653–8139. If you enjoy fishing, you can hire a Boss Charter boat right here for $250 for a half day or $350 for a full day. The boat can carry four passengers, so why not round up three others and share the expense. Call 850–653–8055 for more information.

The Consulate

Continuing north on Water Street for one block, you'll come to number seventy-six, a two-story brick building called the Consulate. For many years, it housed J. E. Grady & Company, once one of the largest commercial establishments on the Gulf coast. Here, canned goods were stacked to the rafters, and pots and pans dangled from overhead beams. To reach them, the clerks used tall ladders. On the floor were sacks of flour and cabbages. Beside them were barrels that might contain almost any kind of imported material. A counter ran the length of one wall. Grady's location, directly across from the city pier, and Apalachicola's importance as a seaport enticed the French government to establish a consulate on the building's second floor.

But, as the railroads drew trade away from Apalachicola, the river

At Apalachicola, the historic Grady's Market has been completely renovated as the Consulate.

traffic dwindled until the building was no longer used. It remained in disrepair until recently when a pair of developers turned it into one of Apalachicola's showplace restorations. Again, the aisles are jammed with goods. And once more, the hardwood floors vibrate as shoppers mill beneath the pressed tin ceiling eagerly examining the goods, many of which are in the high-priced, buy-on-a-whim category.

The second floor contains luxuriously remodeled apartments that certainly would have appealed to the stuffy French diplomats of a hundred years ago. A top-of-the-line two-bedroom suite with a pair of balconies overlooking the river runs $200 per night. A one-bedroom unit with what is quaintly called a garden view costs $140. For more information call 800–824–0416.

The Consulate's rebirth may be representative of Apalachicola's emergence as a tourist town. Real estate values are increasing, and people are buying downtown property at an unprecedented rate. The city, with its authentic historical flavor and access to Gulf fishing and wonderful beaches, has even become the darling of European travel publications, according to *Florida Trend* magazine.

Yet some locals are not happy with this rush toward tourism. Among them are shrimpers who use the docks along the river.

Shrimper's Gripes

After visiting the Consulate, I walked across Water Street to where a shrimp boat was docked. The deck was a jumble of nets and ropes, and a pair of booms rose forty or fifty feet in the air. The vessel's hull was crusty and scarred, the victim of many battles with waves and docks. It smelled of oil, fish, salt, and sweat.

Two burly men sat mending nets. "I've been fishing here since I was sixteen," one of them told me. "It's in my blood. And that boat circling out in the river, that's our cousin." He watched the wavelets crest then disappear. "Our father was in this business before me. He started as a young boy and stayed on until he was disabled by the hard life." He shrugged and scratched his chin. "You just work until you can't no more. What else can you do?"

But the changes coming to the area worried him greatly. "The Chamber is trying to orient the town toward tourists," he noted with more than a trace of bitterness. "They're buying up the docks. We pay seventy dollars a month to tie up here. But they seem to want us out. Towns like Biloxi have fixed up a place for the commercial fishermen. Here, they got no concern. They don't care about us. But we got no place else to go. Don't they realize it was us fishermen who made this

Shrimp boats are active along the waterfront at Apalachicola.

town! We was here first. The Chamber forgets that." He glared at the Consulate.

When he learned I was a writer, he gave full throttle to his frustrations. "We got no protections. They're getting a lot of cheap seafood imported. There's that great sucking sound of American jobs going overseas. Politicians talk about it, but they don't do nothing about it! Tell your readers it's gonna kill us!"

After he cooled down, he told me about the life of a shrimper. "About seventy-five boats operate out of Apalachicola, most from the Scipio Marina just upriver. Nighttime is the best for shrimp fishing. We use nets to get the shrimp. And after we get 'em aboard, we freeze 'em. We go out for two or three weeks at a time. In the spring, the shrimp are in shallow water, five to ten feet, so we fish the reefs off of the Crystal River or the channel at Carrabelle. Other times we have to go seventy miles into the Gulf where we fish 160 feet deep. We're way out of sight of land. We depend on radio to learn 'bout storms and all that." Even so, most shrimpers don't usually let a little rough weather shoo them to port. But those storms can be dangerous. Recently, a shrimper was washed overboard during a storm and his body was found floating in Pensacola Bay.

Along the Waterfront

Upon leaving the shrimpers, I walked along the waterfront. The river is very wide, but shallow. The far shore is mostly marsh, where reeds and salt-tolerant grasses form a dense green matting. Every so often, a shrimp boat would glide along the river. I paused at boat repair shops and commercial seafood processors. Many fishing boats were tied up, their crews lounging on the docks. Most seemed to be quiet, reflective men. Perhaps long days and nights at sea had made them so. Or perhaps they know their way of life is threatened and that, just as when an inevitable storm is approaching, there is little they can do.

Once, Water Street was lined with cotton warehouses. Almost all are long gone. Just two remain: one on either side of Avenue E where it meets Water Street. The one on the north has become the city hall, a fitting tribute to the past.

A Wet Museum

When Water Street ends, turn left two blocks to Market Street and follow it as it arches along the river and near the marina. In centuries past, the wide delta wetlands presented such an obstacle to travel that the Indians living here were called the people on the other side, or the Apalachicola. Today, locals find the name rather cumbersome, so to them the town is simply Apalach.

Continue on Market Street until it, too, ends, and then you should turn left and go a quarter mile to the first building on the left. This is the headquarters of the Apalachicola National Estuarine Reserve. This reserve extends for more than fifty miles up the river, as well as out into the bay to include St. George and St. Vincent Islands. This estuary, where river water forms a unique mixture with sea water, is a vital nursery for creatures that have adapted to this particular environment. One of the National Estuarine Reserve's main functions is to protect these marine resources.

So what's to see here? Tanks, on display Monday through Friday, give visitors the opportunity to become acquainted with the creatures that thrive in the Gulf of Mexico, the Apalachicola Bay, and the river's wetlands. Other exhibits show preserved animals. There is also a display of local shells. Outside, a quarter-mile nature walk leads to the river's floodplain, one of the largest on the entire Gulf of Mexico. Because it's largely undeveloped, you can view it almost as nature laid it out. Fifty species of mammals frequent this huge basin where a thousand varieties of plants grow. The basin contains the highest diversity of amphibians and reptiles in the United States and Canada. You could spend a lifetime roaming this teeming environment and never see more than a fraction of its plants and animals.

The Panhandle Circuit

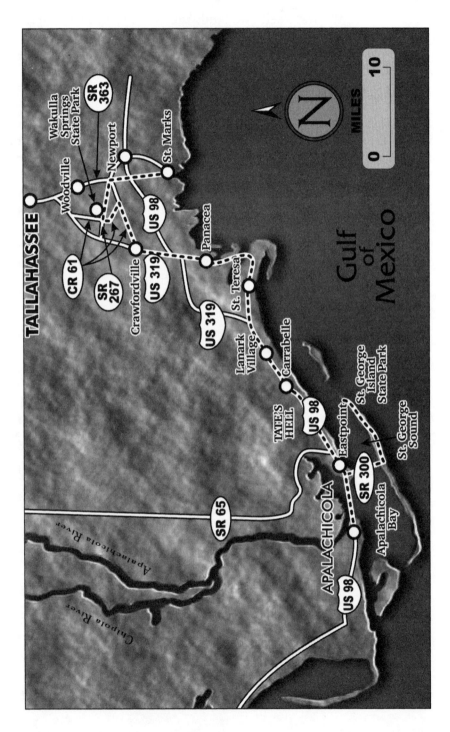

The Forgotten Coast

Apalachicola to Tallahassee • 122 Backroad Miles

The Song of the Road: Overview

This trip will proceed along what many call the forgotten coast. Forgotten though it may be, there are beaches that are among the most beautiful in the world, huge springs for swimming, boat safaris down secluded subtropical rivers, and many forested nature trails. On the way, you'll hear tales of pirates, of castaways, of cannibalism, and even of what must be one of America's most unusual love affairs.

We'll begin on the road to St. George Island. Birds in unbelievable numbers often nest along the causeway. At St. George State Park, the dunes and beaches are almost as pure and white as when they were created by wind and waves thousands of years ago.

From St. George, the road hugs the coast as it edges eastward past the matted jungle called Tate's Hell. Next, we'll enter the picturesque boating town of Carrabelle. Then, we'll visit Lanark Village, the site of one of Florida's largest World War II training camps.

Farther along, we'll stop at Panacea to visit the marine lab and the Gulf setting so well described by lab keeper, Jack Rudloe, in his book *The Living Dock at Panacea*. Next, heading inland, we'll visit Wakulla Springs State Park, where millionaire executive Ed Ball constructed a fancy lodge for the top management of the St. Joe Company, the Panhandle's dominant corporation, then and today. Now, the public park offers lodging, as well as fine swimming in a huge crystalline spring. There is also a spectacular boat excursion down the Wakulla River.

Back on the coast, we'll drive to the village of St. Marks, where the stony ruins of an old Spanish fort recall its capture by the colorful freebooter, Billy Bowles.

Last, we'll drive along the St. Marks Trail, which, for nearly a century and a half, was an active railroad connecting the port at St. Marks with Tallahassee, Florida's capital.

On the Road Again

US 98 leaves Apalachicola by way of the John Gorrie Bridge.

227

The first bridge over the Apalachicola River was constructed in 1936. Until this time, the only way across the river was by means of an unstable, one-car ferry that tended to linger interminably on sandbars at low tide. High tide presented its own difficulties, especially during windy weather when the river could ruffle up whitecaps several feet high. During these times travelers had their choice of spending a few hours, or perhaps a few days, fidgeting in Apalachicola while they waited for a weather change or chancing the obstreperous ferry. "Well, I finally got up nerve enough to risk the ferry," one shaken traveler recounted to a friend. "And I'm telling you, Jim, I was certainly glad I had gone to early Mass that Sunday morning."

The Bridge to Nowhere

When the modern John Gorrie Bridge was built, it received a good deal of criticism. It was very expensive, yet only connected one side of a virtually deserted coast with the other equally as deserted side. Thus, some dubbed it the bridge to nowhere. Today, this nowhere is promoted as the forgotten coast, which means it's still just about nowhere.

The bridge and causeway cross five miles of uninhabited wetlands. For most of its distance, the causeway is low and close to the vegetation. But the bridge soars when it crosses the Apalachicola River. The view from the top presents an inspiring vista extending for many miles. On the right is Apalachicola Bay—a mixture of soft blues penetrated only by the thin white line of another bridge that leads to St. George Island. But you must enjoy the view quickly; there is no pedestrian walkway.

The Bird Bridge

As soon as you descend, watch for SR 300, which leads to St. George Island nine miles south. You may wish that it was farther away, for these nine miles are as scenic as any in Florida. Much of the drive is across shallows where sea gulls speckle the sky and oyster boats fleck the water.

The oyster boats are interesting to watch. To harvest the oyster shells that rest on the bottom in seven feet or so of murky water, the oystermen stand on the decks and manipulate a long pair of wooden poles attached together like scissors. At one end of each pole is a metal rake. As the oystermen move these rakes over the bottom, they listen for the sound and the feel of metal on shells. Then, they clamp the scissors together and pull the shells from the water. This is an age-old method used by their fathers and grandfathers. Yet it's a way of life that is threatened by government regulations.

Not only oyster fishing, but nearly everything else that goes on in St. George Sound (on your left) and Apalachicola Bay (on your right) is closely supervised by the government. Both bodies of water are part of the National Estuarine Research Reserve, whose visitors center is a highlight of a tour of nearby Apalachicola. The estuary is fed by the Apalachicola River, as well as by tidal currents from the Gulf of Mexico. This delicate mixture of fresh and salt water, combined with the shallow depth, provides ideal breeding conditions for oysters and a wide variety of fish and sea birds.

Birds are often numerous along the causeway. Ospreys and eagles soar overhead. Terns, black skimmers, and plovers flit about at ground level. In spring and fall, warblers and other migrating birds rest here before continuing their long journeys.

The grassy areas beside the bridge have become popular nesting places. When the eggs hatch in early summer, chicks by the hundreds emerge. Many wander nonchalantly onto the highway, where they strut and chirp with the joy of the newborn. Most persons find the sight pleasing and stop for a while to watch. But others are unimpressed. "It's despicable," a lady told me. "A few drivers run right over the babies. All they have to do is slow [down] and honk. The little birds don't know any better. I dread coming out here at those times. Oh, those poor little babies!"

Don't let this deter you from visiting the island, for most of the feathered corpses soon wash away, and avian reproduction quickly replaces the dearly departed.

When SR 300 reaches St. George Island, follow it left toward the state park. You're now on a narrow arc of sand twenty-eight miles long. St. George may have been born as an underwater sandbar during a prolonged period of high seas that then became exposed when the sea lowered. Although today wind and waves are carrying the exposed sand westward, the island is nourished by new supplies from the Apalachicola River.

On your way to the state park you'll pass homes on wide lots. A one-acre minimum for home sites was established here several decades ago. The real estate market is very active, both for sales and rentals. If a rental is of interest, you can spend a week in a luxurious beach-front home during the popular summer season (mid-May to Labor Day) for $5,000. On the other hand, inland homes rent for only around $900 per week.

The shifting sands on St. George Island sometimes carry dead trees in their wake.

Development ends abruptly at the state park. Ahead are nine miles of virtually unspoiled landscape. On the left, forested coves reach out into St. George Sound. The water is shallow, and the bottom is paved with oyster shells. These beds are part of the rich fields that make the sound so important to oystermen. A two-and-a-half- mile hiking trail leads through pine and coastal scrub to Gap Point, which provides views of East Cove and the sound.

The seaward side is entirely different. Here, the shore is straight and the sand is as white as talcum. Because the water fairly cries out for swimmers, the park offers bathhouses. Once on the beach, you can see the waves cascading shoreward for miles. Their rumble is sweeter than a lullaby. This is Florida the way it was meant to be. Surely, St. George is what paradise must be like.

But heavenly paradise is one thing and earthly paradise quite another. Take it from Pierre Viaud who vacationed here a number of years ago. Well, it wasn't exactly a vacation, it was a shipwreck.

The Castaways

Viaud (pronounced Vee OH) set sail on a small merchant ship from the French-held island of Haiti in the winter of 1766. It was suppos-

Back bays on St. George Island are ideal for oysters,
but their shells can cut bathers' feet.

edly a routine voyage to New Orleans. Captain La Couture even brought along his wife and young son. In addition, there was a merchant, Viaud's black slave, and a crew of ten. But, as they sailed westward along Florida's Gulf coast, they ran into a fierce storm that wrecked their ship and left them stranded on a barrier island. Shortly, an Indian paddled out in his dugout canoe and offered to transport Viaud, his slave, the merchant, Captain La Couture, and his wife and son to the mainland. There they could make their way to the British fort at St. Marks and return to rescue the crew. They accepted the Indian's offer. Unfortunately, his object was not to save them but to rob them, which he did, leaving them stranded on St. George Island. Yet they were determined to reach the mainland and, upon finding an abandoned Indian canoe, the captain and merchant set out. However, their rotten craft sank just off Gap Point and the two men drowned.

Viaud was left on St. George with his slave, the captain's distraught wife, and her frail son. Their stay on St. George was hateful. "We had much to endure," wrote Viaud in his memoirs. "Cold March nights and sometimes hunger. We spent entire days looking for anything that could be eaten, cursing our luck and asking God to end our torment."

Oysters and other shellfish could be gathered at low tide. But, when the wind blew strong, the tide never ebbed and the shells were not exposed. Then, the castaways existed on roots. Once, when a long-dead porpoise washed up on shore, they were so famished that they ate the putrid flesh, then spent the next five days violently ill.

They finally completed a raft. It was a chancy craft, for they had nothing to secure the logs except vines. In addition, the boy was so sick he could not move. Viaud had no choice except to leave him. Knowing Madam La Couture would stay with her son until he died, Viaud told her he was already dead. "My God," she screamed. "I've lost everything." Then, wrote Viaud, "I took her in my arms and, with the help of my black, carried her to the raft."

The three of them left the island that Viaud called "our dismal refuge." Their goal was to beach the clumsy raft on the mainland, then make their way through the brambles and muck to the fort at St. Marks, sixty miles east. Ahead lay hardship, terror, and cannibalism.

We, too, are headed for St. Marks, so we'll return to this almost incredible, but true story a little later.

Ode to Suburban Sprawl

Aside from the state park, there's plenty to do on the commercial portion of the island. You may want to stop at one of the restaurants on the beach. You can also take a kayak tour—or perhaps just goof around on one of the boats that rent for $30 a day. If you're an angler, you can rent all the gear you need, whether it's for Gulf fishing or surf casting. Bikes are available for peddlers. If you cannot cram all this excitement into one day, you can stay over at one of the three island hotels. The rates are not unreasonable. A night at the St. George Inn, for example, costs $89 in the off season and $198 during the summer. Call 800–367–1680 for more information.

Eastpoint's Oystermen's Joints

Now, it's back over the bird bridge to US 98. After you head right, you'll come almost immediately to the village of Eastpoint. It supposedly has a population of around two thousand, but that's not apparent from the highway. By turning right onto what appears to be the settlement's main street, you'll drive several blocks along the water, passing weather-worn buildings that are almost picturesque. Eastpoint promotes itself as the oystermen's hangout, and, if you care to get out of your car and prowl the street, you'd undoubtedly be rewarded with plenty of oyster-rama. There's at least one Eastpoint restaurant that advertises regularly in Apalachicola. But I can say no more about Eastpoint. It didn't make me want to drop anchor.

Speaking of dropping anchor, only half as many oystermen are dropping anchor at Eastpoint and other oyster ports as did so twenty-five years ago. The problem is the growing prevalence of oyster farms around Seattle and other Pacific areas. To make matters worse, occasional red tides of microscopic algae can taint almost an entire season of Apalachicola Bay oysters. So maybe you should stop at Eastpoint, if only to see an industry before it vanishes.

Tate's Hell

Between Eastpoint and Carrabelle, US 98 hugs the shore, as it arches gracefully from cape to cape. The forest, which grows right down to the water, is almost as thick and tangled as in the days when it became known as Tate's Hell.

Cebe Tate did not know that he would leave his name on this mass of vegetation when he entered it while trying to find stray cattle in 1875. Quickly losing his bearings, he spent several days desperately stumbling through the steamy underbrush. He was justly fearful of snakes and was eventually bitten by a water moccasin. When he stag-

The roadway has been cut through the tangled vegetation known at Tate's Hell.

gered out of the hateful maze, his friends were shocked. Although he was only forty-five years of age, his hair had turned bone white. From that time, the area was known as Tate's Hell. This, at least, is the local folklore as told to William Rogers in *Outposts on the Gulf.*

Pierre's Hell

It was into Tate's Hell that Pierre Viaud, his slave, and Madame La Couture pushed upon beaching their raft after leaving St. George Island. As they fought their way through the forest toward St. Marks, they found it was hell, indeed. "There was swamp almost everywhere," Viaud wrote. Each night they could not pause until they found a low mound that was relatively dry. But these mounds were also favored by wild animals, and only Viaud's fire kept the snarling creatures at bay. The marshes were ideal breeding grounds for insects. "The bites of gnats, mosquitoes, and a host of other insects which we met on the coast so disfigured us that we became quite unrecognizable." And what the bugs didn't accomplish, sharp brambles did. Hunger was an even worse torment.

Their energy lessened every day. Stumbling through the swampy morass of vines, underbrush, and brambles and wading across the treacherous creeks and rivers sapped their strength. They could cover barely two miles a day. More and more, Viaud's eyes fell upon his slave. "You are going to shudder," he confessed, "when reading what remains for me to tell, but, believe me, your horror cannot possibly be as great as mine." One night, as the slave slept, Viaud clubbed and knifed him. Then, he cut up the body and cooked it. This was a vile act, even in the days of brutal slavery, and Viaud lived with the revulsion of it for the rest of his life.

On and on, Viaud and Madame La Couture tramped. When they came to the swampy New River, near what is now Carrabelle, they were forced to make a two-day detour inland before finding a suitable crossing. There, the two of them made a raft. Thereupon, "we stripped off our clothes, making a bundle of them . . . to save ourselves more readily if some accident happened." In case someone might have gotten the wrong idea about the behavior of a naked man and woman alone in the wilderness, Viaud was quick to note: "Our condition made prudish conventions irrelevant. While we traveled together, we were scarcely aware that we were of different sexes." Viaud claimed that the only way he was knowledgeable of La Couture's sex was by her physical weakness. As for La Couture, "she was conscious of mine merely from observing the firmness and courage with which I tried to inspire her." But Viaud's estimation of her was more than a little inaccurate, for he was the one who gave out physically. Then, he was kept alive by La Couture, who scrounged for food along the seashore. Finally, after two and a half weeks, they were rescued by British soldiers in a small boat from St. Marks.

The British took the castaways back to St. George Island, where they picked up La Couture's son, who had somehow managed to survive. The marooned sailors they had left on an adjoining island were gone, probably killed by Indians. At St. Marks, Viaud and La Couture were treated well by the commander, whose records confirm they were actually there. Viaud went back to France, but La Couture returned to her native Louisiana. Nonetheless, she had a deep feeling for Viaud and were it not for her son, Viaud felt, she would have gone with him. "Our farewells were moving," Viaud recalled. "We could not hold back our tears. We promised never to forget each other."

Once he was home, Viaud turned his experiences into a book entitled *Shipwreck and Adventures*, which caused a sensation when it came out two years later. Did Viaud and Madame La Couture ever reunite? No letters have been found, according to Robin Fabel, who did careful research for the recent republication of Viaud's book. Viaud lived only a few years after his book came out. His health had been undermined by his ordeal. As for the hardy French lady, she bought a farm forty miles from New Orleans. But beyond that, she's a woman of mystery. The only reference to her is in a document written twenty years later that pertains to a neighbor's property. In it, she was referred to as the Widow La Couture. Apparently, she never remarried. Did she dream of Pierre Viaud and their strange love affair amid the terrors of Florida's coast? What do you think?

Tate's Hell Is Still Hell

As for the Tate's Hell, it's still there, bordering US 98, as mean as, well, hell. Yet, despite its unsavory reputation, during the latter portion of the nineteenth century, it seemed to smile on humanity as its pine trees fed the numerous turpentine stills that sprouted up in the vicinity. Hell also furnished timber for a sawmill at Carrabelle. The planks manufactured here were used in many north Florida buildings during this time. However, hell is never friendly, and the planks could have accounted for the devilish rash of fires that plagued the region.

Today, Tate's Hell is a Wildlife Management Area under the supervision of state and federal officials, home to wild hogs, coyotes, and skunks. Licensed hunters sometimes tramp the sodden recesses, but they are few. Otherwise, Tate's Hell has been left to fiendishly breed mosquitoes and snakes.

Get Your Thrill at Carrabelle

The high-rise bridge at Carrabelle provides a panoramic view of the spacious Carrabelle River and the numerous pleasure craft at the Moorings Marina. The town's name is said to honor Carrie Arrabelle Hall, niece of the sawmill owner, Oliver Kelley. In the 1870s, Kelley asked her to manage the Island House Inn, which she did with an efficiency and charm that made it a favorite along the coast. But the inn is long gone and today Carrabelle is known for having the world's smallest police station. It's hard to imagine anything less imposing, for it consists simply of an outdoor telephone booth. Usually, a snappy looking police car is parked there ready to handle any untoward frivolities in this sleepy village of 1,300. You'll find this curiosity just over the bridge on the left side of US 98.

But don't get too carried away by the cute booth. The phone's been disconnected for several years and an unused squad car is parked there just for show. The police force, which tops out at three, actually operates out of a cubby in the city hall. Of course, there's no room for a cell, so, if by some fluke, a jailable circumstance occurs, the offender is transported to the county slammer. It's a rather long drive, so the police fervently resist such a drastic step.

Carrabelle has other attractions besides the thrilling telephone booth! Immediately east of historic police-central is Marine Street. By turning south, you can enjoy a half-mile drive along the river to the recently built Riverwalk Pavilion, where you can fish for trout, catfish, and whiting. But you can't use the restroom because there is none. Big time anglers charter boats at the nearby Moorings Marina for exhilarating cruises among the islands and the reefs of St. George Sound and Apalachee Bay. For more information call 850–697–2800.

Carrabelle is also home base for a number of shrimpers. A good place to watch the shrimp boats is from Pirates Landing on Timber Island Road, which runs along the west side of the river. The Tiki Bar, a quaint place that's recently been remodeled, is in the same building. The Tiki serves pretty good food on a deck overlooking the river and the shrimp boats. It opens on weekdays at 11:00 A.M. and

Carrabelle carefully cultivates the claim that this telephone booth is the world's smallest police station.

on Saturdays and Sundays at 7:00 A.M. Closing time is whenever the last person rolls out, usually around 10:00 P.M. or 11:00 P.M.

War and Peace: Lanark Village

Leaving Carrabelle with its defunct police booth, US 98 continues eastward along the coast. In four miles, you'll reach the road to Lanark Village. The settlement began in the early 1900s as a two-story hotel on the Gulf. Today, it's a quiet place favored by retirees.

There was a time when Lanark was quite different. During World War II, Camp Gordon Johnston was erected here. No minor outpost, it was Florida's second largest military installation in terms of number of troops. But it was a dismal location almost unbearably far from civilization (read: girls). According to David J. Coles' article in *Florida Historical Quarterly,* the hastily built barracks had no floors or indoor latrines. Of course, there was also no air conditioning. Popular columnist Walter Winchell dubbed it the "Alcatraz of the Army." Winchell claimed the camp was so bad that even the chaplains went AWOL. But the men made the best of it. The camp newspaper printed a satirical poem:

The rattlesnake bites you, the horsefly stings,
The mosquito delights you with his buzzin' wings.
Sand burrs cause you to jig and dance
And those who sit down get ants in their pants.

The fine beaches were the reason the huge base was established here. This was not to offer the men joyful swimming opportunities, but to train them for hazardous amphibious landings in the Pacific war zone. Water-survival exercises were conducted under the most rugged conditions and live ammunition was often used. Men died in training accidents, although the exact number was kept secret. Sometimes the streets of Carrabelle were cleared and combat troops practiced house-to-house fighting. Operations extended over twenty miles of the coast. Airborne drops were made on St. George Island.

After the war, most of the flimsy military structures were demolished. The more sturdy ones were converted into tourist facilities by the St. Joe Paper Company, which had leased the land to the government. But even these buildings didn't last long. Today, Lanark Village is a tranquil community. All that remains of the war years are the memories of old men, the everlasting beach with its whispering waves—and an unknown number of unexploded shells.

There Was No Saint at St. Teresa—Or Was There?

Continuing on US 98, ten miles east from Lanark is a tiny settlement called South St. Teresa. A Teresa once lived here, and her last name was Hopkins. But no one knows where the holy title came from. It wasn't from any church. Even Allen Morris in *Florida Place Names* doesn't venture a guess. So this leaves us free to conjecture. Was it an honorary designation for a good-hearted lady? Or a wry joke about a lady less than good? Or did a real saint appear to someone in a vision? You won't have much time to speculate, for you'll be in and out of town almost before you can rev up your imagination.

A few miles beyond St. Teresa, the highway crosses the mile-wide Ochlockonee Bay and soon enters the hamlet of Panacea.

Poking Around in Panacea

Panacea is not much today—nor was it much in the past when it was called Smith Springs after the smelly sulfur water that bubbled up from the nether world. Developers thought that anything this revolting must be good for the body, so they built a spa here in 1898.

Then, they renamed the place Panacea, after the Greek goddess of healing. People flocked here, taking the railroad that had just been built between Tallahassee and Carrabelle. But, by the end of the 1920s, people tired of the spa.

Today, if anyone stops here it's because they've read Jack  Rudloe's nature classic, *The Living Dock at Panacea*. Rudloe and his wife, Anne, have spent much of their lives investigating this "wilderness coast," which is also the title of another of Jack's books. To many people, this monotonous, flat expanse of tidal muck, reeds, and coarse marsh grasses that have replaced the sandy beaches has absolutely no appeal. Yet this environment is ideal as a breeding ground for a vast diversity of fish, crustaceans, and other animals. A few can be viewed from the pier at Panacea, but many more can be seen in the Rudloes' 30,000-gallon aquarium, which is open to the public for a $4 admission fee ($2 for children). In this aquarium, you'll see horseshoe crabs, sea horses, shrimp, sea turtles, and an assortment of sharks.

To reach the Rudloes', as well as the pier, which is free, watch for Rock Landing Road on the western edge of town, across from Posey's Motel and Restaurant. Turn south here and continue a short distance to Clark Drive. The Rudloes' are about a block left on Clark Drive. For more information call 850–984–5297.

Rejoice, At Last There's a McDonald's in Crawfordville

From Panacea, continue north on US 98. In a few miles, the road will be joined by US 319. When the roads split, after two miles, stay on US 319. In six miles, you'll enter Crawfordville, the seat of Wakulla County. The county is in the midst of a major population surge, with the number of people almost doubling from ten years ago. But even at 22,000, it isn't exactly overpopulated. Nonetheless, the town can be proud of its school system, which ranked as the state's very best in a recent test of fourth graders' reading skills.

Crawfordville is not incorporated. It is one of the very few county seats to remain under the control of the county commissioners and the sheriff's department. The one-person Chamber of Commerce is in the circa-1885 courthouse—the state's only original, wooden one still dodging termites. As for the town's highlights, the chamber spokesperson said they have just gotten a McDonald's: "We're very excited about that." And what else is there to do in Crawfordville? "Well," she said slowly, "I really can't think of anything off hand."

At Crawfordville, turn east and travel six miles on CR 61 to Wakulla Springs State Park.

Wakulla Springs State Park

Florida has done a wonderful job with its parks, which have recently won the Gold Medal Award as "the best state park system in America." So I was mildly piqued at the park system's literature that told me I was entering "the Real Florida." When I asked the park attendant at the gate (where there's a $3.25 per-car entry fee) what this meant, she answered, after a moment's reflection, that everything here was completely natural. "Even the rooms at the lodge have no television," she added proudly.

I parked in the lot, with the other cars that are part of the real Florida. Oddly, the entrance into the lodge is through the rear of the building. The lobby is spacious, although not what we'd call large in modern terms. At one end is a sandwich and gift shop and at the other, a fine-dining restaurant.

One of the first things you notice about the lobby is the spectacular ceiling enlivened with fanciful paintings done by an artist from the court of the German Kaiser. The lobby is known for its lavish use of marble. It's in the floors and even the chess boards. The gift and sandwich shop's marble bar is claimed to be one of the longest contiguous

The immaculate dining room at Wakulla State Park was a pride of Edward Ball, obstreperous founder of the powerful St. Joe Company.

*Swimming and cruising in the crystalline Wakulla
Spring makes the state park a popular attraction.*

series of slabs in creation. The restroom partitions are also marble, although Edward Ball, who built the lodge in 1935, could have indulged our modesty by making them more than just shoulder height.

Ball envisioned the building as a conference center and overnight lodge for St. Joe Company executives. Thus, he personally supervised its design and construction. Only the finest materials were used. When the building was finished, it was such a masterpiece that during the long periods when company executives were not using the lodge, Ball graciously opened it to the general public.

A long porch runs across the lobby's front. Outside is a wide lawn, and beyond is the famed spring that is the park's central attraction. The spring is one of the largest in the entire state. Its basin occupies three acres. A two-story observation and diving platform overlooks the spring boil. Swimming is allowed in certain areas, although the seventy-degree temperature chills out many visitors. There are also hiking trails in the park, which occupies 2,860 acres.

Along the River of Dreams

The park offers two boat rides, both costing $4.50 for adults and $2.25 for children. One ride features a thirty-minute, glass-bottom glide over the spring's turquoise water. When the water is clear, you can peer all the way down to fossilized mastodon bones. The liquid boils up from four separate conduits in the limestone bedrock. These underground rivers are so long that, although scuba divers have swum nearly a mile down their mysterious channels, they have not gotten close to discovering the rivers' sources.

The other boat ride consists of a forty-minute cruise along the Wakulla River, which is fed by the spring's runoff. This is a voyage that Edward Ball loved to take while wagering with friends on how many alligators they would see.

If you find that, with all the swimming and boating, you've not had time to enjoy the many miles of woodland hiking—or, perhaps, just veranda-sitting—you can stay overnight at the lodge. It's popular, and there are only twenty-seven guest rooms, so you may want to reserve ahead by calling 850–224–5950. The rates range from around $70 to about $100 per night.

The Bulldog of Wakulla Springs

That such a beautiful spot is free of crass commercialism is due to Edward Ball, who oversaw its availability to the public for half a century, until his death in 1981. The state acquired the property five years later. Yet, despite the accolades, Edward Ball, head of the St. Joe Company, was not the sort of person most of us would enjoy being around. But neither would the stocky little man particularly enjoy being around us.

He was "cocky and testy," according to Senator Claude Pepper, who frequently tangled with him. Pepper, an ardent proponent of social change, felt that Mr. Ball "belonged to a by-gone age." Ball, for his part, reviled Pepper and his liberal-oriented colleagues as socialistic nuts. Ball was irascible, ruthless, and consumed with driving ambition, concluded one of his biographers. *Fortune* magazine ran a major article entitled "The Terrible Tempered Mr. Ball." He was anti-unions, anti-taxes, and anti-government interference. Each evening he downed half a dozen whiskeys while muttering "confusion to the enemy"—of whom there were enough for many such toasts.

He married just once, in the 1930s, and ten years later his wife instituted a long and bitter divorce in which she complained that he was completely absorbed in business, as well as being "domineering, self-opinionated and moody." Despite his thorny side, when Edward Ball died at the age of ninety-three, he left his fortune to a foundation that aids sick children and the elderly.

A Relic of the Past: St. Marks

Leaving Wakulla Springs, head east on SR 267. When you reach SR 363, in five miles, turn south. The St. Joe Company owns nearly all the territory from here south to the Gulf and north to Tallahassee. In five miles, you'll reach the village of St. Marks, which consists mostly of a marina, a café on the water, several large storage tanks, and a helter-skelter of miscellany.

Early in the American era, St. Marks was the terminus of a railroad that ran down from Tallahassee, located twenty miles north. Oddly, this railroad had no steam engines, for the thin rails and unstable roadbed were unable to support them. Instead, mules pulled wagons along the wobbly track. The railroad gained acclaim, however, for one seasoned traveler nominated it as "the worst that has yet been built in the world."

Most of the mule wagons were heaped high with cotton—nearly 50,000 bales were freighted from Tallahassee to St. Marks the very first year. In addition, the wagons transported heavy loads of timber, turpentine, and other products from Florida's dense forests. The railroad also brought party-goers from Tallahassee to the crowded St. Marks docks, where they hired Indian guides to canoe them into the bay, which was alive with fish.

For the return trip, the wagons were loaded with an assortment of manufactured goods delivered by ocean-going vessels tied up at St. Marks' docks. Other ships brought grimmer cargoes: slaves wrenched from their homes in Africa. These frightened men, women, and children were hauled to the Tallahassee auction market on the northeast corner of courthouse square.

But the St. Marks harbor was too shallow for large ships. So, as other railroads connected with better ports, St. Marks was used less and less. Although the railroad installed steam locomotives just before the Civil War, by then the town's prosperous days had ended.

Today, all that keeps the village going are the visitors to the old fort and the popular biking-hiking trail at the far end of the fort's parking lot. This was the terminus of the old railroad, and the trail, utilizing the line's former bed, extends to the outskirts of

Tallahassee. Anyone can hike on the trail at no charge. But, if you need a bike, you'll have to drive to Tallahassee for a rental.

Oh, For a Pirate's Life?

Now follow the signs to Old Fort Road, which leads through a wetland to the San Marcos de Apalache State Historic Site. It was here, around 1800, that Indian warriors flying the flag of the Muskogee nation engaged Europeans in two actions that could have had a profound effect on American history. At stake was the future of an independent Indian state.

Florida, at that time, was under the domination of the Spanish, who had constructed a stone fort at this important junction of the Wakulla and St. Marks Rivers. By means of this fort, they controlled trade reaching the upriver Seminoles, Miccosukees, and Creeks. British traders in the Bahama Islands resented being shut out of this part of Florida. So, when a wild-eyed former British officer named William Bowles suggested that, with a little British financial help, he could stir up the tribes and expel the Spanish, the traders listened carefully. Bowles presented a very good case, for he had grown up among the Seminoles and had married an Indian princess, which sort of made

At the fort at St. Marks, the Spanish stored their ammunition in a thick stone building. This is the foundation.

him a chief in his own right. Upon receiving British backing, Bowles began a new nation.

Bowles established his capital at the Indian town of Miccosukee, which we visited in chapter five, located slightly northeast of modern Tallahassee. He even dreamed up his own national flag: a blue cross on a red background with a yellow sun in the upper left corner. He appointed officials from the white adventurers he brought with him. He had plans for schools and the establishment of a handicraft industry. To promote world trade, he intended to establish a free port where Apalachicola is today. Tribes from all over the southeast were invited to come to Muskogee. But first, he had to tend to the pesky detail that the land was claimed by the Spanish. Accordingly, he declared war on Spain.

Gathering a formidable army of over three hundred warriors, Bowles surrounded Fort San Marcos and demanded its surrender. Although the Spanish were protected by sturdy walls and a moat, when Bowles captured a supply boat with cannons, the commandant surrendered. Bowles was jubilant, for he had actually defeated a major European power!

The nation of Muskogee seemed to be a reality.

But the victory was short-lived. A few weeks later, the Spanish were back. They arrived from Pensacola in four armed schooners and five war galleys with nine mean cannons, twenty or more swivel guns, and enough armed men to overwhelm any armed resistance. Bowles and the few Indians who had remained at the fort fled up the St. Marks River. Nevertheless, Billy Bowles continued to harass the Spanish by conducting privateering operations along the Gulf coast. (The modern town of Ft. Walton glorifies him in its annual Billy Bowlegs pirate festival.) But Bowles' British aid dried up when England and Spain signed a peace agreement. The Spanish captured Bowles in 1803 and hauled him off in chains to Havana's dismal Morro Castle. Three years later, in despair, he starved himself to death.

Ruins Tell Many Tales: San Marcos

Even aside from Billy Bowles, St. Marks has had a long and exciting history. In 1679, the Spanish built the first fort: a compact wooden affair at the apex of the St. Marks and Wakulla Rivers. But, after a violent hurricane swept away forty brave soldiers, the Spanish moved farther north and constructed the stone fort whose ruins still exist. In 1763, a treaty gave possession of the fort, along with the rest of

Florida, to the British. It was during their twenty-year occupation that Pierre Viaud and Madame La Couture were given refuge here. In 1818, fiery Andrew Jackson showed up long enough to summarily execute two British civilians for arousing the Seminoles. During the Civil War, the Confederates reinforced the fort.

Fortunately, all of the occupants were litterbugs and today their trash has become valued showpieces in the park museum. (The museum is open Thursday through Monday from 9:00 A.M. to 5:00 P.M. Admission is only $1. Call 850–925–6216 for more information.) You'll see dinner plates with blue flowers—officers must have eaten off of them. And there are liquor and beer bottles whose contents were guzzled by the common soldiers. Prisoners wore the arm shackles on display. There's also a diagram of the fort, which indicates it was shaped like a diamond pointing south toward the confluence of the two rivers. The diagram also shows a moat running from river to river.

Now, take the path running west from the museum to the observation deck on the Wakulla River. The deck overlooks the foundations of the bastion which projected from the fort's main wall. Bowles' captured the Spanish supply ship with cannons near here. Continuing on the path, you'll come to a sign denoting the

The site of the first Spanish fort at St. Marks, demolished by a hurricane, is now used for picnics.

Spanish moat, over which there was a drawbridge. Farther on, you'll pass the remains of the old north wall and the bombproof building where the ammunition was stored. The interior of the fort was on the south, to your right. It was near here that Viaud had his tearful parting with Madame La Couture. Six decades later, young American couples, arriving by rail from Tallahassee, would picnic atop the walls, then dance to violin music in the haunted moonlight.

At this place, the path splits. The left fork heads back to the parking lot. But take the right fork, which leads a quarter of a mile south through a dense hammock, once the fort's vegetable garden, to the point of land looking out on the rivers' confluence. Here, the merged water slides among reeds and marsh grasses to the Gulf of Mexico, four miles distant. This was the site of the Spaniards' first, wooden fort that was swept away by a hurricane. It's peaceful now, so if you'd care to linger, you'll find a picnic table and benches.

You may experience an odd sensation here. The land is flat and shapeless. The two rivers barely move, as if they have used up all their energy just getting this far. Aside from the low hiss of the water, silence pervades the area. If you feel that this is the end of nowhere, long-dead soldiers would certainly have agreed.

Newport Is an Old Port

Leave St. Marks the way you came and when you reach US 98, turn east. In two miles, you'll reach Newport. Once, Newport competed with St. Marks in handling the cotton barged down from the plantation country north of Tallahassee. During its pre-Civil War heyday, shipping supported a population of 1,500. Today, you'll be lucky to see anybody.

On to Tallahassee

At this point, there are two routes available. If you want to end your circuit of the Panhandle at Tallahassee, take SR 363 as described below. If, however, you want to continue on the last segment of our backroads adventure, follow US 98 for 145 miles to Inglis.

I won't glamorize this route. It's through drab flatlands with lots of pines and few backroads. The only true attraction is Cedar Key, which involves a twenty-one-mile detour to the coast on SR 24. On the way, you'll pass the virtually deserted site of Rosewood, whose episode of racial violence during the 1920s was dramatized by the movie of the

Cedar Key's picturesque old buildings are appealing to artists and vacationers.

same name. Cedar Key is a quaint, old fishing and lumber port with a short row of buildings constructed to look seedy hovering over the water. Within these buildings are some fine seafood restaurants. Cedar Key got its start as the western terminus of David Levy's Florida Railroad, along which we traveled briefly in Chapter Four. The railroad brought the town twenty years of prosperity, with its population topping 2,000 in the 1880s. But when the cedar trees gave out, the sawmills closed and the town slid gracefully into the picturesque decay that makes it so appealing today.

 Artists and vacationers enjoy this out-of-the way old village. Fishing is available from the town pier and from rental boats. Many homes and commercial buildings date back to the 1880s. Be sure to pick up a walking tour booklet from the historical society at SR 24 and Second Street. As for accommodations, most have a rustic motif. I am told that the Island Hotel, which is on the National Register of Historic Places, is especially appealing. Rates there vary from $125.00 per night during the February through August in-season to $80.00 at other times. For reservations call 352-543-5111.

If you decide to drive north on SR 363 to Tallahassee, you'll find the St. Marks Trail to your left. This was originally the Tallahassee-St. Marks Railroad. When the railroad was first proposed, the idea was quite novel: imagine a road where vehicles traveled over a pair of iron rails rather than on God's earth. It had never been done in Florida— only in a few places up north where people were harebrained anyway. Yet the line was completed in 1837. Although it was successful during its first few years, it soon lost out to other lines. Somehow it staggered along until the state purchased it in 1984. At this time, the rails were removed and sixteen miles were paved to accommodate the bikers, hikers, and skaters who have made this one of the most popular recreational routes in the state.

The trail ends shortly before SR 363 reaches US 319, which is also known as Capital Circle. Capital Circle skirts the central portion of Tallahassee to provide access to Interstate 10. It's here that our Panhandle circuit ends.

The Exotic Nature Coast

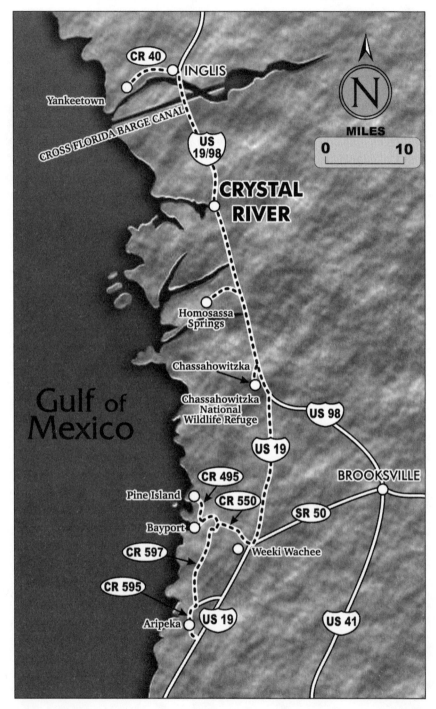

The End
of the World
Inglis to Aripeka • 91 Backroad Miles

The Song of the Road: Overview

This chapter explores ninety-one miles along the lower reaches of the Big Bend region of the Gulf coast. It's probably Florida's most unusual and least visited area. Locally known as the Nature Coast, it's a world of limitless salt marshes. In many places, you can look for miles and never see anything except reeds, grasses, and long-legged birds. To me, it seemed as if I was in some far distant future when all the hills had worn away and oceans and land had merged. It was like the world at the end of time.

We'll enter this strange world at the village of Inglis, where a county road leads west to Yankeetown, with its canopy of trees and a charming restaurant on the Withlacoochee River. From there, we'll head out through the salt marshes and palmetto hammocks, pausing at Bird Creek, the site of an Elvis Presley movie. Finally, we'll reach a tranquil little beach and fishing site on the Gulf of Mexico.

Returning to Inglis, the way will lead south past the impressive, though abandoned, Cross Florida Barge Canal. At Crystal River, we'll stroll among mysterious earthen formations left by long-vanished Native American peoples. Also at Crystal River, we'll visit a gigantic spring frequented by manatees during the winter. Boaters take visitors out to watch the large, lumbering animals that some call sea cows. You can even swim among them, if you have a hankering to do so.

Farther down the highway is Homosassa Springs, known for its spectacular underwater viewing gallery. Nearby are the haunting stone ruins of an old sugar mill where slaves once labored.

Next, we'll enter the Chassahowitzka National Wildlife Refuge. A side road leads to a minuscule settlement, from which you can take a rental boat into the refuge. A flock of threatened whooping cranes makes its winter home deeper into the wilderness, far from where humans are allowed.

Then, passing Weeki Wachee, renowned for its clear spring

enlivened by colorful mermaid shows and short river cruises, we'll head over to the coast once more. The road leads through a wide marsh to Bayport, where there is picnicking and dockside fishing beside a quiet cove that once resounded to Yankee cannons bombarding Confederate earthworks. If you crave a swim in the Gulf of Mexico, you can make a short excursion to Pine Island.

From here, we'll continue south through an almost limitless expanse of needlerushes to Hernando Beach Park, where you can fish from the long pier or leap into the Jenkins Creek swimming hole.

Finally, we'll drive through the village of Aripeka, almost lost in the vast salt marsh of the Nature Coast.

On the Road Again

We begin at the Gulf coast town of Inglis, a little place of barely 1,400 people. Its downtown, at US 19/98 and CR 40, consists of several gas stations and a convenience store. The town's name dates back to the day a Scottish sea captain named Inglis paused here to do some trading. The settlers adopted his name though there wasn't much reason to do so. But anything was better than Blind Horse, the designation the town had been laboring under.

For a while, the community thrived, but after the phosphate industry died, Inglis' fame, such as it was, rested on its reputation among scientists as the premier location in all of North America for snake fossils. Then, one day, Elvis Presley decided to make a movie at Bird Creek, five miles out on CR 40. After he was gone, the town designated CR 40 as the *Follow That Dream Highway*, after the title of Elvis' movie. That's about the sum of Inglis' fame. Except, of course, for the fact that Inglis is probably the only town in America where Satan is banned by official decree.

Satan Is Not Allowed Here

Driving west on CR 40, the village seems to have almost as many churches as people. The religious nature of Inglis must have put it high on Satan's hit list, at least according to the town's forceful lady mayor. Such was Her Honor's apprehension that, early in 2001, she wrote a proclamation that she and a pastor placed on four sturdy posts planted at each of Inglis' highway entry points. This proclamation, which found its way onto the national news services, read in part: "Be it known from this day forward that Satan, ruler of darkness, giver of evil, destroyer of what is good and just, is not now, nor ever again will be, a part of this town of Inglis. Satan is hereby declared powerless, no longer ruling over, nor influencing our citizens." Satan evidently saw the signs and took umbrage, for they vanished not long after being installed.

Yankeetown

Bordering Inglis on the west is Yankeetown, whose population is even smaller than that of its neighbor. From CR 40 watch for Riverside Drive, the second street after the Yankeetown Elementary School. Turn left here to enjoy one of the most pleasant streets in all of Florida. Trees arch over the roadway, which curves and wiggles just as if it were far out in the country. It's worth parking your car and strolling along this comforting byway, stopping, perhaps, at the Winding River Garden Park to enjoy the quiet murmur of the Withlacoochee River, which has received the designation of one of Florida's Outstanding Waterways. Shrimp boats frequent the river on their way to and from the Gulf of Mexico, a few miles downstream.

If the tiny settlement of less than a thousand seems almost separate from the rest of Florida, its history accounts for this. Yankeetown originated as a small enclave of Northern sportsmen in the 1920s. The location along the river was an ideal base for fishing cruises into the

Yankeetown's main street wends beneath an archway of live oaks.

nearby Gulf. Southerners found the newcomers rather standoffish, and so, with a hint of derision perhaps, called the place Yankeetown.

 Farther along Riverside Drive is the rustic Isaac Walton Lodge. Although a fixture in Yankeetown since the Roaring Twenties, it recently burned to the ground and has been rebuilt as a restaurant. The dining room not only has spacious windows looking out on the river, but offers excellent food as well. Meals are served Tuesday through Saturday between 11:30 A.M. and 2:30 P.M. and 5:00 P.M. to 9:00 P.M. and Sunday 3:00 P.M. to 8:00 P.M. Call 800–611–5758 for more information.

 Boat tours also leave from the lodge. For $35 you can enjoy a leisurely, two-hour excursion. The boat holds up to six people, and for more than two there is an additional charge of $5 each. Reservations are required, so call the lodge if you're interested.

West from the Isaac Walton Lodge, Riverside Drive passes the Riverside Marina, with cottages, sailboats, and a ship's store. Lawn chairs line the docking area.

Welcome to a Strange World

Just beyond the marina, Riverside Drive returns to CR 40. As you turn west on CR 40, the coastal wilderness settles in. You're entering the essence of what locals call the Nature Coast. It's probably like nothing you've ever seen. The vista is long and wild, and

A shrimp boat ascends the Withlacoochee River near Yankeetown.

the predominant vegetation is black needlerush, which receives its dull color from last year's dead spikes. The plants are not dead, however, for fresh green shoots are working their way up from the muck below.

This is just a small segment of the vast salt marsh that extends along the Big Bend area for two hundred miles. It's an old, tired world where the land and the sea intermingle so languidly that it's sometimes difficult to determine where one ends and the other begins. Tidal ooze creeps between the needlerushes, which are almost the only plants able to filter out enough salt to exist. In places, where the land is a little higher, cedars and palmettos form island hammocks that seem like derelict galleons.

Elvis at Noon

This may seem to be a strange place for Elvis Presley to make a movie. But the landscape made an exotic backdrop, and once Hollywood had transformed a few acres along murky Bird Creek into a broad sandy beach, the setting became idyllic.

You must watch for the bridge over Bird Creek, since not only does it lack an Elvis marker, it has no name indication at all—officials who did not relish Elvis-watchers must have seen to that. Just be aware, it's the first bridge beyond Yankeetown.

The set for *Follow That Dream* was immediately north of the bridge on the east side of the creek. Today, the area is overgrown with weeds, cabbage palms, and a few cedars. But in 1961, it had a beautiful, Hollywood-style, quarter-mile beach with a one-story wooden house and a short fishing pier jutting into the creek. This was the homestead of kindly Pop, his handsome, but sexually innocent son, Elvis, and an assortment of orphans, including a beguiling young lassie played by Anne Helm.

At Bird Creek, Elvis may have been at the height of his career. Although he was only twenty-six, he was famous and had been featured on virtually every top TV variety show in the land. He had already made so much money that he had purchased the impressive Graceland mansion in Memphis as a gift for his mother, whom he adored. Priscilla Beaulieu, beautiful and devoted, would become his wife in a few years. However, that did not keep co-star, Anne Helm, from falling in love with him while they were making the movie.

Anne found Elvis to be a charming young man, wholesome and unsullied by the sycophants who latched onto him. "I fell in love with him," she wistfully recalled years later. "I just thought he was the best! We had a lovely romance. It was sweet and tender. I wouldn't change it for a moment." She remembered the last scene they had together. It was in the evening on the porch of the little house beside Bird Creek. "He sang a song called 'Angel' to me. We were really saying goodbye in our personal life." Returning to civilization after the movie was over, Anne noted with a sigh, "was very hard because we came to all the fanfare and all the crazy ladies and . . . it was different."

As for Elvis, in the years that followed, he would lose his boyish luster. He hardened and became disillusioned with life. He developed insomnia and took sleeping pills to rest. During the daytime, he lacked his old vigor, so he took pep pills to liven him up. He began dressing in the gaudy costumes that have since made him a caricature. His weight soared to more than two hundred pounds. He died of apparent heart failure alone on his bathroom floor. The year was 1977. He was forty-two years old.

The Creatures of the Salt Marsh

Beyond Bird Creek, the road becomes little more than an elevated platform above the tidelands. Black needlerushes extend into hazy infinity, their monotony broken only by a scattering of palmetto hammocks. The air is usually still and hot and smells of salt, muck, and humidity.

Although it may seem that animals can't survive in this harsh environment, they do. Plant detritus provides food for several hundred species of micro-algae and micro-plankton. These tiny organisms, in turn, are consumed by animals, such as fiddler crabs. The crabs dig deep burrows that aerate the muck and permit nutrients to reach the needlerush roots.

Other animals, too, live in the salt marsh. Several dozen species of birds spend some time here, including cattle egrets, marsh wrens, and seaside sparrows. Their principal foods are insects and spiders. The most frequent mammals found here are the raccoons that live on the forested fringes and forage in the marsh for terrapin eggs.

Land's End

The road rambles westward. It seems as if it will stretch forever as it pushes through a landscape that could have been here since the world's creation. Finally, the road ends at a boat ramp that leads into the Gulf of Mexico. There are almost always small,

Black needlerush and palmetto hammocks create an unusual landscape along the two-hundred-mile Nature Coast.

A wind-shaped cedar marks the merging of the Withlacoochee River with the Gulf of Mexico at Bird Creek Park near Yankeetown.

private fishing boats cruising the Gulf. In the western haze are island platforms, including one that was once Port Inglis, which was abandoned when the phosphate trade ended. To the south, the shoreline reaches toward the horizon, a vista marred only by the distant cooling towers of the Crystal River Energy Complex. The Gulf is nearly always placid, for it is so shallow along Florida's Big Bend that seagrass flats extend out thirty miles into the sunset. The water ripples against the shore so softly that scientists denote this coast as one of zero wave energy.

 Some anglers try their luck from the banks of the Withlacoochee River, which glides softly into the Gulf at this point. Wind-sculpted cedar trees grace the river shore.

 A short side road leads to a Levy County park. The park has a beach of imported sand where non-supervised swimming is allowed. But there are few takers for fear of stingrays. A better swimming location is at a tiny beach beside the river.

An Impressive Fiasco: The Cross Florida Barge Canal

Returning to Inglis, head south on US 19/98. Shortly after leaving town, you'll come to a lofty bridge over the Cross Florida Barge Canal. To get a close view of this huge undertaking, go over the bridge and then turn left onto a short road that leads to a parking area at the southeast foot of the bridge.

The canal was meant to provide a shortcut between the Gulf and the Atlantic. The canal would have also offered a scenic waterway through central Florida for pleasure boaters, which would greatly benefit the landlocked communities along the 185-mile route. Although this project was launched during the Franklin Roosevelt era, work was halted when preparations for the Second World War made manpower unavailable. However, agitation for the canal continued and construction was resumed in 1964. By the time the US 19/98 bridge was opened, two other bridges had been constructed, as well as twenty-five miles of canal, one dam, and three of the five boat locks.

Evidently, there was to have been a formal completion ceremony here, for there is a large boulder on a pedestal in the parking area with a flat space where a plaque was to have been installed. The stone waits, but the plaque will never appear. In 1971, naturalists convinced President Richard Nixon that the project would imperil the vital Floridan aquifer beneath it. Accordingly, the president stopped construction. After subsequent presidents Gerald Ford and Jimmy

Carter refused to resume work, the project was declared dead. Ultimately, the federal government gave the cross-state strip of canal land to the State of Florida, which has begun converting it into a series of parks.

Nuclear Time Bomb?

Now, continue south on US 19/98. During Seminole days, this land was thick with cedars. But, after the Indians were disposed of, American settlers found that the cedars were ideal for roof shingles. So sawmills went up and the trees came down.

In a few miles, you'll see high-tension wires draping across the highway. Enough mega-volts are coursing through them to satisfy the needs of thirty-two counties reaching from Tallahassee on the north to St. Petersburg on the south and Orlando on the east. The electric lines belong to the mighty Crystal River Energy Complex, which, with 1,200 workers, is Citrus County's largest employer. The complex boasts five complete generating plants, including one run by nuclear fuel.

The company assures us a nuclear accident cannot happen, for the uranium is far too diluted to pose a danger, being only three to five percent enriched compared to almost one hundred percent enrichment for bomb-grade uranium. Nor is the uranium stored as a whole but in tiny pellets the size of pencil erasers. The pellets cannot react together because each one is encased in heat resistant ceramic. Furthermore, the reactor in which the pellets are stored is surrounded by nine-inch-thick steel. And around the reactor is a massive containment building made of concrete three feet thick laced with steel rods.

Nonetheless, we may be excused if we have disquieting memories of Chernobyl and Three Mile Island. Accidents and acts of terrorism do occur. So perhaps you'll feel relief as the high-tension wires grow smaller in your rearview mirror.

The World of 500 B.C.

Just beyond the energy plant is the road to the Crystal River State Archaeological Site. Follow the signs for two miles, heading west.

As early as 500 B.C., Native American tribes constructed villages along the north bank of the Crystal River, where clams and other mollusks could be found in abundance. Over the years, the shells and camp refuse, as well as decayed leaves and wind-blown dirt, accumu-

A modern stairway ascends an ancient ceremonial mound at the Crystal River Archaeological Park.

lated in large mounds. Gradually, these mounds took on religious significance and temples were built on them. Then, the site became the sacred ceremonial center for this portion of Florida. Although the area was abandoned before the arrival of the Spanish, today fourteen acres have been set aside as the Crystal River State Archaeological Site.

The park offers a mile-and-a-half walkway past burial and temple mounds. The most imposing is Temple Mound A, which rises thirty feet above the Crystal River. The summit is reached by way of a wooden stairway, which probably follows an ancient ceremonial ramp. If the view today is inspiring, think what it must have been like for the Indian holy men and women centuries ago when the mound was three times loftier!

The various Indian groups who inhabited the site over a period of more than 1,600 years left many artifacts, some of which are on display in the park museum. Here are the clay pots in which they stored their food, and the arrowheads they used to hunt deer and other animals. Here are the pendants with which they adorned their bodies, and the pins with which they fashioned their hair. And here is a pipe flute made of four reeds, the longest of which is eight inches and the shortest about four. The reeds are replicas, but archaeologists know they existed, for the copper with which the original reeds were wrapped has been found in numerous burial sites and was described by early Spanish observers at the Fort Walton site that we visited in chapter nine. Although we can recreate the flutes, we will never be able to recreate the melodies that once vibrated over the mounds.

Where Manatees Come Calling: Crystal River

The town of Crystal River is on US 19/98 immediately south of the archaeological site. Seldom has a town been so cut and mutilated by a federal highway as Crystal River. Before the recent completion of the Suncoast Parkway, cars on US 19/98 created a bedlam of noise and fumes. Many of them are gone now, but the broad expanse of cement remains like a dry arroyo. It's a shame, for, otherwise, Crystal River is a pretty little town. And it really does have a river of crystalline water. This river was created by a spring that is among the largest of all Florida's twenty-seven first-magnitude springs. Indeed, the spring is so immense it that emerges in the form of Kings Bay: a mile and a half long and half a mile wide with an island in the middle.

The major attractions here are the manatees. Manatees are large, sluggish mammals distantly related to elephants. Crystal River is one of the few places in the United States where swimming

At Crystal River, resorts and restaurants look out on one of Florida's largest springs.

with them is sanctioned. The water is a cool, but comfortable, seventy-two degrees, and there are often upwards of three hundred manatees lounging about during the winter.

One of the most favorable accesses to the spring is from the grounds of the Best Western Resort at the north end of town. Here, sightseeing boats leave from the Crystal River Dive Center. For $15, you can either watch the manatees from the boat or actually snorkel beside them. There's also scuba diving, for which equipment can be rented. Although October through March is the best time for manatees, the tours run year-round. Most leave at 8:00 A.M., since morning is the most favorable time for contact. The operators urge reservations, especially for weekend trips. Call 352–795–6798.

For open-air dining directly on Kings Bay, you might enjoy the restaurant next to the dive shop. It's open seven days a week and serves breakfasts as early as 7:00 A.M. and dinners until 8:00 P.M.

Just a Memory

Although the Crystal River is a joy, it's not what it once was. "The Crystal River I remember from my youth stands in stark contrast to how it appears today," wrote Frank H. Adams in *Florida Wildlife* magazine. Then, the water was so clear that "it seemed like we were riding on shimmering air." When Adams scuba dove into the spring's cavern, "our air bubbles danced on the ceiling, looking like so many puddles of mercury held aloft by magical forces." Three decades later he found the water murky and the cavern dim.

Research by the Southwest Florida Water Management District suggests that the water's pollution is caused by nitrates seeping into the aquifer from outlying septic tanks, cattle waste, and the fertilizers dumped on farms, golf courses, and lawns. And it will probably get worse, for when Citrus County officials attempted to obtain approval for a penny sales tax increase for sewer and storm-drainage improvements, voters flushed it down by a two-to-one tally.

The Woman's Club vs. Wild Cattle

As you leave Crystal River on US 19/98, you might be surprised to learn that, in the old days, this was a quiet country road. About the only trespassers were the cattle that roamed freely over all of Florida's unfenced roads right up until 1950. Although there were many complaints, it is said that the real momentum for abolishing the open-range policy, at least in this part of the state, came when a cow entered the grounds of the Crystal River Woman's Club and calmly munched a prized sapling the ladies had planted that very day!

Homosassa Springs

From Crystal River, continue on US 19/98 to Homosassa Springs. This is the second of the four major springs along this portion of the Nature Coast. (The others are at Crystal River, Chassahowitzka, and Weeki Wachee.) Although the spring at Homosassa is only a fifth the size of that at Crystal River, it is still large enough to form a runoff river a hundred yards wide.

The Seminoles named Homosassa for the place where the wild pepper grows. The spring was to their liking, for the water was rich with fish, and oyster beds were thick along the river bottom. When war with the whites broke out in 1835, grim Seminole warriors stalked the woods, ready to challenge anyone who dared dispute their right to be here. But the courage of the Seminoles could not be enforced by numbers, and, by the 1840s, they had either been herded beyond the Mississippi or forced into the dismal Everglades.

This mural at the Welcome Center in Homosassa Springs depicts the manatees that flock here during the winter.

Homosassa Springs State Park

The park's visitors center is beside US 19/98. It opens at 9:00 A.M., seven days a week, and the last $3.50-ticket is sold at 4:00 P.M. From the center, you'll reach the park by way of a twenty-minute electric pontoon boat ride through the heart of a lush hardwood hammock. Alligators bask along the canal's bank. Wood ducks and anhinga are often close by, and osprey nests are visible in the distance.

However, you may prefer to drive to the park, for there is more to see in Homosassa than the spring. If so, drive west on Hall's River Road, which crosses US 19/98 just north of the visitors center. (The Greater Nature Coast Welcome Center is on the corner.) When you come to the fork, take the road on the left, which is West Fishbowl Drive. Shortly, you'll come to the parking lot. If you get there early, you can have breakfast at the park's snack shop, which opens at 7:30 A.M.

Homosassa Springs' major attraction is the fishbowl. From this underwater viewing chamber, visitors gape at the scores of fish, which belong to some thirty-two species, gliding in the flood of spring water. Manatees often cavort past the window, revolving like bloated torpedoes. "They know people are watching," a ranger told me. "Sometimes they'll come right to the glass and look in."

The park also has popular animal shows, some involving manatees, others featuring alligators. These shows begin at 10:45 A.M. and run for forty-five minutes, with the last at 3:15 P.M. The park is open seven days a week from 9:00 A.M. until 5:30 P.M. But since these times are subject to seasonal change, check with the park by calling 352–628–5343. One word, if you want to swim with the manatees, don't. While the animals don't seem to mind, the park prohibits it.

Fame, Fortune, and Failure

From Homosassa Park, continue west on the road that soon becomes Yulee Drive, named in honor of David Levy Yulee, whose ruined sugar mill is a state historic site. It is directly beside the road and admission is free. Now, you can't beat that combination.

The remains of the stone walls stand silent, yet vibrant with whisperings from the past. Here is the iron furnace where sweating slaves once fed the flames that converted water into steam. Here are the ponderous steam-driven gears that turned the wringers through which other slaves guided sugar cane stalks—ever fearful they themselves

The ruin of an antebellum sugar mill is an attraction at Homosassa Springs.

might be caught in the unforgiving wringers. Here is the thirty-foot-high chimney through which smoke from the furnace drifted over the jungle and out into the surrounding cane fields where more slaves, laboring beneath the scorching sun, cut the stalks, loaded them onto ox carts, and drove them to the mill.

To one side are five large iron saucers in which the sweet juice, wrung from the cane stalks, was boiled until all that was left was a gooey paste of raw sugar and molasses. The slaves, both men and women, placed the mixture in barrels and carried them to the curing room, where they were stored for a month until the molasses had dripped into separate containers. Then, the barrels of brown sugar and of molasses—the latter eventually made into rum—were carted to the nearby canal, which still exists, for shipment to U.S. and European ports.

The mill owner, David Levy Yulee, was a brilliant and dynamic person. His leadership abilities caused him to be one of the elite chosen to write Florida's first state constitution at St. Joseph in 1839. When Florida achieved statehood four years later, Yulee was elected to the United States Senate, becoming the first Jew in the nation's history to hold this office. Although his looks were anything but impressive, with an oversized head and a too-prominent jaw, he and his vivacious wife, Nancy, became highly popular in Washington society.

It was during his years in the Senate that Yulee established his sugar plantation at Homosassa. Here, using a thousand slaves, he cultivated a huge estate of more than five thousand acres. While his slaves lived in shacks, he luxuriated in a large mansion on a beautiful island in the Homosassa River. He used the profits from his plantation to help build a railroad from Fernandina to Cedar Key, Florida's first reliable transportation line.

After the Civil War broke out, Yulee used his mansion as a storehouse for smuggled Confederate ammunition. But, while he was away, soldiers from a federal gunboat burned his house to the ground. At the war's end, after Yulee's slaves were freed, his plantation and sugar mill fell into ruin. So, too, did his railroad. Not only were his fortunes wrecked, but Yulee spent more than a year imprisoned for his part in the war. He died a disillusioned old man in 1886.

The Village of Homosassa

Homosassa is unusual among Florida's tourist towns, for no major highway runs through it. Instead, it is isolated by the Homosassa River, salt marshes, and the regenerated forest. The village's narrow streets wend this way and that as they follow the contours of the land and of the Homosassa River. Although its population is less than three thousand, it has its own subculture replete with artists' shops, marinas, seafood restaurants, and charter fishing services.

Yulee Drive ends at the riverfront, where there's a homespun motel, as well as pontoon boats that take visitors on leisurely hour-and-a-half (or longer) trips along the river, often affording glimpses of alligators, ospreys, herons, anhingas, and other creatures. The village's two flagship restaurants are here. On this side of the river is Barnacle Ray's Yardarm and, on the other side, is Crump's, which can be reached courtesy of a friendly little ferry boat.

The Whooping Cranes of Chassahowitzka

Seven miles south of Homosassa Springs, off of US 19/98, is the settlement of Chassahowitzka. It's a locale that some find more interesting as a name, which means the pumpkin opening place, than as an attraction. But for people who wish to do a little exploring in a trackless wilderness, head down Miss Maggie Drive past modest homes to the Chassahowitzka River Lodge, where canoes may be had for paddling along the scenic, spring-fed Chassahowitzka River.

A flock of several dozen whooping cranes spends the winter deep in the recesses of the Chassahowitzka National Wildlife Refuge. These birds are part of only two migratory flocks in existence. (The other winters in Texas.) The birds are part of a program intended to save the species, which at one time was down to just fifteen migrating birds. In order to teach the whoopers to migrate, chicks were raised in Wisconsin by handlers dressed in silly bird costumes. They were brought up to regard an ultra-light aircraft with wings shaped something like a crane's as their mother. The trickery worked so well that when "mom" took off for Florida in the fall of 2001 her children dutifully followed. They arrived five weeks and 1,200 miles later at Chassahowitzka. Then, the following spring, nature took over, and the birds made the migratory flight back to Wisconsin without assistance. It's a miraculous success story that will be repeated as more young birds are trained. Eventually, they hope to have a migratory flock of a hundred birds.

You probably won't see any of these magnificent cranes with seven-foot wing spans, unless you're fortunate enough to be at Chassahowitzka at the precise moment the birds take off for Wisconsin in the spring or return in the fall. Their route leads over Crystal River, where sighting them on the wing and in formation brings great excitement.

Just be wary of canoeing too far on your own, for I am told the swamp is a bewildering maze of islands, bayous, marshes, and mystery. It's also forbidden to have any contact with the whoopers, should you chance upon them.

Al Capone at Chassahowitzka

The primitive remoteness of Chassahowitzka appeals to many people. One of the region's most illustrious visitors, Al Capone, found this to be just the kind of escape he wanted. He took time out from his trying position as Chicago's premier gangster to vacation here during the 1930s. Good ole Al was rather highly regarded by many of the Chassahowitzka's Depression-era inhabitants. He regaled them with food and liquor—paid for courtesy of bootleg booze and selective slaughters in Chicago.

Miss Maggie of Chassahowitzka

A more wholesome memory is that of Miss Maggie, for whom the entry road is named. Born Maggie Smith in 1901, she became Citrus County's first woman commissioner when her husband died in office. But townsfolk remember her best as the affable shopkeeper of a little store near the head of the Chassahowitzka River. Here, she became such an institution that, in 1982, just fifteen months before her death, she was presented with an Amiability Award by officials of the Chassahowitzka National Wildlife Refuge.

Black Bears or Garbage Bags?

A few miles south of Chassahowitzka, US 19/98 splits. Stay on US 19, which passes through the edge of the Chassahowitzka National Wildlife Refuge. Now, most of the commercial mish-mash is gone and the landscape has reverted to a semi-wilderness of sand and pines, particularly on the west side, which a few miles back becomes a swamp. Aside from the whooping cranes, the most publicized residents within the refuge are black bears, many of which, apparently, would prefer to be on the dry side of US 19, for periodic road signs warn motorists to watch for their crossings. This is more difficult than it might seem, since the animals usually shuffle across the highway at night, when they appear to be large, wind-blown garbage bags. Thus, the toll of rundown bears continues to mount. Neither do automobiles fare well in such unexpected encounters.

The Fast Life and Early Death of Centralia

The land along US 19 originally supported towering cypress. But, as Florida was settled, timber companies discovered that these forests could furnish lumber for the burgeoning region. Thus, in 1910, the Tidewater Cypress Company constructed a large sawmill on the northeast corner of what is now US 19 and CR 476. Quickly, the work force grew to 1,500 men, who, with their wives and children, lived in a company town called Centralia. To feed and clothe them, Tidewater Cypress built a cavernous commissary that sold everything from grits and chawin' tobacco to red suspenders and diapers. The community even boasted a theater that showed only slightly dated silent movies.

But the mill gobbled up the cypress so voraciously that, in a decade and a half, the forest was nothing but rotting stumps. Then, Centralia was abruptly abandoned. Within a few years, all the buildings had rotted away.

The Glitzy Gals of Weeki Wachee

After a dozen and a half miles, US 19 reaches the junction of CR 550, which is dominated by the Weeki Wachee Springs water park. Here, from a below-ground gallery, spectators can watch "underwater babes"—as they were ballyhooed in the 1940s before babe-liberation transformed them into mermaids. These pretty young ladies cavort in the almost transparent water coursing up through a massive spring. To watch this cavorting, management charges $16.95 for adult spectators, who, you may be surprised to learn, include eleven year olds. The entry fee is $12.95 for kids—all the way down to three-year-old tots, who are deemed able to appreciate babes when they see them.

From its opening in 1947 well into the 1970s, cars lined up to get into Weeki Wachee, one of Florida's major attractions. But, with the growing popularity of Disney World and the other theme parks, Weeki Wachee's appeal dried up. Today, it is barely making a go of it.

The admission fee also covers a delightful thirty-minute voyage along the Weeki Wachee River, as well as some animal shows, and, during the summer season, use of Buccaneer Bay beach, where you can swim in the spring. Thus, you can get your money's worth—if you have the time and if the weather is right. Otherwise, the park is rather expensive for a short visit and you may want to bypass the watery women of Weeki Wachee.

Back To the Salt Marsh

After leaving Weeki Wachee, head west on CR 550 into the wilderness where backroads travelers belong. The two-lane highway travels over land that rises and falls like ocean swells. Scrub live oaks are the main vegetation. There is little indication of civilization except for a few realtors' signs. As the road gently descends to the coastal flatland, the small oaks are displaced by the black needlerush that has laid claim to the marshy world along the Gulf. In a few miles, you'll come to CR 597 (Shoal Line Boulevard). Pass it by; we'll return in a while. Soon, you'll be at a crossroads occupied by the Bayport Inn. The Bayport is old and wooden, with a certain air of decrepitude. It's just the type of place you'd expect in this backwater world.

Bayport: the Inn and the Lost Town

The Bayport Inn features a cheaply rustic bar where fishermen are the main patrons. Beer is the drink of choice, which should be downed to the accompaniment of country music on the jukebox. The bar is rather dark and smells of brews and deep-fried fish. If the weather is right and the waitresses in a good mood, they'll serve you gator tail on the outdoor deck in the rear. Here, you can look out on black needlerushes that reach to the edge of infinity. The only distraction is a row of cabbage palms and a weathered mannequin sitting in a battered fishing boat waiting for the big one that will never come.

For you tenderfeet, the Bayport Inn also has a quite respectable dining room that is open weekdays after 4:00 P.M. and weekends at noon. For reservations call 352–596–1088.

From the Bayport Inn, continue on CR 550 through the rushes. After the road turns south past Coogler's Bayou, the land becomes somewhat higher, allowing a fringe of trees to arch over the road. You'll pass a boat launching area with restrooms before the road ends at Bayport Park, where a lonely fishing pier looks out towards the Gulf of Mexico. Water laps listlessly against the pier legs as the damp breath of the salt marsh pants around you. It's a drab setting, all gray and olive green. Some people find it oppressing and some find it eerie, but to others it has a pungent appeal, almost as if they were transported to another planet where life is forming in a primordial soup.

It may seem impossible that anything important ever happened in this virtually deserted corner of Florida, but once there was a thriving port here with docks, warehouses, and even a rambunctious hotel. During the Civil War, Bayport became the center for goods smuggled past Union ships patrolling the coast. Its importance was such that it even rated a bombardment. After the war, the port continued to be active until the railroads passed it by. Then, the commerce vanished, the town was abandoned and the buildings were left to decay—which they promptly did.

Refuge Amid the Marshes: Pine Island

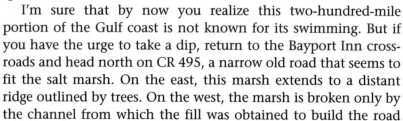

I'm sure that by now you realize this two-hundred-mile portion of the Gulf coast is not known for its swimming. But if you have the urge to take a dip, return to the Bayport Inn crossroads and head north on CR 495, a narrow old road that seems to fit the salt marsh. On the east, this marsh extends to a distant ridge outlined by trees. On the west, the marsh is broken only by the channel from which the fill was obtained to build the road bed in the 1920s. In a mile, Pine Island appears as a low hump on the

Pine Island is set amid a vast, black needlerush salt marsh.

left. In another mile, the road bends toward the island and crosses a little bridge before doubling back to pass a dozen or so picturesque homes. Once, Pine Island supported a beautiful stand of longleaf pines, but, during World War II, the trees were felled so as not to interfere with the anti-submarine radar station built here.

The road ends at McKethan County Park, where there is a beach of real sand. The sand is not native to this mucky coast and must be replenished yearly. Nonetheless, this is a first-rate park with picnic facilities, outdoor showers, public restrooms, and a snack shop. Just don't expect the rolling surf of the Atlantic. Admission is only $2 per car.

Empire of the Needlerushes

Now, go back to the Bayport Inn and head east on CR 550 to CR 597 (Shoal Line Boulevard). Here, you should turn south, which is the only direction the road goes. Scattered along the boulevard are the homes of Weeki Wachee Landing. Boating seems to be the main appeal of this area, for there are several channels where private craft are docked. Beside the bridge over the Weeki Wachee River, a nice restaurant called the Upper Deck overlooks the water. On the other side of the bridge is the Rogers Park Public Boat Ramp. This area was once thick with cypress and cedars, but the trees were gobbled up in the 1880s and 1890s by one of

The old swimming hole thrives again at Jenkins Creek in Hernando Beach.

Florida's largest sawmills, which stood on the river near here. Today, the forest is regenerating itself, for much of the land upriver is protected by the Weeki Wachee Preserve.

Just beyond the bridge, you'll come to Hernando Beach Park. If you love dreamy vistas, turn west to the long fishing pier beside Jenkins Creek. Here, you can gaze over a landscape composed mostly of needlerushes and sky. The atmosphere is often hazy, for this is a marshy region where salt-scented air mixes with vapors from plant debris. Nature hovers close and heavy. It's not a place in which one would care to be lost, but, from the safety of the pier, there is an undeniable thrill to the scene.

For people who wonder where the beach is, drive across Shoal Line Boulevard to the eastern section of the park. Here, a swimming platform extends into Jenkins Creek, which must be spring-fed for it is clear and clean. Sometimes manatees swim this far inland. Along one bank, imported sand has been spread to form a small lounging beach for sunbathers. There are restrooms, and, not far away, a forty-foot-high tower that offers a rewarding overlook.

Hernando Beach

Shoal Line Boulevard continues south accompanied by a

water-filled ditch from which the roadbed was formed. Soon, you'll come to the small community of Hernando Beach. The homes here sell at a premium. Each is on a channel leading directly to the Gulf of Mexico, which, though unseen, is about a mile west. As you pass a marina, a yacht club, and a large, three-story lodging for boats, you'll have no doubt that boating is a big activity here.

Hernando Beach dates back to 1959 when Charles Sasser used draglines to scoop out channels from the salt marsh. Then, he utilized the dredgings as land for development. Sasser had the good fortune to complete his operation before the passage of the environmental laws in the 1970s that probably would have prevented this dredge-and-fill community.

Trail's End

As you head south once more on Shoal Line Boulevard, the forest closes in. This area was marked for a large development not long ago, but last-minute efforts by conservationists thankfully brought these wetlands into the possession of the public. Now, hopefully, the forest will thrive here forever as part of the Oak Sound Nature Reserve.

Oak Sound ends where CR 595 joins Shoal Line Boulevard. Turn right at the corner and continue along the salt marsh fringed with palmettos. The road crosses a series of tidal creeks. Black needlerushes, with points as sharp as bayonets, march over the wetlands in a never-ending parade of power.

Passing over Hammock Creek, you'll be in Aripeka, a map-dot named for an otherwise forgotten Seminole brave. When Aripeka was on the Old Dixie Highway, it was a chic resort village. But there is no evidence of glamour today. Instead, the tiny village is home to a few artists and crafters, along with some long-time residents who love the secluded place. You'll be out of Aripeka before you can draw more than a few breaths, so why not park and stroll along the wayside for a while. There's nothing much else to do in the place. But for Aripekans it's enough.

As CR 595 leaves Arikepa, it makes an abrupt turn east. At this point, the Old Dixie Highway branches off to continue along the Gulf toward the town of Hudson. Wishing to continue on the backroads, I followed Old Dixie for a few hundred yards—until loose sand began scraping ominously beneath my fenders. So I rejoined CR 595, which quickly ended at US 19 and civilization.

Epilogue

It's been fun traveling the byways as I did the research for the three Best Backroads volumes. During six years I've meandered over more than three thousand miles of backroads, visited some 350 villages and small towns, and talked to hundreds of ordinary folk, from timber haulers to shrimp fishermen. I've gotten to appreciate the tremendous diversity of Florida.

Too often, visitors, as well as Florida residents, know the state only from its glittering beach-front resorts and the manufactured splendor of theme parks. But there's an entirely different Florida along the backroads where artificiality is gone. The people are, somehow, more real. And the landscape is what nature made, not what Disney created.

I've loved almost every minute of my travels. And, although the backroads books have been completed, there is still so much more to see, so many more byways to travel, stories to hear, people to meet, and landscapes to admire.

So now I'll be on my way once more. Maybe I'll meet you out there on the backroads. 'Bye for now.

Bibliography

Bell, C. Ritchie and Bryan J. Taylor. *Florida Wild Flowers and Roadside Plants.* Chapel Hill, NC: Laurel Press, 1982.

Boone, Floyd E. *Florida Historical Markers & Sites.* Gulf Publishing, 1988.

Bowden, Jesse Earle. *Gulf Islands, The Sands of All Time.* Eastern National Park and Monument Association, 1994.

Campbell, Kenneth M. *A Geologic Guide to the State Parks of the Florida Panhandle Coast.* Tallahassee, Florida: Florida Geological Survey Leaflet, L 13, 1984.

Carswell, E. W. *Holmesteading: The History of Holmes County, Florida.* Chipley, Florida: self-published, 1986.

Carswell, E. W. Washington, *Florida's Twelfth County.* Chipley: self-published, 1991.

Carter, W. Horace. *Nature's Masterpiece at Homosassa: Where the Salt Grass Joins the Sawgrass.* Tabor City, NC: Atlantic Publishing, 1981.

Danese, Tracy E. *Claude Pepper and Ed Ball.* Gainesville, FL: University of Florida Press, 2000.

Dunn, Hampton. *Back Home: A History of Citrus County.* Clearwater, FL: Citrus County Bicentennial Steering Committee, 1976.

Ellsworth, Lucius, and Linda Ellsworth. *Pensacola: Deep Water City.* Tulsa, OK: Continental Heritage Press, 1982 and 1986.

Fabel, Robin F. A., ed. *Shipwreck and Adventures of Monsieur Pierre Viaud.* Pensacola, FL: University of West Florida Press, 1990.

Federal Writers' Project. *The WPA Guide to Florida.* New York, NY: Pantheon, 1984 (reprint of original 1939 edition).

Fishman, Gail. *Journeys Through Paradise: Pioneering Naturalists in the Southeast.* Gainesville, FL: University of Florida Press, 2000.

Gannon, Michael V. *The Cross in the Sand: The Early Catholic Church in Florida, 1513-1870.* Gainesville, FL: University Presses of Florida, 1965.

Gannon, Michael, ed. *The New History of Florida*. Gainesville, FL: University of Florida Press, 1996.

Hann, John H., and Bonnie McEwan. *The Apalachee Indians and Mission San Luis*. Gainesville, FL: University Press of Florida, 1998.

Head, Clarence M., and Robert B. Marcus. *The Face of Florida*. Dubuque, IA: Kendall/Hunt, 1984 and 1987.

Hewlett, Richard Greening. *Jessie Ball duPont*. Gainesville, FL: University of Florida Press, 1992.

Hunt, Bruce. *Visiting Small-Town Florida*. Sarasota, FL: Pineapple Press, 2003.

Hunt, Bruce. *Florida's Finest Inns and Bed and Breakfasts*. Sarasota, FL: Pineapple Press, 2001.

Kendrick, Baynard. *Florida Trails to Turnpikes, 1914-1964*. Gainesville, FL: University of Florida Press, 1964.

Keuchel, Edward F. *A History of Columbia County*. Tallahassee, FL: Sentry Press, 1981.

King, M. Luther. *History of Santa Rosa County: A King's Country*. No publisher given, 1965 and 1972.

Lane, Ed, ed. *Florida's Geological History and Geological Resources*. Special Publication No. 35. Tallahassee, FL: Florida Geological Survey, 1994.

Lattimer, Dick. *All We Did Was Fly to the Moon*. Gainesville, FL: Whispering Eagle Press.

Long, Ellen Call. *Florida Breezes*. Gainesville, FL: University of Florida Press, 1962 (facsimile of original 1883 edition).

Mason, Raymond K., and Virginia Harrison. *Confusion to the Enemy: A Biography of Edward Ball*. New York, NY: Dodd, Mead, 1976.

McCarthy, Kevin M., ed. *The Book Lover's Guide to Florida*. Sarasota, FL: Pineapple Press, 1992.

McKinnon, John L. *History of Walton County*. Gainesville, FL: Kallman Press, 1968 (reprint of original 1911 edition).

Milanich, Jerald T. *Laboring in the Fields of the Lord: Spanish Missions and Southeastern Indians.* Washington, DC: Smithsonian Press, 1999.

Morris, Allen. *Florida Place Names.* Sarasota, FL: Pineapple Press, 1990.

Myers, Ronald L., and John J. Ewel, eds. *Ecosystems of Florida.* Orlando, FL: University of Central Florida Press, 1990.

Muir, John. William Frederic Bade, ed. *A Thousand-Mile Walk to the Gulf.* Boston, MA: Houghton Mifflin, 1998.

Muir, John. Edwin Way Teale, ed. *The Wilderness World of John Muir.* Boston: Houghton Mifflin, 1982.

Nelson, Gill. *Exploring Wild North Florida* and *Exploring Wild Northwest Florida.* Sarasota, FL: Pineapple Press, 1995.

Paisley, Clifton. *The Red Hills of Florida, 1528-1865.* Tuscaloosa, AL: University of Alabama Press, 1989.

Peek, Ralph L. "Lawlessness in Florida, 1868-1871." *Florida Historical Quarterly,* (April 1962). Vol. 40, p. 164-185.

Portier, Michael. "From Pensacola to St. Augustine in 1827." *Florida Historical Quarterly,* (October 1947). Vol. 25, p. 135-167.

Quinn, Jane. *Minorcans in Florida: Their History and Heritage.* St. Augustine, FL: Mission Press, 1975.

Randazzo, Anthony F., and Douglas S. Jones, eds. *The Geology of Florida.* Gainesville, FL: University of Florida Press, 1997.

Remini, Robert V. *Andrew Jackson and the Course of American Empire: 1767-1821.* New York, NY: Harper and Row, 1977.

Rogers, William Warren, and Erica R. Clark. *The Croom Family and Goodwood Plantation.* Athens, GA: University of Georgia Press, 1999.

Rogers, William Warren. *Outposts on the Gulf: Saint George Island and Apalachicola from Early Exploration to World War I.* Pensacola, FL: University Presses of Florida, 1986.

Rudloe, Jack. *The Living Dock at Panacea.* New York, NY: Knopf, 1979.

Scott, Thomas M. *A Geological Overview of Florida.* Open File Report No. 50. Tallahassee, FL: Florida Geological Survey, 1992.

Shofner, Jerrell H. *Jackson County, Florida—A History.* Marianna, FL: Jackson County Heritage Association, 1985.

Sikes, Bob. *He-Coon, The Bob Sikes Story.* Pensacola, FL: Perdido Press, 1984.
Taylor, Walter Kingsley. *Florida Wildflowers in their Natural Communities.* Gainesville, FL: University Press of Florida, 1998.

Tebeau, Charlton W. *A History of Florida.* Coral Gables, FL: University of Miami Press, 1980 (revision of original 1971 edition).

Waitley, Douglas. *Best Backroads of Florida.* Volumes 1 and 2. Sarasota: Pineapple Press, 2001 and 2002.

Waitley, Douglas. *Roadside History of Florida.* Missoula, MT: Mountain Press, 1997.

Wallechinsky, David. *The 20th Century.* New York, NY: Little, Brown & Company, 1995.

Walters, Ed, and Frances Walters. *The Gulf Breeze Sightings: The Most Astounding Multiple Sightings of UFOs in U.S. History.* New York, NY: Morrow, 1990.

Womack, Marlene. *Along the Bay: A Pictorial History of Bay County.* Panama City, FL: Pictorial Heritage, 1994.

Index

If you enjoyed reading this book, here are some other Pineapple Press titles you might enjoy as well. To request our complete catalog or to place an order, write to Pineapple Press, P.O. Box 3889, Sarasota, Florida 34230, or call 1-800-PINEAPL (746-3275). Or visit our website at www.pineapplepress.com.

The first two volumes in Doug Waitley's *Best Backroads of Florida* series also offer day trips along Florida's less-traveled byways. You'll explore some of the state's least-known towns and learn a little local history along the way in these paperback guides. **Volume 1** (ISBN 1-56164-189-8) covers Florida's central region, and **Volume 2** (ISBN 1-56164-232-0) highlights the state's lower coastal and lake regions.

Visiting Small-Town Florida by Bruce Hunt. Newly Revised. From Carrabelle to Bokeelia, Two Egg to Fernandina, these out-of-the-way but fascinating destinations are well worth a side trip or weekend excursion. ISBN 1-56164-278-9 (pb)

The Exploring Wild series: A series of field guides, each with information on all the parks, preserves, and natural areas in its region, including wildlife to look for and best time of year to visit. The entire state of Florida is covered in the four-volume set.

> *Exploring Wild North Florida* by Gil Nelson. From the Suwannee River to the Atlantic shore, and south to include the Ocala National Forest. ISBN 1-56164-091-3 (pb)
>
> *Exploring Wild Northwest Florida* by Gil Nelson. The Florida Panhandle, from the Perdido River in the west to the Suwannee River in the east. ISBN 1-56164-086-7 (pb)
>
> *Exploring Wild South Florida* by Susan D. Jewell. The new third edition includes over 40 new natural areas and covers Broward, Collier, Dade, Hendry, Lee, Monroe, and Palm Beach Counties. ISBN 1-56164-125-1 (pb)

Florida's Finest Inns and Bed & Breakfasts by Bruce Hunt. From warm and cozy country bed & breakfasts to elegant and historic hotels, author Bruce Hunt has composed the definitive guide to Florida's most quaint, romantic, and often eclectic lodgings. With photos and charming pen-and-ink drawings by the author. ISBN 1-56164-202-9 (pb)

Historical Traveler's Guide to Florida by Eliot Kleinberg. Visit Henry Plant's Tampa hotel, the wreck of the *San Pedro,* and Ernest Hemingway's Key West home. Here are 57 travel destinations in Florida of historical significance. ISBN 1-56164-122-7 (pb)

Historic Homes of Florida by Laura Stewart and Susanne Hupp. Seventy-four notable dwellings throughout the state—all open to the public—tell the human side of history. Each home is illustrated by H. Patrick Reed or Nan E. Wilson. ISBN 1-56164-085-9 (pb)

Haunt Hunter's Guide to Florida by Joyce Elson Moore. Visit 37 haunted sites, each with its "haunt history," interviews, directions and travel tips. ISBN 1-56164-150-2 (pb)

Houses of St. Augustine by David Nolan. A history of the city told through its buildings, from the earliest coquina structures, through the Colonial and Victorian times, to the modern era. Color photographs and original watercolors. ISBN 1-56164-0697 (hb); ISBN 1-56164-075-1 (pb)

Ghosts of St. Augustine by Dave Lapham. The unique and often turbulent history of America's oldest city is told in 24 spooky stories that cover 400 years' worth of ghosts. ISBN 1-56164-123-5 (pb)

200 Quick Looks at Florida History by James Clark. Florida has a long and complex history, but few of us have time to read it in depth. So here are 200 quick looks at Florida's 10,000 years of history from the arrival of the first natives to the present, packed with unusual and little-known facts and stories. ISBN 1-56164- 200-2 (pb)

Guide to the Gardens of Florida by Lilly Pinkas. This comprehensive guide to Florida's gardens includes detailed information about featured species and garden facilities as well as directions, hours of operation, and admission fees. Learn the history and unique offerings of each garden, what plants to see and the best time of year to see them. Traveling outside of Florida? Check out *Guide to the Gardens of Georgia* and *Guide to the Gardens of South Carolina* by the same author. **Florida** ISBN 1-56164-169-3 (pb); **Georgia** ISBN 1-56164-198-7 (pb); **South Carolina** ISBN 1-56164-251-7 (pb)